JavaScript Bitmap Graphics
with Canvas

First Edition

Ian Elliot

I/O Press
I Programmer Library

Ian Elliot JavaScript Bitmap Graphics With Canvas

1st Edition

ISBN Paperback: 9781871962628

First Printing, 2019
Revision 0

Published by IO Press   www.iopress.info
In association with I Programmer   www.i-programmer.info

Preface

JavaScript is a language that has evolved to be fast enough and sophisticated enough to be used for graphics applications right in the browser. Of the two approaches to graphics – vector and bitmap – the canvas is the simpler and more useful with regard to using existing bitmap sources. This book is about how to use Canvas in ways that you might not have thought possible.

Like many books and online resources, it covers the basics of using Canvas, but it also goes into many of the skills that you need to make good use of these facilities. For example, a graphics application often needs to download or upload files, but exactly how to do this in a modern way is difficult to find out. If you do upload a file then you might want to work with it at the pixel level and this requires working with raw binary data. How do you do this in JavaScript, which tries hard to keep data types hidden from the programmer?

There is also the issue of how do you keep graphic processes from bring your application to a halt – as far as the user is concerned. You need to keep graphics on a separate thread or use the GPU to get the job done – or both!

I have tried not only to cover the mechanisms of using canvas, but the background knowledge needed to make using them easier and more successful.

My grateful thanks are due to Sue Gee and Kay Ewbank for their input in proof-reading the manuscript. As with any highly technical book there are still likely to be mistakes, hopefully few in number and small in importance, and if you spot any do let me know.

Ian Elliot

September 2019

3

This book is part of the I Programmer Library and extracts from it, and its companion volume, can also be found on the website:
www.i-programmer.info

To keep informed about forthcoming titles visit the I/O Press website:
www.iopress.info.

This is also where you will find live listings for all programs, errata, update information and can provide feedback to help improve future editions.

Table of Contents

Chapter 1

JavaScript and Graphics

JavaScript doesn't have any graphics commands, functions or facilities of its own. In fact, as a language it knows nothing about graphics. However, when it is used with HTML in a web page it has access to all of the graphics facilities it could possibly need. In many ways, interacting with the HTML that creates a web page is nothing but graphics.

As JavaScript graphics depends on the facilities provided by HTML, and ultimately by the browser, it has many different ways of creating graphics. You can work with individual HTML elements such as divs, color them, fill them with patterns and set outlines. If you move on to the graphics facilities provided by CSS then you can do almost anything but it might be difficult to find out how. CSS/HTML do not form anything that looks like a traditional graphics system.

There is, however, an object within HTML that is designed to provide JavaScript with something that does look more like a traditional graphics system in both 2D and 3D – the canvas object. The canvas object provides a 2D bitmapped graphics system that you can draw on. It also provides a 3D bitmapped graphics system via WebGL. Both of these are the subject of this book, but 3D graphics is such a big topic that all it can provide is an introduction to using WebGL in 3D mode and slightly more detailed look at the unusual topic of WebGL in 2D mode.

Canvas provides a bitmap approach to graphics. The alternative is to use a vector approach and this is what SVG is all about. Unlike Canvas, SVG is more like an extension to HTML. You can create SVG graphics without using JavaScript because it is defined in terms of tags.

But first, what is the choice between bitmap graphics and vector graphics all about?

Bitmap v Vector

Why two graphics types?

There has been confusion over different types of graphics formats for as long as there have been graphics applications and the web is no exception.

Until recently nearly all the graphics you would find in a web page were bitmap graphics - jpeg, png and gif format images are all bitmaps.

A bitmap is essentially just a file containing a list of color values for each pixel in the image. Generating a bitmap image is just a matter of writing a program that sets pixels to specific colors.

In a bitmap everything is a pixel.

What is a vector format?

The simple answer is that a vector format is a program that draws a bitmap. For example, if you want to display a circle in a web page then the simple and most direct way of doing it is to insert a picture of a circle in .GIF or .JPG format, i.e. a bitmap of a circle. An alternative way of doing the same job is to write a program that draws a circle, i.e. setting the pixels required, when the web page is loaded and this would be referred to as a vector format.

The advantage of the vector format is that the program that draws the circle is a lot smaller than the file of pixels it generates. Also, as the circle is drawn each time it is needed, it can use whatever bitmap resolution is available. This means that vector drawings are resolution-independent and can scale. The disadvantage of vector drawing is that it takes processor time and this can be significant for a complex graphic.

There is also the small matter of creativity. Bitmaps can be "painted" using brushes that modify the color of the pixels they pass over. With a bitmap you paint areas. With a vector drawing, on the other hand, you draw geometric outlines and then use fill tools or operators to achieve blocks of color. Vector drawing is more like technical drawing, but don't underestimate it for creative work - it can produce amazing results.

Then there is the small matter that photos are bitmaps not vectors. That is, when you take a selfie, or any other image, the file format is naturally a bitmap. This means that if you are going to process the image to modify it in almost any way then you are going to have to work with bitmaps.

Canvas is JavaScript's bitmap component and SVG is JavaScript and HTML's vector drawing language. SVG has lots of HTML tags that allow you to create static and animated graphics. SVG objects are also exposed in the DOM, allowing you to write scripts that draw vector graphics on an SVG surface. So

with SVG you have a choice of HTML or JavaScript to create and/or
manipulate the graphic.

With Canvas you have only JavaScript as a way of working with bitmaps.
To confuse the issue further, there is also CSS, Cascading Style Sheets, which
is also very much involved in controlling the way things look on an HTML
page. Many of the facilities that CSS provides – such as color names – are
used with Canvas and CSS is so powerful that many of the things that you
can do with canvas you can achieve just using CSS. Just because it is
possible, however, doesn't mean it is the right way to do things. Canvas has a
simple and direct approach to using bitmap graphics and in most cases it is
the best choice when you want to work with images.

So reasons for using Canvas include:

- Creating bitmap graphics within a web page that can even be used
  within the web page without having to be downloaded from the
  server.

- Sprite-based animation for games and general presentation.

- Image processing.

- Dynamic data display.

In addition, knowing how Canvas works and how you can push it in new
directions is sure to suggest more creative uses.

What's in this Book?

The big division in Canvas use is generating graphics and processing bitmaps.
In the first you are more concerned with drawing shapes, lines, text and so
on, to create original graphics. In the second you are more concerned with
some combination of loading, modifying and saving bitmap files. This
distinction is reflected in the two parts of this book. The first explains the
commands that allow you to create a canvas element and then draw on it to
create rectangles, circles and so on. The second is about bitmaps and working
at the pixel level.

Part I starts out with the basics – the canvas element and the fundamental
ideas of a path and its stroke and fill properties. These simple ideas can be
remarkably sophisticated when you allow for the possibilities of paths that
include "holes" and the use of vector paths to define complex shapes.

From here we learn about transformations which are on the face of it just
ways of changing the co-ordinate system in use, but they are so much more.
Understanding transformations is a key idea in organizing and using "unit"

shapes as the building blocks for complex graphics. Text is the next topic and it is surprisingly complex if you care about getting things exactly right. Again a meeting of Canvas and SVG is required to get the best results.

To round off we look at the amazing range of possible clipping, compositing and effects that Canvas offers. This also leads us into the second part of the book as these can be seen as bitmap effects.

Part II begins with a look at the Image object and using it as a source of bitmaps. This naturally entails considering the asynchronous nature of image loading and saving and here we use `async` and `await` to make things really simple. Bitmaps have a natural role to play in animation and the ideas of sprite-based animation are introduced and explored. This inevitably involves a lot of work and is best not done on the UI thread. To keep your programs responsive, you have to learn how to use web workers and Offscreencanvas and these ideas are explained in detail.

Getting deeper into bitmap processing means being very clear about bit manipulation in general and how to store and work with raw data in typed arrays. You also need to know how to load and save bitmaps using files, blobs and the new Fetch API. Once you know all this, you are ready to implement any image processing you may care to think up.

The final two chapters are about "other" graphics system you can use with Canvas, WebGL. This is usually thought of as a 3D graphics system, and indeed it can be, but fundamentally it is a 2D graphics rendering system which can be used to create 3D graphics if you arrange things correctly. The first of these chapters explains how WebGL is usually employed as a 3D graphics display. The second shows how to use it to implement 2D graphics – a topic rarely explored.

All of the programs in the book are presented on its web page at www.iopress.info. The majority are available as live web pages where you can see the program in action and view the source. The exceptions are programs that upload to the server which cannot be implemented live without modifications to meet the various privacy laws that exist in different regions.

Developing With JavaScript

You don't need to use an IDE to create JavaScript applications, but it helps. There are many to choose from but one of the easiest to get started with, but most overlooked, is NetBeans. Once you have it set up, you can try out complete HTML/JavaScript projects using its built-in web server or a standalone web server that you have already set up. It includes advanced debugging options and is ideal for learning new APIs and Frameworks.

Can I Use?

There are many features of Canvas and related technologies that are not supported by older browsers. You can forget making your programs work with Internet Explorer 6-8 and browsers of a similar age as they simply don't support the canvas element. Even later browsers, such as IE 9 and 10, only support the basic Canvas features. If you need to check what works with what browsers then the standard way of finding out is to use https://caniuse.com, but be careful to check out the exact feature you are interested in and not just the "basic support" category. At the time of writing Can I Use estimates that 98.9% of users have access to basic Canvas, but this drops to 62.8% if you ask for the availability of OffscreenCanvas.

In general it is reasonable to say that Chrome, both desktop and Android, is ahead of the pack in supporting new features. Firefox puts in a good effort at keeping up and so does Safari, apart from a few areas (WebGL 2 for example) where it seems to ignore the feature altogether. What features you allow yourself to use mostly depends whether Apple device users are part of your target audience.

If you are building cutting edge web pages/applications you can't expect to have a 100% audience. You are going to have to show a, hopefully small, minority of your users a "best viewed in X" notice.

Part I – Canvas Drawing

In this part of the book we look at how to draw on a canvas element and so generate new graphics.

Chapter 2

Getting Started With Canvas

The HTML5 canvas object provides bitmap graphics to JavaScript. You can use Canvas to create graphics applications, animation and a completely custom UI if that's what you are interested in. It also supports 3D graphics by way of WebGL, a topic we'll return to in Part II, and in this chapter we look at how 2D Canvas is used.

A 2D Drawing Context

The canvas object is essentially a bitmap drawing surface. (If you want vector drawing then you need to look at SVG.) As such, the canvas object provides a drawing context which specifies how the bitmap will be drawn. At the moment there are two types of drawing context, a 2D one and a 3D one. The 3D drawing context is more complicated and perhaps best used via a framework. So we will concentrate on the 2D context.

Creating a drawing context is a two-step process. First you have to create a canvas object and use its `getContext("type")` to retrieve a `CanvasRenderingContext` object of the specified type. Once you have the drawing context you can use its methods and properties to draw on the surface. You can think of the canvas object as the bitmap that you are going to draw on and the Context as the collection of functions and properties that let you draw on it.

The 2D drawing surface has its origin (0,0) at the top left corner. The x axis increases to the right and y values increase going down the page.

The size of the drawing surface is specified as the height and width parameters in pixels.

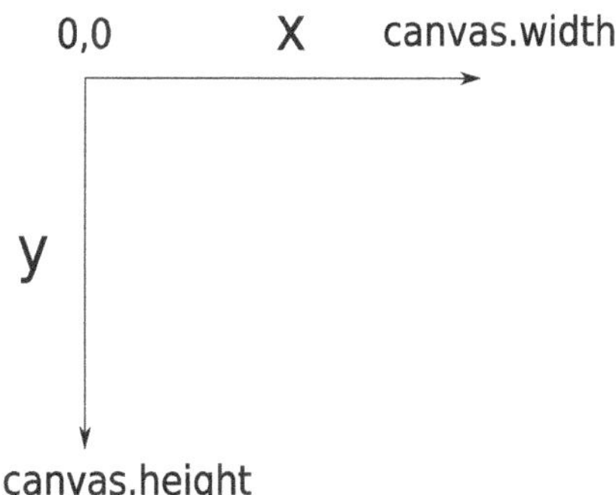

All drawing commands use pixel co-ordinates, but notice that fractional co-ordinates can be used and these shade pixels according to their proximity to the location - i.e. anti-aliasing techniques are used – see Chapter 4. Any drawing operation that specifies pixels outside of the canvas area are simply clipped to fit – see Chapter 7. In many cases you can use negative values to indicate distances to the left and up the screen respectively and positive to the right and down.

Creating a Canvas Object

To create a canvas ready for use the usual method is to embed a `<canvas>` tag where you want it to appear:

```
<canvas id="Canvas" width="300" height="300">
</canvas>
```

This creates a 300x300 pixel canvas and displays it. Note that there is no Canvas constructor within JavaScript.

The usual method of getting the drawing context is to use the DOM to retrieve the canvas object and then call the `getContext` method:

```
var c = document.getElementById("Canvas");
var ctx = c.getContext("2d");
```

Once you have the drawing context you can get on with using it via its drawing methods and attributes. For the whole of this book the variable `ctx` can be assumed to be a 2D drawing context belonging to some canvas object.

For example, to draw a rectangle:

```
ctx.fillStyle = "rgb(200,0,0)";
ctx.fillRect(10, 10, 55, 50);
```

Dynamic Canvas Creation

As there is no Canvas constructor within JavaScript if we want to work with
the canvas object completely in code we have to create our own constructor.
First create the canvas object and set its size:

```
var c = document.createElement("canvas");
c.width = "300";
c.height = "300";
```

You can now draw on the bitmap, but it won't actually be displayed until you
add the canvas object to the DOM, for example:

```
var ctx = c.getContext("2d");
ctx.fillStyle = "rgb(200,0,0)";
ctx.fillRect(10, 10, 100, 50);
document.body.appendChild(c);
```

Notice that this approach allows you to work with a canvas behind the scenes
and only show it when you are ready, if ever.

This dynamic approach is so useful that it is worth defining a function to
create a simple constructor or factory method for canvas:

```
function createCanvas(h,w){
 var c = document.createElement("canvas");
 c.width = w;
 c.height = h;
 return c;
}
```

With this function our program now reads:

```
var c=createCanvas(100,100);
var ctx = c.getContext("2d");
ctx.fillStyle = "rgb(200,0,0)";
ctx.fillRect(10, 10, 100, 50);
document.body.appendChild(c);
```

If you do want to display the canvas as soon as it is created you can use
something like:

```
var c=document.body.appendChild(createCanvas(100,50));
```

and if you never want to refer to the canvas object again you could even
write:

```
var ctx =document.body.appendChild((100,50)).getContext("2d");
```

It is worth knowing that the context object has a read-only property which
gives the canvas object. That is:

```
var c=ctx.canvas;
```

is the associated canvas object. This means that you usually never have to
store a reference to the canvas object.

The `createCanvas` function will be used in the rest of this book.

Styling Canvas

There is a subtle point to take note of in that the canvas object also has `style` properties. In particular, the `style` `height` and `width`, if specified, set the size that the canvas will be displayed at.

The canvas `height` and `width` properties specify the number of pixels in the rendering surface, i.e. the size of the bitmap, and if you specify a `style` size the pixels are scaled to fit the space you allocate. This is exactly the same as when you use an `<img>` tag - the bitmap has a physical size, so many pixels by so many, and the height and width you specify allocates the space used to display the bitmap.

In short, think of the `width` and `height` as specifying the size of the bitmap in pixels, and the `style` `width` and `height` as the space that it will be displayed in - with scaling applied if necessary.

Notice that this means that a single pixel in the canvas bitmap could correspond to a number of pixels in the display.

For example:

```
<canvas id="Canvas"
    width="300" height="300"
    style="height:600px;width:600px;">
</canvas>
```

This creates a canvas object 300 pixels by 300 pixels and displays it scaled to 600x600 pixels. What this means is that each pixel that you draw on the bitmap is displayed as four pixels on the page. This is exactly what happens when you load an image 300x300 pixels and then display it at 600x600.

You can also style the display like any normal image. That is, if you treat the canvas object as if it was a bitmap being displayed in an `<img>` tag, then you can apply the usual attributes – `margin`, `border` etc. Notice that how you style a canvas object has no effect on how you draw on the canvas, only on how it displays. Think of a Canvas object as an image that you can style as you would any image and you should have no problems.

Fallback

Older browsers don't necessarily support the <canvas> tag, but it is easy to provide a fallback display. Just put whatever you want to appear in between the <canvas> and closing </canvas> tag. Older browsers will render what is between the tags and ignore the tags. Browsers that support Canvas will ignore what is between the tags.

This means that you always need to include the closing </canvas> tag as otherwise everything following the opening tag will be ignored – a common bug.

Notice that you can put anything between the tags to act as the fallback, including an image that shows something like what the canvas object would have shown if it was supported.

```
<canvas id='Canvas" width="300" height="300">
  <img src="fallback.png" />
  canvas not supported
</canvas>
```

Events

The canvas object reacts to all the usual events including all of the mouse events. For example, you can set a click handler using:

```
ctx.canvas.addEventListener('click', function (e) {
    console.log("Clicked");
});
```

You can discover the location of the mouse event using the `offsetX` and the `offsetY` properties of the event object. These give you the location in pixels in the canvas co-ordinate system of the mouse event.

For example to display the location that the mouse was clicked you can use.

```
ctx.canvas.addEventListener('click', function (e) {
   console.log("Clicked "+ e.offsetX+","+ e.offsetY );
});
```

You should be able to see that it is easy to use this to allow the user to draw on a Canvas or interact with it in any way you need.

Summary

- The <canvas> tag creates a canvas object within the DOM and this can be accessed and used by a JavaScript program.

- The <canvas> tag has to have a closing </canvas> tag and you can include text between the two that will only be shown if the browser doesn't support Canvas.

- You can size a canvas element in terms of number of pixels, and using CSS style, by the space it takes on the page. The image will be scaled to fit and this can make one canvas pixel correspond to more or fewer pixels on the page.

- Canvas supports a number of drawing contexts, but the one that we use the most is a simple 2D graphics context which supplies easy-to-use drawing methods.

- You can easily create a canvas object in code and add it to the page or just use it behind the scenes.

- The drawing context has a canvas property which gives you access to the canvas object that it is associated with.

- A canvas element is also an HTML element and can be used in the standard way.

- The canvas element responds to all of the usual mouse events and you can easily obtain the pixel co-ordinates of the location of the click from the event object.

Chapter 3

Drawing Paths

Now that we have a canvas object and a drawing context it is time to find out how to draw on the bitmap. What methods you have available depends on the drawing context you selected, but the most common is the 2D context. You might be surprised to learn that this doesn't have a huge range of drawing commands and nearly everything you want to do has to be achieved using a custom path. In fact, the only predefined shape that is available is the rectangle and we will look at this at the end of the chapter. First let's find out about the more general idea of a path.

Paths

In general the drawing methods work by creating a path which you can then fill or stroke (draw as an outline). You can think of a path as a specification for drawing an outline which is stored in a `Path` object.

You can create a `Path` object using its constructor:

```
var myPath=new Path2D();
```

The `Path` object has a range of methods which are used to specify the path. Usually the first method used is the `moveTo(x,y)` call which sets the start of the path to the specified position i.e. `x,y`. Following the `moveTo` you can start to draw straight lines using the `lineTo(x,y)` method.

For example to draw a triangle you might use:

```
var myPath = new Path2D();
myPath.moveTo(50, 50);
myPath.lineTo(100, 100);
myPath.lineTo(0, 100);
myPath.lineTo(50, 50);
```

This defines the path shown in the diagram:

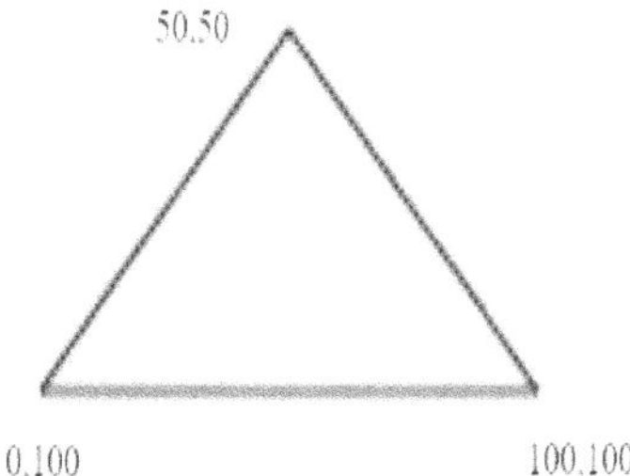

You can't see the path at the moment – it is just a set of co-ordinates and instructions to draw lines. To see the path you have to render it to the canvas object using one of the drawing context's methods. You can use `fill()` to create a filled shape or `stroke()` to just draw the path as an outline. `Fill` and `stroke` are the subject of Chapter 4.

So to draw our path using the default stroke setting the entire program is:

```
var myPath = new Path2D();
myPath.moveTo(50, 50);
myPath.lineTo(100, 100);
myPath.lineTo(0, 100);
myPath.lineTo(50, 50);
ctx.stroke(myPath);
```

Once you have defined a `Path` object you can use it as many times as you want to draw the same shape. If you change the last line to:

```
ctx.fill(myPath);
```

the result is a triangle filled with the default fill color.

Notice that while you can use expressions in the path specification, these are worked out and stored. This means that the path always has a fixed location and shape. We will find out how to use paths at different locations in Chapter 5.

You can use additional `moveTo` function calls to create a disconnected path. Think of `moveTo` as moving a pen to a new location with the pen up and off the paper and `lineTo` as moving with the pen down. For example:

```
var myPath = new Path2D();
myPath.moveTo(50, 50);
myPath.lineTo(100, 100);
myPath.lineTo(0, 100);
myPath.lineTo(50, 50);
myPath.moveTo(50, 110);
myPath.lineTo(0, 60);
myPath.lineTo(100, 60);
myPath.lineTo(50, 110);
ctx.stroke(myPath);
```

draws two disconnected paths in the shape of a star:

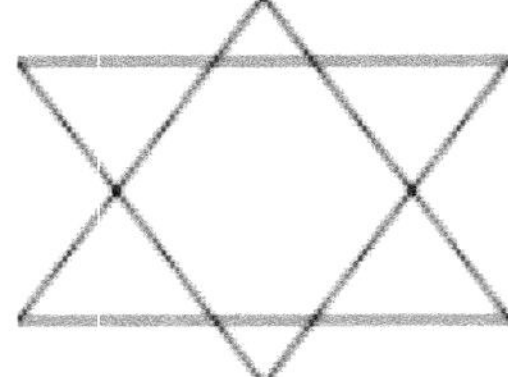

The two triangles are sub-paths of the complete path.

You can see that the need to create a line that moves back to the start of a sub-path is needed to create any closed path. The `closePath` function will draw a line from the current position back to the start of the current sub-path.

So we can write the star path program as:

```
var myPath = new Path2D();
myPath.moveTo(50, 50);
myPath.lineTo(100, 100);
myPath.lineTo(0, 100);
myPath.closePath();
myPath.moveTo(50, 110);
myPath.lineTo(0, 60);
myPath.lineTo(100, 60);
myPath.closePath();
ctx.stroke(myPath);
```

Notice that each `closePath` call closes the current sub-path. It is also very important to be clear that `closePath` doesn't in any sense end the sub-path. You can carry on drawing and extend the sub-path from its initial position. For example, if you change the first sub-path to:

```
myPath.closePath();
myPath.lineTo(50, 0);
```

the sub-path continues and you get:

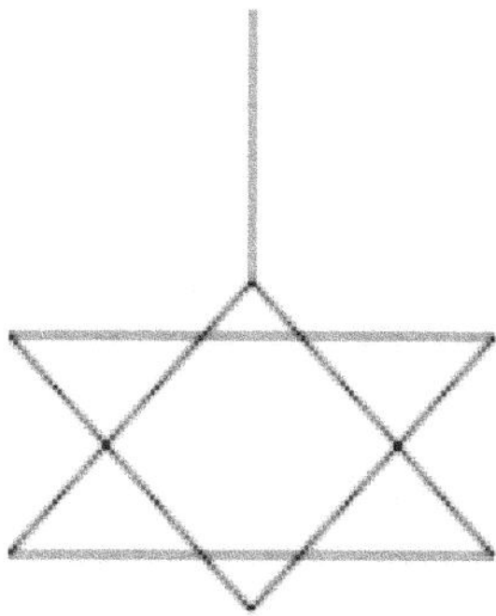

That is, `closePath` draws a line back to the starting point of the sub-path and nothing else. To start a new sub-path you need to use a `moveTo` call.

The Default Path Object

It has to be admitted that using a `Path` object is not the way that Canvas is mostly introduced. Instead, the drawing context is used directly without any mention of a `Path` object, but a `Path` object is still being used. The drawing context has a current, or default, `Path` object that you can use to create a path.

It is often said that you start a path using the `beginPath()` method of the drawing context, but this actually clears the default path ready for you to create a new one.

For example the star path can be written as:

```
ctx.beginPath();
ctx.moveTo(50, 50);
ctx.lineTo(100, 100);
ctx.lineTo(0, 100);
ctx.closePath();
ctx.lineTo(50, 0);
ctx.moveTo(50, 110);
ctx.lineTo(0, 60);
ctx.lineTo(100, 60);
ctx.closePath();
ctx.stroke();
```

Notice that now no `Path` object is explicitly created, we are simply using the default `Path` object. If you call path methods on the drawing context then the default path is used. This is initially simpler but less flexible.

Using the default `Path` object is slightly more efficient than creating a single custom `Path` object, but the difference is small – around 5%. There is also the matter of reuse of paths. If you need to draw two paths repeatedly then you could use the default object, set the first path, then use `beginPath` and set the second path. Alternatively you could create a `Path` object for the first path and a `Path` object for the second path and then simply use `stroke(path1); stroke(path2)`.

Using a separate `Path` objects is about 30% faster than changing the default `Path`. All timings are based on Chrome 71 and you should regularly check that JavaScript optimizations haven't changed the position.

In most cases it is better from an organizational point of view to use explicit `Path` objects irrespective of efficiency.

The Rectangle

The simplest drawing function is:

```
rect(x,y,w,h)
```

which draws a path starting at (x,y), the top left corner of the rectangle, of width w and height h.

You can specify negative values for w and h and this changes which corner of the rectangle (x,y) specifies. That is, for a negative w, (x,y) is the top right corner; for negative h, it is the bottom left, and if both are negative it is the bottom right. Of course, all of this changes if you change the co-ordinate system with a transformation - see Chapter 5.

There are two things to be aware of when using rect. The first is that it starts a new sub-path. It is as if there was a moveTo(x,y) in front of the call. If you continue to draw after the rectangle, the path continues from the top left corner.

For example:

```
var path1 = new Path2D();
path1.rect(200,400,20,50);
path1.lineTo(300,500);
```

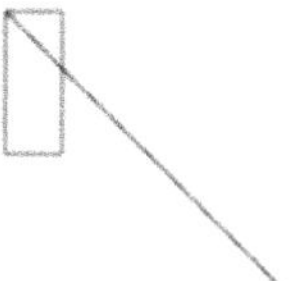

As well as the rect function there is also the strokeRect function and the fillRect function of the drawing context. These work in exactly the same way as rect but they are only available on the drawing context and they fill or stroke the rectangle using the current fill or stroke style.

These two functions are sometimes convenient when you don't want to go to the trouble of creating a path and filling or stroking it as a separate operation. See the end of this chapter for more information.

Circles and Ellipses

The `lineTo` function draws straight lines and sometimes this is enough. You can approximate almost any shape with short straight lines. For example, here is a short program that draws a circle using straight lines:

```
var path1 = new Path2D();
var x = 200;
var y = 200;
var r = 100;
path1.moveTo(x, y + r);
var inc = 0.5;

for (t = 0; t < 2 * Math.PI; t =t+ inc) {
    path1.lineTo(x + r * Math.sin(t), y + r * Math.cos(t));
}
path1.closePath();
ctx.stroke(path1);
```

The circle is drawn using the standard equation for a circle and the number of line segments is controlled by `inc`. It requires polar co-ordinates:

x= r*cos t + cx

y= r*sin t + cy

which give a point on the circle of radius r centered on cx,cy at angle t.

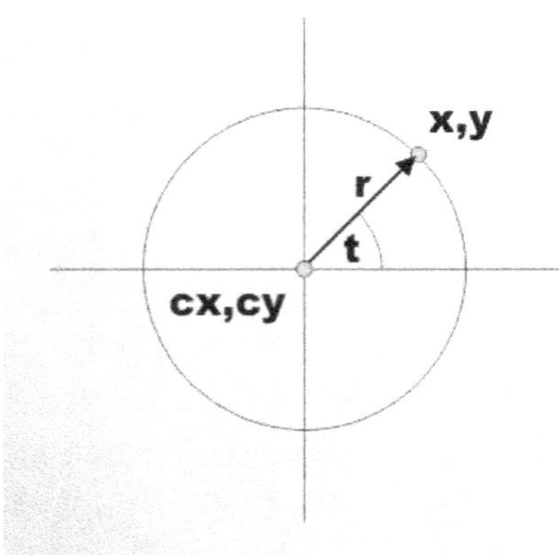

When inc is `0.5` the result is a polygon approximation to a circle:

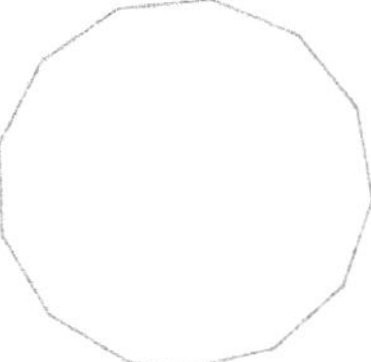

As inc is decreased the number of sides increases and the shape looks more and more like a circle. For inc set to `0.1` the result is a reasonable looking circle:

If you want a simpler approximation to a circle, or of part of a circle, you can use:

```
arc(x,y,radius, start angle, stop angle, direction)
```

The center of the circle with radius r is at x,y and start angle and stop angle determine how much of the circle is drawn. The angles are in radians and this often causes problems because we are not as familiar with radians as with degrees. All you need to know is that if d is in degrees d/180*Math.PI is the angle in radians. The angles are measured in a clockwise direction from the positive x axis. Direction is true if you want to draw in an anti-clockwise direction and false for a clockwise direction – the default is false/clockwise.

To draw the same circle in the previous example all you need is:

```
var path1 = new Path2D();
var x = 200;
var y = 200;
var r=100;
path1.arc(x, y, r, 0, 2*Math.PI);
ctx.stroke(path1);
```

The angle is from 0 to 2π, which is a full circle.

The arc function uses the same method to draw the circle as the earlier function, i.e. it uses line segments, but it is optimized and adjusts to the number of pixels available.

A subtle point is that the circle drawn forms part of the current path. That is, it isn't a disconnected sub-path. A line will be drawn from the end of the current line to the start point of the circle and a line will be drawn from the end of the circle to the start of the next line.

For example:

```
var path1 = new Path2D();
var x = 200;
var y = 200;
var r = 100;
path1.moveTo(0, 200);
path1.arc(x, y, r, 0, 2 * Math.PI);
path1.lineTo(300, 0);
ctx.stroke(path1);
```

This puts the start point to 0,200, draws a line to the start of the circle and, when the circle is complete, draws a line from the end point to 300,0:

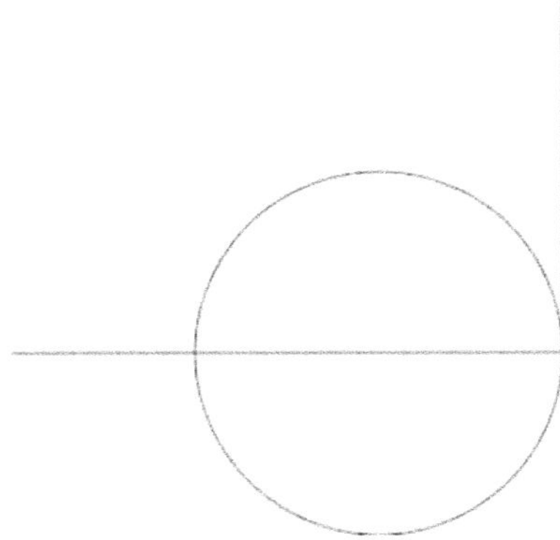

If you only draw part of the circle what is happening becomes clear.

If you change the arc call to:

```
path1.arc(x, y, r, 0, Math.PI/2);
```

which draws a quarter of a circle, you can see the lines drawn to the start and end points:

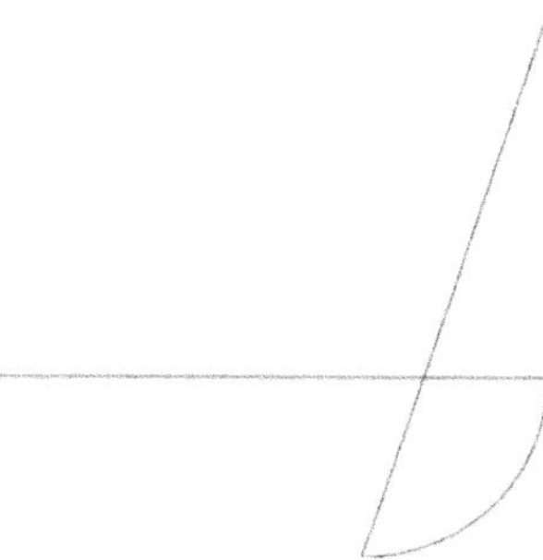

If you want the circle to be a sub-path disconnected from any other sub-path then use a moveTo the start point and a moveTo the start of the next sub-path. For example, adding two moveTo calls creates three sub-paths – two lines and the quadrant:

```
var path1 = new Path2D();
var x = 200;
var y = 200;
var r = 100;
path1.moveTo(100, 150);
path1.lineTo(150, 300);
path1.moveTo(300, 200);
path1.arc(x, y, r, 0, Math.PI / 2);
path1.moveTo(200, 200);
path1.lineTo(400, 400);
ctx.stroke(path1);
```

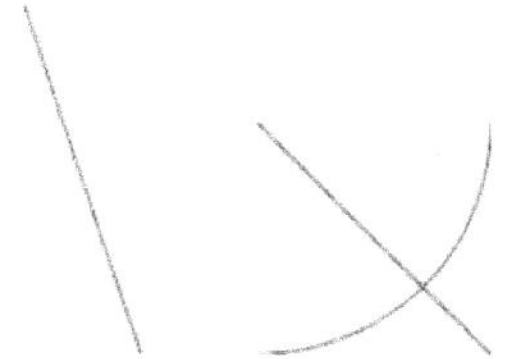

Finally, notice that any arc that you draw isn't closed. You can close it using the closePath function.

For example:

```
var path1 = new Path2D();
var x = 200;
var y = 200;
var r = 100;
path1.arc(x, y, r, 0, Math.PI / 2);
path1.closePath();
ctx.stroke(path1);
```

which closes the quarter circle to give:

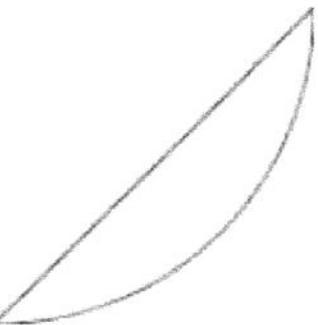

If you were expecting a more traditional closed quadrant then to achieve this you need to add some lines from the start and end to the center of the circle:

```
var path1 = new Path2D();
var x = 200;
var y = 200;
var r = 100;
path1.moveTo(x,y);
path1.arc(x, y, r, 0, Math.PI / 2);
path1.lineTo(x,y);
ctx.stroke(path1);
```

which produces:

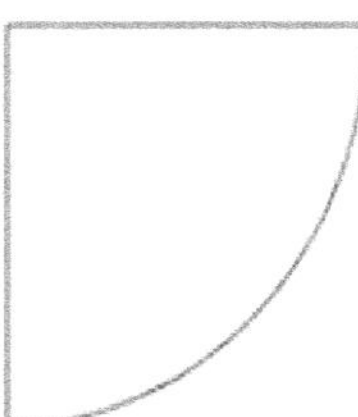

Ellipse

The `ellipse` function is a generalization of the arc function. It draws part of
an ellipse as specified by start and stop angles as in the case of the `arc`
function. The difference is that you can now specify a horizontal and a
vertical radius and a rotation angle:

```
ellipse(x,y,rx,ry,rot,start angle, stop angle, direction);
```

This draws an ellipse centered on x,y with horizontal radius rx and vertical
radius ry. The `start angle`, `stop angle` and `direction` parameters work in
the same way as in the `arc` function. The `rot` parameter rotates the entire
ellipse so that you can draw something more general.

For example:

```
path1.ellipse(300,200,150,50,0,0,Math.PI*2);
```

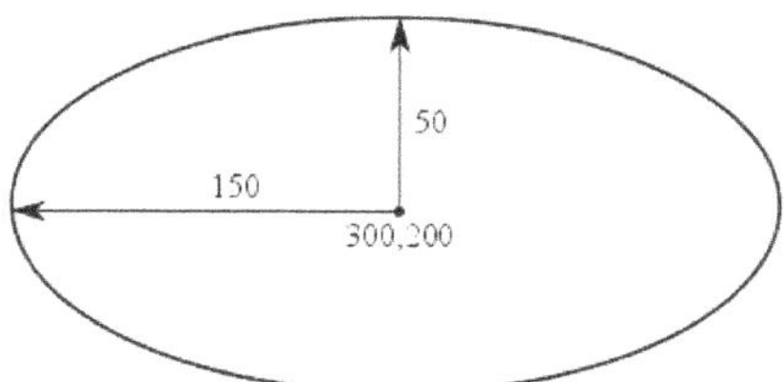

In this case the rotation angle is zero so the horizontal and vertical radii are in
their default orientation. If we specify a rotation angle of 45 degrees:

```
path1.ellipse(300,200,150,50,Math.PI/4,0,Math.PI*2);
```

The x radius is tilted at 45 degrees:

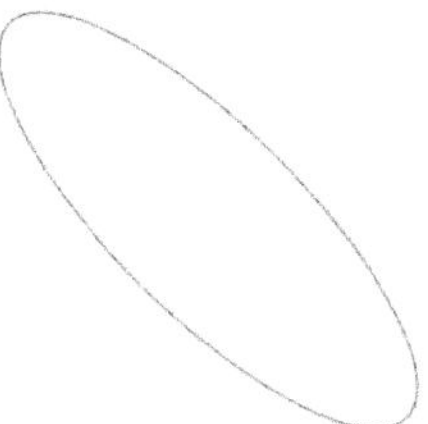

The only other thing to be aware of is that ellipse continues the current path.
A line will be drawn from the current position to the starting point of the
ellipse and the final point becomes the starting point of the rest of the path.

The arcTo Function

The `arcTo` function draws a circle or circular arc, but it is slightly more complicated to understand than the `arc` function.

The `arc` function draws an arc at a specific center, radius and angles. The `arcTo` function draws part of a circle of a specified radius, but at a position and with angles governed by two "control" points.

The key to understanding `arcTo` is to realize that there are actually three points involved in drawing the curve that `arcTo` specifies – the start point, i.e. where the current path has got to, and the two given control points. The arc is constructed at the given radius so that it is tangent to the lines formed by the start and the first control point and the first control point and the second control point:

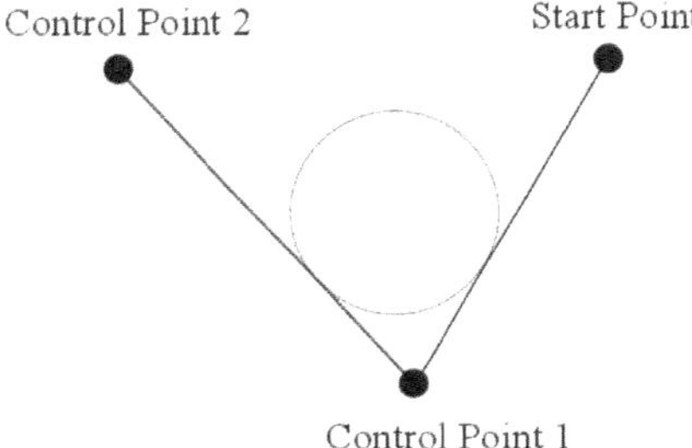

You can see how the circle of a given radius can be moved until it is tangent to both lines. In the diagram the complete circle is shown but only the circular arc from the first tangent point to the second is actually drawn. Also the line from the start point to the start of the arc is drawn but not the line from the end of the arc to the second control point:

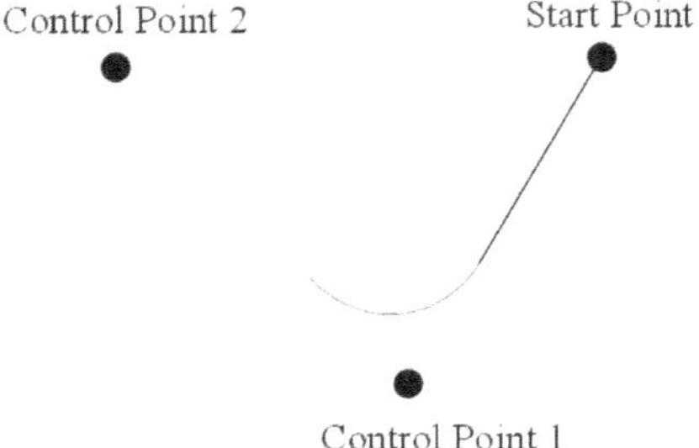

If you want to draw the line to control point 2 then you simply use `LineTo`.

Notice that the radius of the circle controls where along the lines the circle is placed. As the radius gets smaller the circle moves to be closer to control point 1. As the radius gets bigger it moves away from control point 1. If you make the radius very big then it might be tangent to the lines projected back away from control point 1:

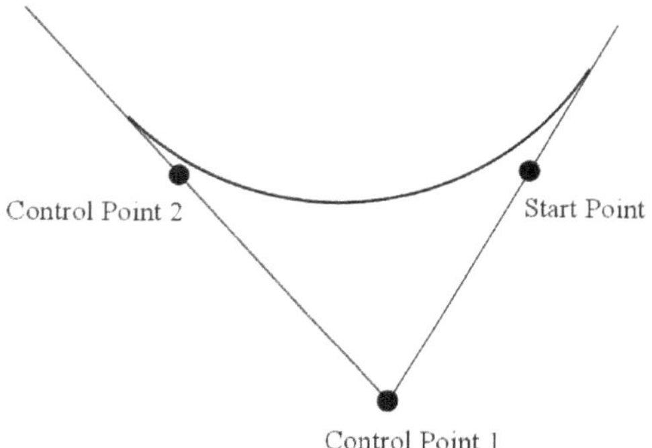

Which is probably not what you want or expect.

For example:

```
path1.moveTo(200, 120);
path1.arcTo(200, 230, 50, 120, 20);
path1.lineTo(50,120);
```

produces:

where circles have been drawn to mark the start and control points.

The main use of the `arcTo` command is to draw polygons, usually rectangles, with rounded corners. It is surprising that canvas doesn't have a built-in function for rectangles with round corners, but it is easy to create.

To draw a rectangle with its top left corner at 100,100 of width 200 and
height 300 you would use:

```
path1.moveTo(100, 100);
path1.arcTo(200, 100, 200, 300, 20);
path1.arcTo(200, 300, 100, 300, 20);
path1.arcTo(100, 300, 100, 100, 20);
path1.arcTo(100, 100, 300, 100, 20);
```

This simply moves to the starting point and then draws each side with a
rounded corner. This doesn't quite work because the initial `moveTo` starts the
top side where the sharp corner should be. This doesn't matter if you fill the
shape but if you stroke it then you will see a "tail":

The solution is to start the top side from the end of the arc, i.e. from `x+r`.

It is easy to turn this into a general function that will draw a rectangle with
top left corner at a specified point at the given height, width and radius.

```
function roundRect(x, y, h, w, r) {
  var path = new Path2D();
  path.moveTo(x+r, y);
    path.arcTo(x+w, y, x+w, y+h, r);
    path.arcTo(x+w, y+h, x, y+h, r);
    path.arcTo(x, y+h, x, y, r);
    path.arcTo(x, y, y+h, y, r);
    return path;
}
```

For example:

```
var path1=roundRect(50,100,300,200,40);
ctx.stroke(path1);
```

Bezier Curves

The most sophisticated of the path creation functions are the two Bezier curve functions. A Bezier curve is a smooth curve that you can use to approximate complex curves. They were invented by Pierre Bezier in the 1960 to give Renault cars their smooth curvy bodies. There are different types of Bezier curves with different properties. What is important to realize is that a Bezier curve isn't an exact shape like a circle or an ellipse. They are generally created by interactive adjustment of their parameters to give a pleasing shape. For example you might interactively adjust a Bezier curve until it was the shape of a face, then another to be the shape of a nose and so on. The big problem with using Bezier curves with Canvas is that you have to specify them in the function call and getting the parameters right can be very tricky. More on how to do this later.

Canvas supports two types of Bezier curves - quadratic and cubic. The names tell you the highest power that occurs in their implementation. Put simply, cubic Bezier curves are potentially wigglier than quadratic Bezier curves. You can achieve the same overall curve using either type, but you might need more quadratic curves to do the job. In most cases the slightly more complicated cubic curve is the better choice.

To specify the curvature of a Bezier curve you need to specify a starting point, a finishing point and a number of control points. A quadratic Bezier curve has a single control point and it acts like an attractor for the curve pulling it towards it. At the start point the curve is tangent to the straight line between it and the control point. The same is true at the end point where the curve is tangent to the line between it and the control point.

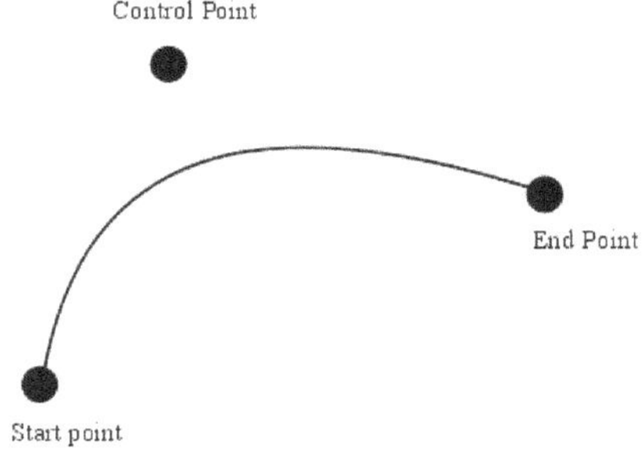

To draw a quadratic Bezier curve you use the `quadraticCurveTo` function `quadraticCurveTo(cpx,cpy,x,y)`, where the start point is the current point, the end point is `x,y`, and the control point is `cpx,cpy`. For example:

```
path1.moveTo(10,10);
path1.quadraticCurveTo(200,50,100,100);
```

draws a curve between `10,10` and `100,100` with a control point at `200,50`. You can see the result below with the control point marked as a circle.

The cubic Bezier curve works in much the same way but now there are two control points:

```
bezierCurveTo(cp1x,cp1y,cp2x,cp2y,x,y);
```

This draws a cubic curve between the current point and `x,y` using `cp1x,cp1y` and `cp2x,cp2y` as the control points. The action of the control points is more complicated and the first control point affects the curve more close to the start point and the second control point affects it near the end point. The curve is tangent at the start point to the straight line between the start and the first control point, and tangent at the end to the line between the end point and the second control point.

For example:

```
path1.moveTo(10,10);
path1.bezierCurveTo(200,20,20,200,200,300);
```

produces a curve with two wiggles:

where again the two control points have been marked with circles.

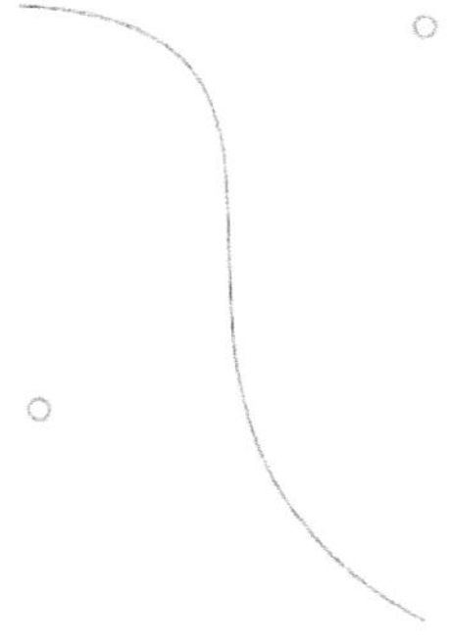

As promised, the cubic Bezier curve can wiggle more than the quadratic. You couldn't produce this sort of curve with a quadratic because you only have one control point which attracts the curve. With a cubic curve you can "pull" the curve in two different directions.

The big problem with both forms of the Bezier curve is how to specify the control points. You could write a utility that allowed you to draw interactively and so set the control points, but there is a much simpler and better approach. First, however, we need to find out about another way to specify a path.

Using SVG Paths

You don't have to know anything about SVG paths to make use of the notation that it introduces to specify a path. The basic idea is that there is a set of single letter commands that you can include in a string and these define the path.

For example, M means moveTo and so a string "M50,50" means the same thing as

```
moveTo(50,50);
```

The commands available that are the direct equivalent of function calls are:

- Mx y = moveTo(x,y)
- Lx y = lineTo(x,y)
- Qx1 y1 x y= quadraticCurveTo(x1.y1,x,y)
- Cx1 y1 x2 y2 x y = bezierCurveTo(x1,y1,x2,y2,x,y)
- Z = closePath()

You can use a string specifying the path in the Path2D constructor.

For example:

```
var path=new Path2D("M50 50 L100 100");
```

creates a path that is identical to:

```
var path=new Path2D();
path.moveTo(50,50);
path.lineTo(100,100);
```

You might ask at this point what is the advantage? The string notation is much more compact than the function calls. In addition it goes beyond what the function calls can do. For example, if you use the same string commands in lower case then the co-ordinates are all taken to be relative to the current position. This is very useful as to get relative forms of the function calls you have to do arithmetic.

If you change the previous example to:

```
var path=new Path2D("m50 50 l100 100");
```

it creates a path that moves to `cx+50, cy+50` where `cx` and `cy` `is` the current position and then draws a line 100 pixels horizontally and 100 pixels vertically, i.e. to `cx+50+100,cy+50+100`.

There are also two additional line drawing commands:

- `Hx` is a "horizontal line to" command
- `Vy` is a "vertical line to" command

which only require you to supply an x or a y co-ordinate. For example "H50" draws a line from the current position to `50,cy`.

The commend for drawing an elliptical arc command is `A`:

- `Arx ry rot size sweep x y`

This draws an arc, with radii `rx` and `ry`, between the current point and `x, y`. The `rot` parameter controls the rotation of the radii. The `size` and `sweep` flags are confusing at first, but not when you realize that there are usually two ellipses that connect two points – a big arc and a small arc.

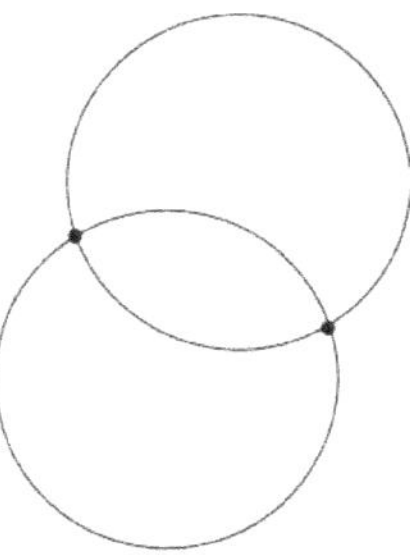

Which of these four possible arcs do you want to use to connect the start point to the end point? This is what the `size` and `sweep` flags are for. The `size` flag either selects the small arcs or the large arcs. In this case `large` or `small` is measured using the angle specified by `sweep`. If you set `size` to `0` then you select the two small arcs:

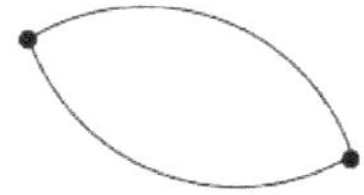

If you set `size` to `1` you select the two large arcs:

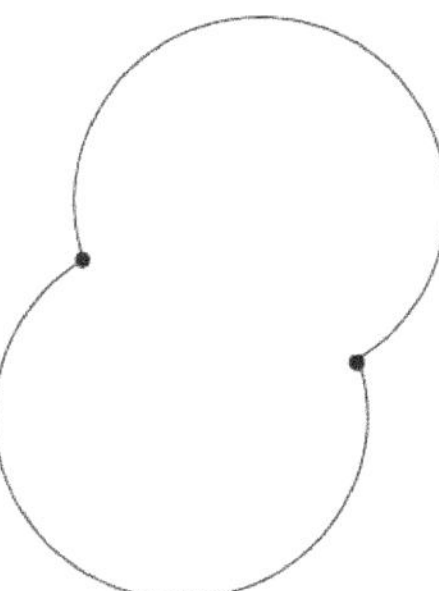

Now we just have to select which of the pair of arcs to use. This is what the `sweep` flag is for. One of the pairs of arcs will run clockwise from the start to finish point and the other runs anticlockwise. If the point on the left of the diagrams is the start point setting `sweep` to `0` selects the anticlockwise arcs:

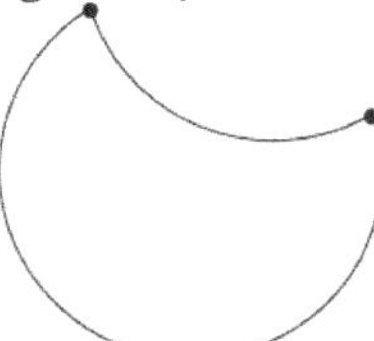

Setting sweep to 1 selects the clockwise arcs:

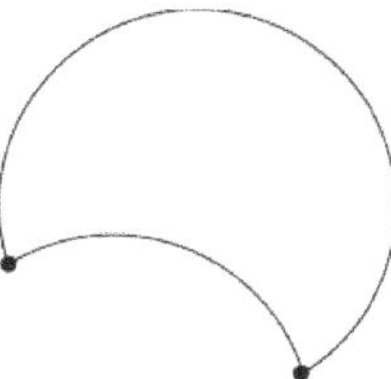

You can now appreciate that by setting size and sweep together you can pick out just one of the possible arcs. For example:

```
path1=new Path2D("M50 50 A40 40 0 0 0 100 80");
```

draws an arc from `50,50` to `100,80` with radii equal to `40`. As both the `size` and `sweep` flags are `0` this selects the small anticlockwise arc:

If you change the string to:

```
path1=new Path2D("M50 50 A40 40 0 1 1 100 80");
```

i.e. `size` and `sweep` set to 1, it draws the large clockwise arc:
This is a very flexible approach to drawing arcs, but it suffers from one major problem – how do you draw a complete circle or ellipse?

To specify a complete circle or ellipse the start and end point have to be the same and this doesn't work. If you try:

```
path1=new Path2D("M100 80 A40 40 0 1 1 100 80");
```

nothing is drawn as there are an infinity of circles that pass through the same point – you need a second point to fix the position.

There are a number of solutions to this problem but no accepted best solution. One possibility is to specify the start and end points a small distance apart and then close the path. A possibly better solution is to draw two half circles or ellipses. For example:

```
path1=new Path2D("M100 80 A40 40 0 0 1 180 80 A40 40 0 0 1 100 80");
```

This draws a perfect circle by drawing a semicircle from `x,y` to `x+2r,y` and then another from the current point back to `x,y` where `r` is the radius and `x,y` is the left edge of the circle.

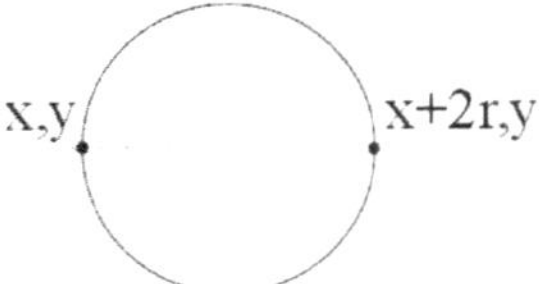

If you want to use `x,y` as the center then the method is move to `x-r,y`, draw a semicircle radius `r` to `x+r,y` and then close the path by drawing a semicircle to `x-r,y`.

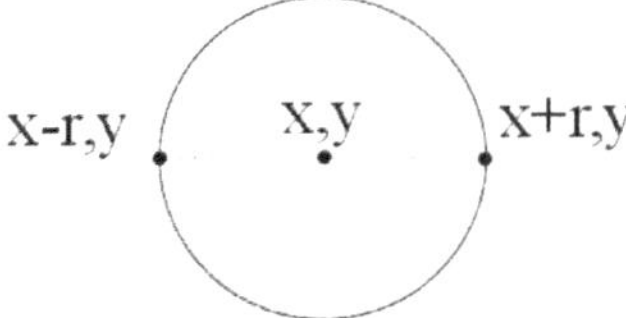

It is worth restating that all of these commands have relative versions corresponding to the same command letter but in lower case.

Bezier and String Paths

We have already discovered that you can specify both sorts of Bezier curve using a string path:

- ◆ `Qx1 y1 x y = quadraticCurveTo(x1.y1,x,y)`
- ◆ `Cx1 y1 x2 y2 x y = bezierCurveTo(x1,y1,x2,y2,x,y)`

There are two additional commands that sometimes make things easier.

- ◆ `Tx y = smooth quadratic Bézier curveto`
- ◆ `Sx2 y2 x y  = smooth curveto`

In each case these commands are to be used after the usual quadratic or cubic commands and their purpose is to continue the curve smoothly. If you use them following any other command then the missing control point is taken to be the current position.

What does smooth mean in the case of a quadratic Bezier? The answer is that the control point for the second part of the curve has to be on a line through the first control point and the end point. The reason is simply that the curve has to be a tangent to this line as it approaches the end point and the only way it can be continued in a smooth way is if it continues to be at a tangent to the same line as it leaves the first end point.

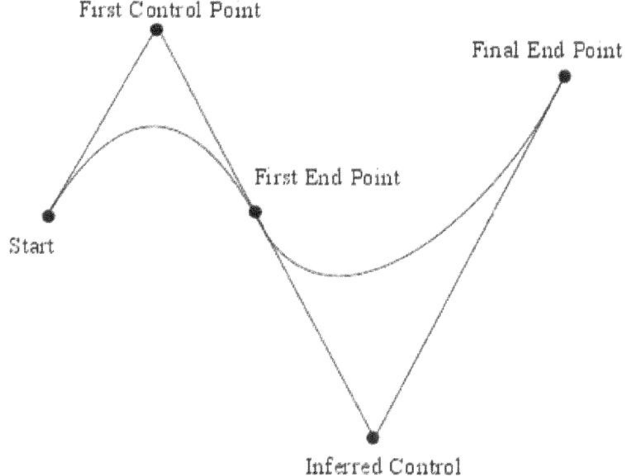

You can see that the only degree of freedom you have in the curve, if it is to be smooth, is the position of the final end point. The curve continues in the same direction through the first end point, but then smoothly turns towards the final end point.

For example:

```
path1=new Path2D("M50 100 Q75 50 100 100 T200 50");
```

produces:

The command:

```
Sx2 y2 x y
```

continues a cubic Bezier curve in the same way as T and you only specify the
second control point and the end point. In this case the control point inferred
to make the curve smooth is on the line that connects the second control
point to the first end point and at an equal distance from that end point. As
the curve has to be tangent to this line as it approaches and leaves the first
end point, you can see that this does give a smooth curve. Notice that now we
have more control over how the curve is continued because we have the final
end point and its control point.

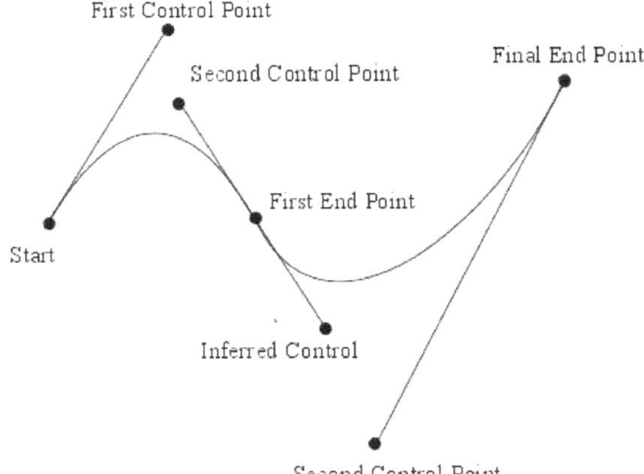

For example:

```
path1=new Path2D("M50 100 C100 50 150 200 200 100 S250 50 300 100");
```

produces:

Creating Bezier Paths

Bezier paths are powerful but they are difficult to draw by just programming.
In most cases if you want a circle or an ellipse, or even a simple shape such as
an arrow, you can put together the commands needed to create it. When it
comes to more complex shapes then you need help. There are a number of
different ways of obtaining or creating Bezier paths.

The first is tc use one of the many SVG icons that are available for free on the
web. For example the following is a search icon and this is the path tag that
creates it.

```
<path d="M31.008 27.231l-7.58-6.447c-0.784-0.705-1.622-1.029-2.299-
0.998 1.789-2.096 2.87-4.815 2.87-7.787 0-6.627-5.373-12-12-12s-12
5.373-12 12 5.373 12 12 12c2.972 0 5.691-1.081 7.787-2.87-0.031
0.677 0.293 1.515 0.998 2.299l6.447 7.58c1.104 1.226 2.907 1.33
4.007 0.23s0.997-2.903-0.23-4.007zM12 20c-4.418 0-8-3.582-8-8s3.582-
8 8-8 8 3.582 8 8-3.582 8-8 8z"></path>
```

To use this you simply put the path drawing commands into a string and
create the path:

```
path1=new Path2D("M31.008 27.231l-7.58-6.447c-0.784-0.705-1.622-
1.029-2.299-0.998 1.789-2.096 2.87-4.815 2.87-7.787 0-6.627-5.373-
12-12-12s-12 5.373-12 12 5.373 12 12 12c2.972 0 5.691-1.081 7.787-
2.87-0.031 0.677 0.293 1.515 0.998 2.299l6.447 7.58c1.104 1.226
2.907 1.33 4.007 0.23s0.997-2.903-0.23-4.007zM12 20c-4.418 0-8-
3.582-8-8s3.582-8 8-8 8 3.582 8 8-3.582 8-8 8z");
```

which produces:

The only real problem that can occur is that the path uses absolute
positioning. In the example above you can see that there is an `M31.008
27.231` at the start and an `M12 20` towards the end. The first is easy to deal
with as it can simply be removed as the rest of the instructions will then be
relative to the current position. The second is slightly more difficult. It
follows a z command which closes the first curve and moves the current
position back to the start, i.e. `31.008, 27.231`. Relative to this the point
`12,20` is at `-19.008 -7.23`. So the second move command can be made
relative.

The complete string is:

```
path1=new Path2D("M100 100 l-7.58-6.447c-0.784-0.705-1.622-1.029-
2.299-0.998 1.789-2.096 2.87-4.815 2.87-7.787 0-6.627-5.373-12-12-
12s-12 5.373-12 12 5.373 12 12 12c2.972 0 5.691-1.081 7.787-2.87-
0.031 0.677 0.293 1.515 0.998 2.299l6.447 7.58c1.104 1.226 2.907
1.33 4.007 0.23s0.997-2.903-0.23-4.007zm-19.008 -7.23c-4.418 0-8-
3.582-8-8s3.582-8 8-8 8 3.582 8 8-3.582 8-8 8z");
```

where the absolute move has been added to the start to draw the icon at
`100,100`. Having a completely relative path allows you to set the position of
the entire path very easily.

An alternative way of creating complex Bezier curve paths is to use an editor.
InkScape is a full function SVG editor which you can use to draw a shape and
read off the path as a string.

For example if you use the Bezier tool to draw a rocket ship outline:

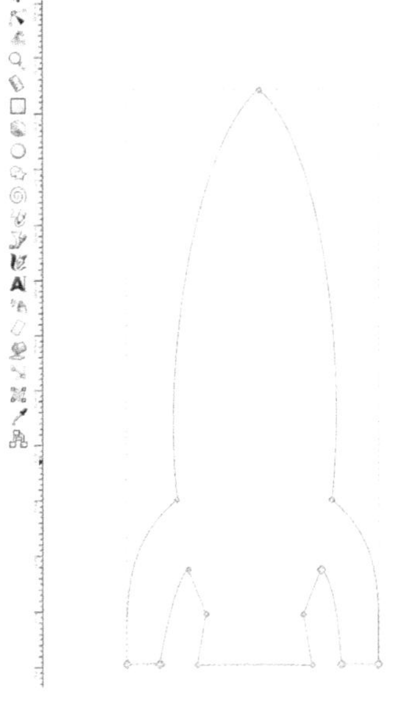

You can use the command `Edit,XML editor` to open the XML editor window. In this you can find the path that corresponds to the shape and copy the d property:

Copying the path to a string gives:

```
path1=new Path2D( "m 98.684674,206.63833 c 2.891926,-25.77092
-1.958475,-65.0136 -13.037221,-73.92172 -11.072474,8.90817
-17.526591,48.1508 -14.634563,73.92172 -9.479011,8.46903
-9.015897,17.40218 -9.068381,29.71617 l 5.92022,-0.074 c 0,0
2.493141,-15.15787 5.105513,-16.98251 l 3.15542,8.06751
-1.537022,9.15649 c 13.277647,-0.17974 7.242537,-0.17974 20.52018,0
l -1.537022,-9.15649 3.15552,-8.06751 c 2.979241,2.08093
3.605942,17.00168 3.605942,17.00168 l 6.61799,0.0548 c -0.0526,-
12.31399 1.21238,-21.24714 -8.266576,-29.71617 z");
```

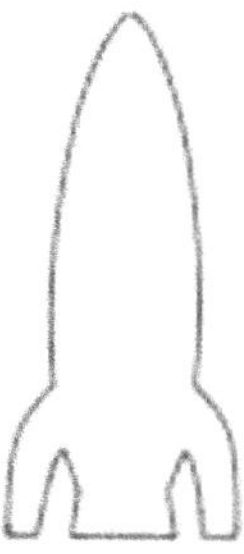

All of the commands after the first m are relative so you can position the rocket anywhere you want it by changing the initial m co-ordinates.

There are many other graphics editors which can be used to create paths. Usually the end product isn't as neat as a hand-crafted path but it is much easier.

Using Multiple Paths

One way of approaching Canvas graphics is to break the drawing down into separate paths which you use to create the final image. You can duplicate paths using the constructor:

```
Var path2= New Path2D(path1);
```

creates `path2` as a copy of `path1`. You can then make additions to the copy using the standard path functions.

The `addPath` function can also be used to merge paths:

```
path2.addPath(path1);
```

adds `path1` to `path2`. This is more useful than you might expect because you can also specify a transformation matrix:

```
path2.addPath(path1,transform);
```

This means you can move, scale and rotate the path being added. To make use of this you need to know how to specify a transformation matrix, which is a topic we cover in Chapter 5.

In many cases it is simpler to use multiple paths to draw on the canvas directly rather than combining them into a single path before rendering.

Drawing Without Paths

There are four canvas methods that draw directly without the use of a path. The first is `fillRect`, the second is `strokeRect`, the third is `clearRect`, and the fourth is `fillText`, which is discussed in Chapter 6.

They all work by changing pixels in the canvas without creating or modifying a path.

For example:

```
ctx.fillRect(x,y,w,h);
```

draws a rectangle in the current `fillStyle` with its top left corner at `x,y` with width `w` and height `h`.

Similarly:

```
ctx.strokeRect(x,y,w,h);
```

draws the same rectangle but using the current `strokeStyle`.

The clearRect command:

```
ctx.clearRect(x,y,w,h);
```

is slightly strange in that it doesn't just clear a rectangle of pixels to a specified color but to transparent black - `rgba(0,0,0,0)`.

If you try it cut you might conclude that it clears the rectangle to white, but this is a misinterpretation. As it clears the rectangle to 100% transparency, what you see is the default white of the web page behind it. If you place the canvas on a colored or patterned background this is what you see when you clear a rectangle. The main use of `clearRect` is in animation where it is used to provide a cleared canvas ready for the next frame to be drawn onto it.

It is important to note that any color with 100% transparency is regarded as a background pixel.

Summary

- The fundamental way to draw on a canvas object is to define a path – an outline of a shape.

- Once you have a path you can use `stroke`, which draws a line along the path, or `fill` which fills the path with a solid color or pattern.

- You can avoid creating a path object by using the default `Path` object associated with the canvas. In most cases it is better to define path objects as these are reusable.

- The basic path creation methods are `rect`, `arc`, `ellipse` and two types of Bezier curve.

- You can also use the SVG path command which has many advantages. It is more like a mini-language for describing shapes.

- In many cases it is easier to use an application such as InkScape to draw paths and then transfer them to your program using an SVG path string.

- There are also a few methods that draw directly to the canvas without creating a `Path` or interacting with the default `Path`.

- The `clearRect` method clears the area to transparent black which is the default color for "background" pixels.

Paths are mathematical abstractions – lines of zero width and no color connecting mathematically exact points in a co-ordinate system. To convert a path into something physical it has to be rendered to the canvas bitmap. There are two way to do this, `stroke` and `fill`. The `stroke` function simply colors the outline of the path whereas the `fill` colors all of the points in the interior of the path. This all sounds easy and obvious, but in practice it is subtle and you need to understand it to get control of what exactly is happening.

For both `fill` and `stroke` a fundamental is how to specify color. So this is where we have to start.

Color

Color relies on using the CSS color data type and you can specify a color by one of the standard CSS color names. The big problem is that the names available for use have been added to over time. In CSS level 1 there were only 16 colors whereas in CSS level 3 the full X11 set was added. If you want to specify a color using a name then look up the full list on the web – you are safe to use black, white, red, green, yellow, blue, etc.

If you want to specify an exact or a custom color then specify the amount of Red, Green and Blue to mix to get the color. The only complication is that it is usual to use hexadecimal notation. A hexadecimal digit is one of 0 to 9, A, B, C, D, E and F. Two hex digits specify an eight-bit number, i.e. in the range 0 to 255, and a color value is two hex digits for each of Red, Green and Blue.

To indicate a hex color value you precede the number by # and so a color value is of the form `#RRGGBB`. For example, `#FF0000` is red, `#00FF00` is green, `#0000FF` is blue and `#FFFFFF` is white. You can use lower case if you want to. Many colors are specified using RGB hex notation and many color pickers will give you the color using the same format.

If you don't like hexadecimal values then you can use the alternative `rgb`
function. This will accept an R, G, B value specified in decimal, i.e. `0` to `255`,
or using a percentage. For example:

`rgb(255,0,0)`

and:

`rgb(100%,0,0)`

are both red.

In addition to specifying color using the RGB system, you can also specify it
using the HSL system. HSL stands for Hue, Saturation and Lightness and
many find it a more intuitive system. In this case Hue is an angle on the color
wheel specified in degrees (the default), radians, grads or turns. Saturation
and Lightness are specified as percentages. To specify a color using HSL you
use the `hsl` function.

For example:

`hsl(120,50%,70%)`

is a shade of green.

Alpha

As well as specifying color you can also specify an alpha value which
indicates the transparency of the color. You can add an alpha value to either
the `rgb` or the hsl function. Alpha ranges from `0.0` (fully transparent) to `1.0`
(fully opaque). There are also older `rgba` and `hsla` functions which work in
the same way as `rgb` and `hsl` but require an alpha value as the fourth
parameter.

For example:

`rgb(255,0,0,0.5);`

and:

`rgba(255,0,0,0.5);`

both set a color of pure red with a transparency of 50%.

You can also set an alpha value when using hexadecimal notation in the
format `#RRGGBBAA`. In this case alpha varies between `00` (fully transparent) and
`FF` (fully opaque).

If you leave out the alpha value `FF` is the default.

For example:

```
#FF0000FF
```

and:

```
#FF0000
```

both set a pure red with no transparency.

As well as setting alpha values for particular colors you can also set it globally for all colors – more of this later.

You can also set a global alpha value that is used to draw all objects:

```
ctx.globalAlpha=value;
```

After this you only have to specify an RGB value or a color name and the chosen alpha value will be used automatically.

Stroke and Fill Color

Now that we know how to specify a color we can see how to set the color of the stroke and fill. All you have to do is is specify the color using the CSS color strings described in the previous sections as the value of the drawing context's `strokeStyle` or `fillStyle` property.

For example:

```
var path1 = new Path2D();
path1.arc(20, 200, 20, 0, 2 * Math.PI);
ctx.fillStyle = "#FF0000FF";
ctx.strokeStyle = "#00FF00FF";
ctx.fill(path1);
ctx.stroke(path1);
```

This draws a red filled circle with a green outline. Notice that the color specification is a string. This doesn't seem so unreasonable for a hexadecimal specifier, but even if you use a function it still has to be a string.

For example:

```
ctx.fillStyle = "rgb(255,0,0,1.0)";
```

specifies the same color. The `rgb` and `hls` functions may look like functions, but they are used as strings.

If the color functions have to be used as strings how can we set a computed color?

Before ES2015 the only way of doing this would be to use string handling functions to construct the color specification.

For example:

```
var red=Math.random()*255;
ctx.fillStyle = "rgb("+ red.toString()+",0,0,1.0)";
```

This creates a random integer between 0 and 255 and then builds a string that uses it as the red specification in the rgb function. You don't need the toString call as JavaScript will convert the number into a string automatically. Each time the program is run you will see a different shade of red.

After ES2015 a simpler method is to use string template literals. A template is like a string literal but you have to use backticks rather than single or double quotes. You can also enclose any expression in ${} and it will be evaluated and its toString function used to convert to a string and add it to the rest of the literal.

For example:

```
var red=Math.random()*255;
ctx.fillStyle = `rgb( ${red},0,0,1.0)`;
```

is equivalent to the previous string expression.

Stroke Properties

There are a set of properties of the drawing context which change the way a path is stroked starting with the most fundamental which sets the width of the stroke:

```
ctx.lineWidth = value;
```

The value is the width in the co-ordinate system. By default this is set to 1.0 and the stroke is drawn equally each side of the path. That is, the path defines a line centered on the path with half the width to either side. Because of the way antialiasing works, this has some unexpected consequences, see the next section.

The lineCap property sets the way a line ends. The possible values are butt, round or square. The only real problem with lineCap is working out exactly what the types correspond to. The default, butt, simply ends the line where you specify, using a straight edge, round puts a small semicircle on the end, so lengthening the line by its LineWidth, and square does the same thing, but with a square.

You can see the effect of `lineCap` using the following program:

```
ctx.lineWidth = 10;
var path1 = new Path2D();
path1.moveTo(100, 300);
path1.lineTo(500, 300);
ctx.lineCap = "butt";
ctx.stroke(path1);
var path2 = new Path2D();
path2.moveTo(100, 320);
path2.lineTo(500, 320);
ctx.lineCap = "round";
ctx.stroke(path2);
var path3 = new Path2D();
path3.moveTo(100, 340);
path3.lineTo(500, 340);
ctx.lineCap = "square";
ctx.stroke(path3);
```

This draws three lines, each with a different `lineCap`:

You can see that the round and square `lineCap`s really do make the line

longer. The round cap is useful if you want a decorative line, an underlining
say, but what is the use of the square `lineCap`? The answer is the way two
disconnected lines meet. For example, if you draw a right angle to the same
point using two butt ends the result has a small square missing:

If you use square ends however the result is a sharp corner:

Notice that this only applies if the two lines are not connected, i.e. not part of a closed sub-path. If the lines are connected then what controls the way that they connect is the `lineJoin` property, which can be set to any of `bevel`, `round` or `miter` (default). The `miter` join is usually what you expect to happen when lines join – their outside edges are extended to where they meet:

The problem with miter joins is that for lines that meet at very sharp angles the miter can be very long – often longer than the lines themselves. To keep this under control there is another drawing context property you can set, `miterLimit`. This sets the maximum distance between the inner and outer corners if the miter was drawn. The default is `10` and if the `miter` is longer than this it isn't drawn and a `bevel` is used:

This raises the question, what is a `bevel`? It simply draws a line between the two outer corners of the lines and fills in the triangle:

Finally `round` draws a disc centered on the common endpoint with a radius equal to the thickness of the lines.

For example:

```
var path1 = new Path2D();
path1.moveTo(100, 300);
path1.lineTo(500, 300);
path1.lineTo(100, 350);
ctx.lineJoin = "miter";
ctx.lineWidth = 10;
ctx.miterLimit = 100;
ctx.stroke(path1);
```

draws:

If you set `miterLimit` to 10 the result is:

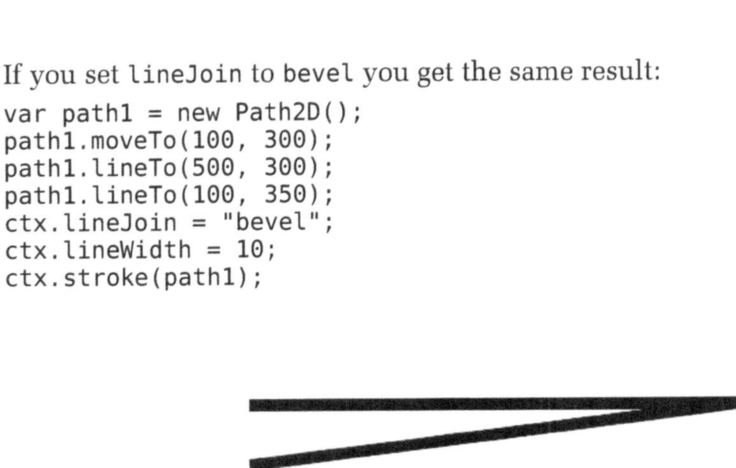

If you set `lineJoin` to `bevel` you get the same result:

```
var path1 = new Path2D();
path1.moveTo(100, 300);
path1.lineTo(500, 300);
path1.lineTo(100, 350);
ctx.lineJoin = "bevel";
ctx.lineWidth = 10;
ctx.stroke(path1);
```

Changing `lineJoin` to "round"

```
ctx.lineJoin = "round";
```

gives the following result:

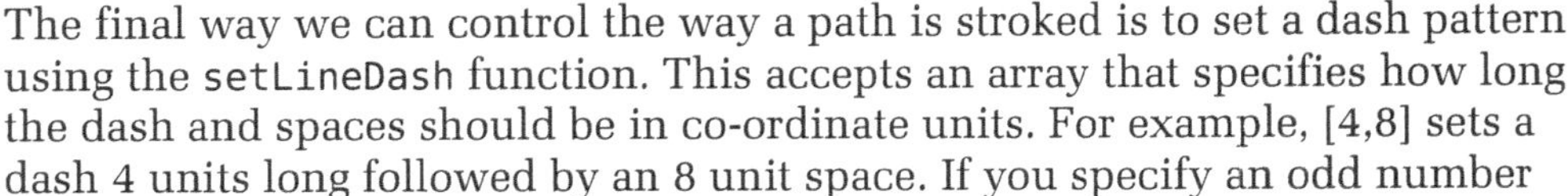

The final way we can control the way a path is stroked is to set a dash pattern using the `setLineDash` function. This accepts an array that specifies how long the dash and spaces should be in co-ordinate units. For example, [4,8] sets a dash 4 units long followed by an 8 unit space. If you specify an odd number of elements in the array, the array is doubled in length to make it even. For example, [4,8,2] becomes [4,8,2,4,8,2]. You can also specify the current dash array using the `getLineDash` function. To set the line back to solid use an empty array:

```
ctx.setLineDash([]);
```

There is one last control you can use, the `lineDashOffset`. This starts the dash pattern at the co-ordinate given by the offset. Notice that the offset is relative to the dash pattern and just indicates where to start the pattern.

For example:

```
var path1 = new Path2D();
path1.moveTo(0, 50);
path1.lineTo(300, 50);
ctx.setLineDash([4, 16]);
ctx.stroke(path1);
```

draws a line with dashes of 4 pixels followed by a 16-pixel space.

■ ■ ■ ■ ■ ■ ■ ■ ■ ■ ■ ■ ■ ■ ■ ■

If we set the offset to 4 then the pattern starts with the 16-pixel space. If we set it to 2 then the pattern starts halfway though the first 4-pixel dash:

❙ ■ ■ ■ ■ ■ ■ ■ ■ ■ ■ ■ ■ ■ ■ ❙

Although we have yet to deal with animation, the "marching ants" program is too good to miss. All that happens is that you animate a line by changing the dash offset by one each time. For example:

```
var ctx = document.body.
              appendChild(createCanvas(600, 600)).getContext("2d");
var path1 = new Path2D();
path1.rect(0, 50, 200, 200);
var offset = 0;
ctx.setLineDash([4, 2]);
function march() {
    offset = (offset+1) % 16;
    ctx.clearRect(0, 0, ctx.canvas.width, ctx.canvas.height);
    ctx.lineDashOffset = offset;
    ctx.stroke(path1);
    requestAnimationFrame(march);
}
march();
```

This repeatedly draws the dashed line after changing the offset by one. The effect is very good for so little effort.

Antialiasing

If you draw a horizontal line between two integer co-ordinates you would
expect that all the pixels between the two lines would be set and no other
pixels. This isn't what happens as antialiasing is applied.

In many cases you can simply ignore antialiasing and accept that it provides
better looking graphics than you would achieve without its help. However,
there are times when you draw something that just doesn't look as you
expect. This usually occurs when the shape you are drawing is the size of a
few pixels. If you draw nothing but large shapes then antialiasing is your
friend. First we need to know how antialiasing works and how it produces the
final bitmap pattern that you see displayed.

The idea of antialiasing is to spread the color value over all of the pixels that
intersect with the location. For example, if you assign black to a point 3,3
then this is the location of a single pixel and that pixel is set to black. Now
imagine you assign black to a point 3.5,3.5. This intersects four pixels - which
pixel do you set to black? One possible answer is all four. A better answer is
to assign each the amount of color that overlaps with them. In this case a
quarter of the color is in each of the four pixels, so each is set to a shade of
gray. This is antialiasing and when you are drawing large shapes it makes
things look smoother by hiding the pixel boundaries.

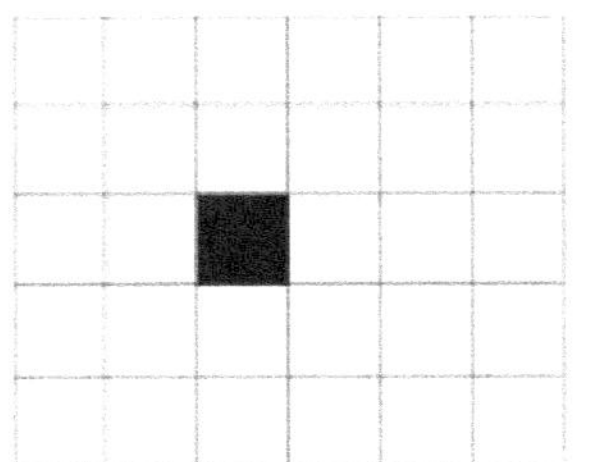 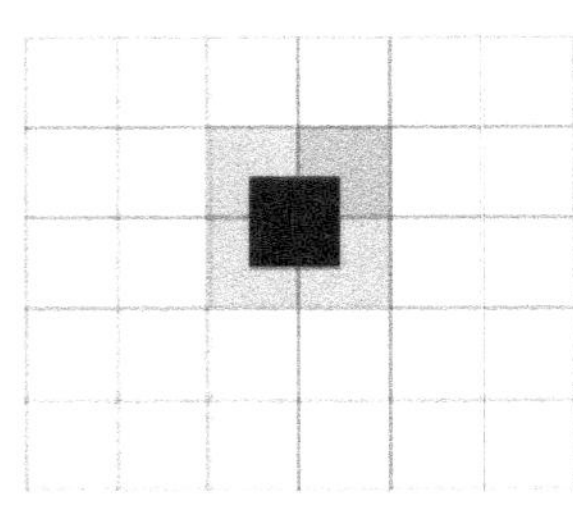

You can see antialiasing in operation by drawing a line at an angle.

Without antialiasing the line would consists of a very obvious staircase of black pixels as shown on the left. Viewed at a distance that makes the pixels small, the antialiased line looks a lot better than the jagged line. For this reason antialiasing is turned on by default and there is no way to turn it off.

As well as knowing how it works, you also have to be aware that it can have some unexpected effects. Returning to the question posed at the start of the section, what happens when you draw a straight horizontal line between integer co-ordinates? In this case you would not expect antialiasing effects because the path passes though just one row of pixels. But it does have an effect because when you draw a line of thickness t, the line is drawn with the path centered, i.e. t/2 on one side and t/2 on the other side.

Consider:

```
var path1 = new Path2D();
path1.moveTo(100, 200);
path1.lineTo(500, 200);
path1.moveTo(100, 210.5);
path1.lineTo(500, 210.5);
ctx.lineWidth = 1;
ctx.fillRect(250, 205, 1, 1);
ctx.stroke(path1);
```

This draws two parallel lines. The only difference is that the first one is exactly on a pixel co-ordinate row and the other is halfway between two rows. The first line actually overlaps two rows of pixels, as can be seen in the diagram below. Where the solid line shows is where it intersects with two rows of pixels. Antialiasing spreads this over two rows and the result is a line two pixels wide and in gray. The second line is in the middle of a pixel row and hence it only affects a single line of pixels – it is a one pixel wide black line.

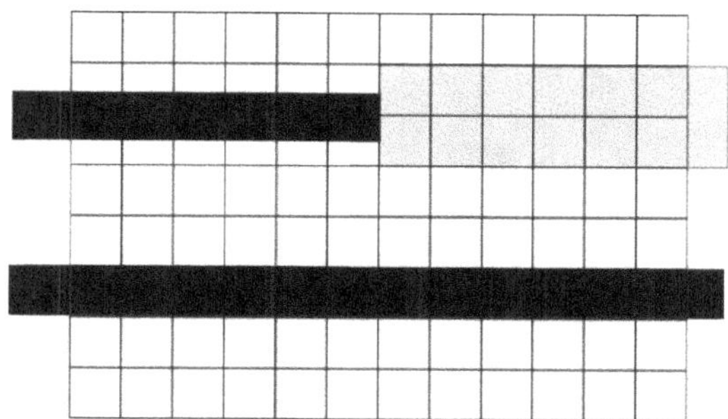

You can see that this happens in practice from the following screenshot, where the dot between the lines is a single pixel for scale:

The anti-aliasing problem occurs for fills just as much for stroke, but as the majority of the interior of a shape encompasses whole pixels it is only visible at the edges.

For example is you want to draw a single pixel you might try using:

```
ctx.fillRect(50, 50, 1, 1);
ctx.fillRect(50.5, 60.5, 1, 1);
```

The first instruction draws a filled rectangle with top left corner at 50,50 and the second with the top corner at 50.5 and 60.5. Both rectangles are one pixel in size but the results are different:

The reason should be fairly obvious. The first co-ordinate places the rectangle over a single pixel. The second places it in the middle of a group of four and hence these are shaded gray.

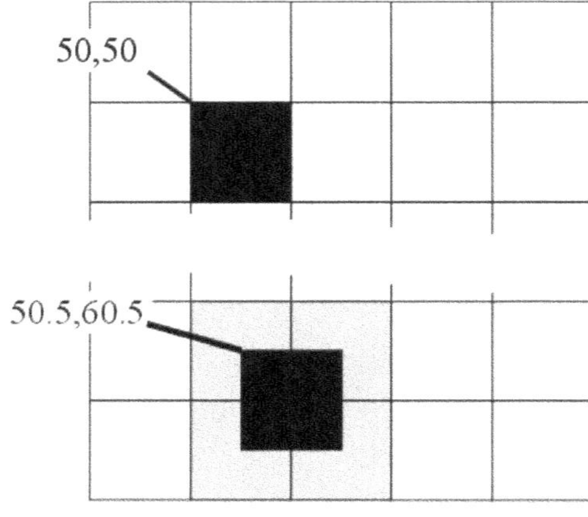

You can also appreciate that if you draw a line that is one pixel wide as part of an animation what the line looks like depends on where it is drawn and this can make a moving object look as if it is sparkling. The effect of antialiasing also depends on any scaling being performed and this includes both transformations that you might apply and any zoom the user has applied to the browser.

Notice that when drawing a line using the default co-ordinate system, co-ordinates like 1.5,0.5 pick out individual pixels, but when filling, integer co-ordinates pick out whole pixels.

You cannot turn antialiasing off and it is also used by the browser rendering engine.

Fill, Stroke and the Painter's Algorithm

You can combine a fill and a stroke and the effect that you get depends on the order that you perform them in. The basic principle is very simple - anything drawn after a given graphic will overwrite the graphic if they share pixels. This is generally called "the painter's algorithm" because it is exactly what happens with physical paint – new paint covers up old paint. The way that new color is applied to pixels is in general more complicated than simply covering up the old, but this is the default behavior.

For example if you try:

```
var path1 = new Path2D();
path1.rect(50, 50, 200, 100);
ctx.lineWidth = 10;
ctx.strokeStyle = "black";
ctx.fillStyle = "lightgray";
ctx.fill(path1);
ctx.stroke(path1);
```

then what you will see is a gray rectangle with a 10-pixel outline as the rectangle is filled and then the outline is drawn over it. If you change the order of the fill and stroke functions then the result is a gray rectangle with a 5-pixel outline as the fill now covers the inner portion of the stroke.

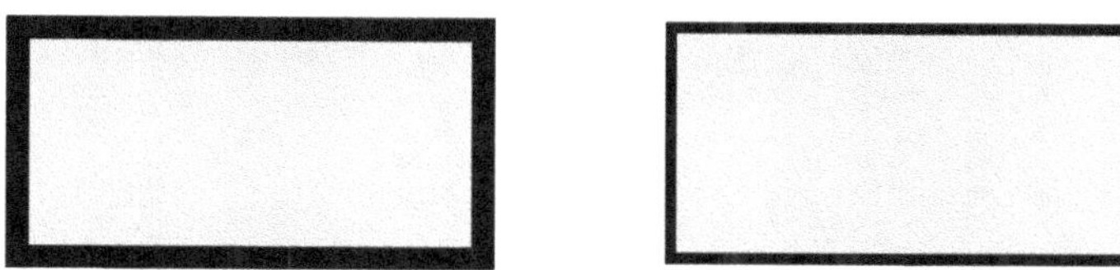

Holes and Fill

A path can intersect with itself and in this case the question is how is the path filled? This can seem like a complicated question, but it is answered very simply. A point is either inside or outside of the path. If it is inside then it is part of the fill and if it is outside of the path it isn't filled.

For simple connected paths, the question can be answered quite easily. If you pick a point and draw a line from it to infinity, a ray, if the line intersects with the path once the point is inside; if it intersects twice it is outside. More generally a point that has a ray that intersects an odd number of times is an interior point and if it intersects an even number of times it is an exterior point.

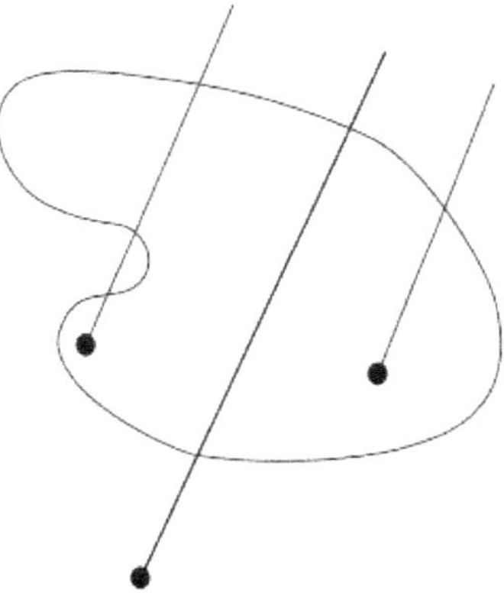

This is called the odd-even rule and you can use it to determine how paths are filled. For example, consider the star path made of two triangle sub-paths. Is the central area a hole or part of the interior? Using the odd-even rule you can see that the central area is an exterior region and should not be filled.

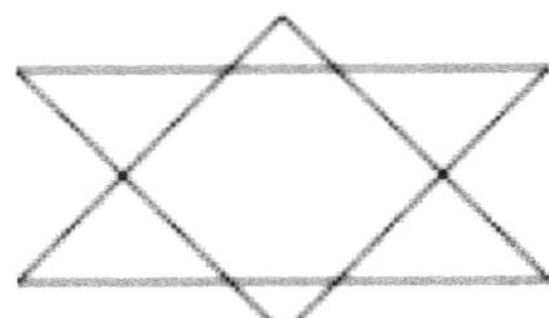

If you set the "evenodd" option in the fill then this is exactly what you see:

```
var Path1 = new Path2D();
Path1.moveTo(50, 50);
Path1.lineTo(100, 100);
Path1.lineTo(0, 100);
Path1.lineTo(50, 50);
Path1.moveTo(50, 110);
Path1.lineTo(0, 60);
Path1.lineTo(100, 60);
Path1.lineTo(50, 110);
ctx.stroke(Path1);
ctx.fill(Path1, "evenodd");
```

The odd-even rule is just one of the possible ways of defining the interior of a complex path. The non-zero winding rule is another, that also happens to be the default for the fill function. It works in the same way, but now we also take into account the direction that the path takes around a point.

The basic idea is that if the path winds around a point in the same direction then it is inside. The motivation comes from the physical intuition that if you surround a nail by a piece of string, representing the path, then if the nail is inside the path you cannot pull the string off the nail, but if it is outside the string is not "hung" on the nail. If you count a clockwise intersection with the path as +1 and an anticlockwise intersection with the path as -1 then the winding number is the sum of the values. For example in the example below the path intersects the ray once in the clockwise and once in the anticlockwise direction hence its winding number is zero and it is outside of the path.

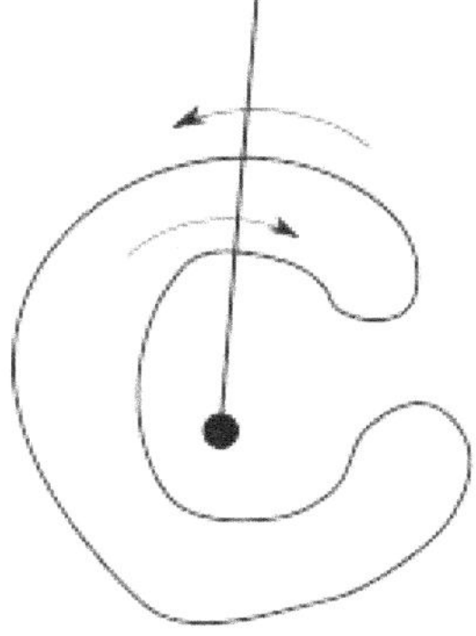

For connected curves a winding number of zero makes sense, but for disconnected curves things are slightly arbitrary. It is often believed that the non-zero rule fills in "holes" whereas the "odd-even" rule doesn't. This isn't exactly true.

For example, if we change the star path fill rule to:

```
ctx.fill(Path1, "nonzero");
```

then the hole is filled:

However, this is only because the two disconnected paths are drawn in the same sense – i.e. anticlockwise. If the second triangle is changed to:

```
Path1.moveTo(50, 110);
Path1.lineTo(100, 60);
Path1.lineTo(0, 60);
Path1.lineTo(50, 110);
```

it is drawn in the opposite sense to the first triangle and the winding number of a point in the middle is now zero and hence the hole is not filled:

So what happens to a "hole" in a shape depends on which way you draw the disconnected path that fills it.

How do you work out the fill rule to use in any given case?

Most often you simply try it out and see. If a hole that you want to have unfilled is being filled then you can either change the direction you draw it in or try the odd-even rule.

For example, consider the space ship path introduced in the previous chapter.
We could add a "port hole" by adding a circle path to it:

```
var Path1 = new Path2D("m 98.684674,206.63833
c 2.891926,-25.77092 -1.958475,-65.0136 -13.037221,
  -73.92172 -11.072474,8.90817 -17.526591,48.1508 -14.634563,
  73.92172 -9.479011,8.46903 -9.015897,17.40218 -9.068381,29.71617
l 5.92022,-0.074
c 0,0 2.493141,-15.15787 5.105513,-16.98251
l 3.15542, 8.06751 -1.537022,9.15649
c 13.277647,-0.17974 7.242537,-0.17974 20.52018,0
l -1.537022,-9.15649 3.15552,-8.06751
c 2.979241,2.08093 3.605942,17.00168 3.605942,17.00168
l 6.61799,0.9548
c -0.0526,-12.31399 1.21238,-21.24714 -8.266576,-29.71617 z");
var Path2 = new Path2D();
Path2.arc(85, 180, 10, 0, 2 * Math.PI, 0);
Path1.addPath(Path2);
ctx.fill(Path1, "nonzero");
```

If we fill the path using the non-zero rule then the hole will not be filled if the
circle is drawn in the same direction as the outer path:

However, if you change the `arc` function to:

```
Path2.arc(85, 180, 10, 0, 2 * Math.PI, 1);
```

i.e. draw the circle in the opposite direction, then the port hole will be filled
in.

Gradient Fills

As well as solid colors you can also define fills that are gradients between a range of colors in both linear and radial configurations. Although these are described here as fills they can be applied to `fillStyle` or `strokeStyle`.

A linear gradient is created using:

```
var grad=ctx.createLinearGradient(x1,y1,x2,y2);
```

where `x1,y1` and `x2,y2` are the start and end points of the gradient line. The gradient line gives the angle that the gradient is at and the distance over which the colors change. To specify the actual colors involved you need to set any number of color stops:

```
grad.addColorStop(p,color);
```

where `color` specifies the color and `p` the proportion along the gradient line that the color is applied, i.e. `0` is the starting point, `1` is the end point and `0.5` is the mid point.

For example:

```
var gradient = ctx.createLinearGradient(0, 0, 400, 0);
gradient.addColorStop(0, 'green');
gradient.addColorStop(1, 'red');
```

defines a gradient starting at `0,0` and ending at `400,0`. The color at `0,0` is `green` and at `400,0` is `red`. Notice that the gradient is defined relative to the global co-ordinate system and not relative to any path that you might apply it to. As a demonstration of this consider drawing a set of rectangles each shifted in the x direction:

```
var path1 = new Path2D();
path1.rect(0, 0, 400, 100);
path1.rect(100, 110, 400, 100);
path1.rect(200, 220, 400, 100);
path1.rect(300, 330, 400, 100);
path1.rect(400, 440, 400, 100);
var gradient = ctx.createLinearGradient(0, 0, 400, 0);
gradient.addColorStop(0, 'green');
gradient.addColorStop(1, 'red');
ctx.fillStyle = gradient;
ctx.fill(path1);
```

Notice that only the first rectangle is filled with the complete gradient. The final rectangle is just red because it is beyond the gradient's end point.

You can think of this as defining a gradient across the entire canvas and whatever you fill gets the portion of the gradient at its location.

Setting multiple color stop points makes some special effects easier. For example:

```
var path1 = new Path2D();
path1.rect(0, 0, 400, 100);
var gradient = ctx.createLinearGradient(0, 0, 400, 0);
gradient.addColorStop(0, 'darkred');
gradient.addColorStop(0.08, 'red');
gradient.addColorStop(0.5, 'white');
gradient.addColorStop(0.92, 'red');
gradient.addColorStop(1, 'darkred');
ctx.fillStyle = gradient;
ctx.fill(path1);
```

creates the illusion of a curved surface with light coming from the front:

Notice that you can increase the rate at which a color falls off by adding more
color stop points. For example to make the white area in the middle of the
rectangle wider all you have to do is use two white color stops:

```
gradient.addColorStop(0, 'darkred');
gradient.addColorStop(0.08, 'red');
gradient.addColorStop(0.4, 'white');
gradient.addColorStop(0.6, 'white');
gradient.addColorStop(0.92, 'red');
gradient.addColorStop(1, 'darkred');
```

There is also a radial gradient fill, but it is slightly different from any radial
fill you may have encountered in graphics programs. At first it might seem
that the way that the radial fill is implemented is complicated, but underlying
it is a very simple algorithm. The fill is defined by two circles at given centers
and radii:

```
var grad=ctx.createRadialGradient(x1,y1,r1,x2,y2,r2);
```

The two circles don't have to be one inside the other, although in most
examples they are. What happens is that the first circle is drawn and then a
sequence of circles are drawn on the line connecting their centers, shrinking
or growing until we reach the second circle. For example, if the first circle is
smaller the sequence is something like:

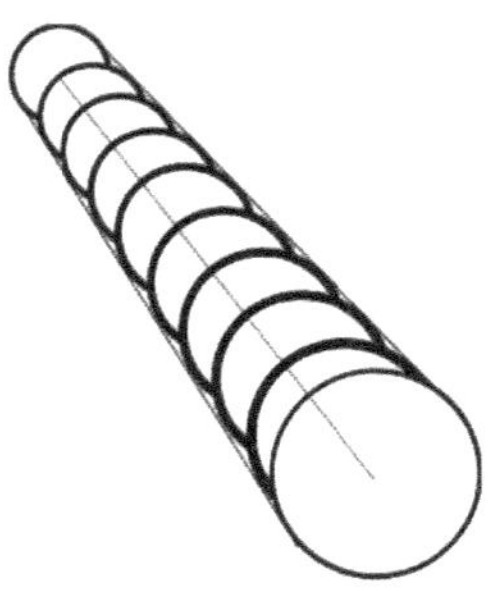

In practice the circles are filled and drawn much closer together. Of course, the color of the circles is also changed according to the specified stop colors. Also, if the fill is needed beyond the area shown, the sequence is extended with the circles growing larger or smaller, but staying in their final color.

This is easy to understand after a simple example:

```
var path1 = new Path2D();
path1.rect(0, 0, 400, 300);
var gradient = ctx.createRadialGradient(50, 50, 30, 150, 150, 80);
gradient.addColorStop(0, 'red');
gradient.addColorStop(.5, 'white');
gradient.addColorStop(1, 'blue');
ctx.fillStyle = gradient;
ctx.fill(path1);
```

In this case the first circle is small and to the top left and the second is larger and to the bottom right. You can see the result in the diagram below where the position of the circles has been indicated so that you can see how things work:

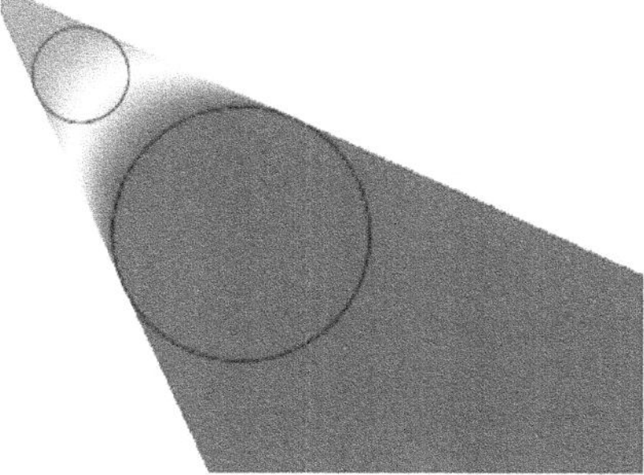

Notice that as the rectangle being filled is larger than the area of the two circles, the sequence continues with circles smaller than the first and larger than the second.

In most cases a radial fill isn't specified with two circles positioned as above. The most common arrangement is to have the first circle large and the second smaller and positioned within the first.

For example:

```
var path1 = new Path2D();
path1.rect(0, 0, 400, 300);
var gradient = ctx.createRadialGradient(100,100, 100, 100, 100,20);
gradient.addColorStop(0, 'red');
gradient.addColorStop(.5, 'blue');
gradient.addColorStop(1, 'white');
ctx.fillStyle = gradient;
ctx.fill(path1);
```

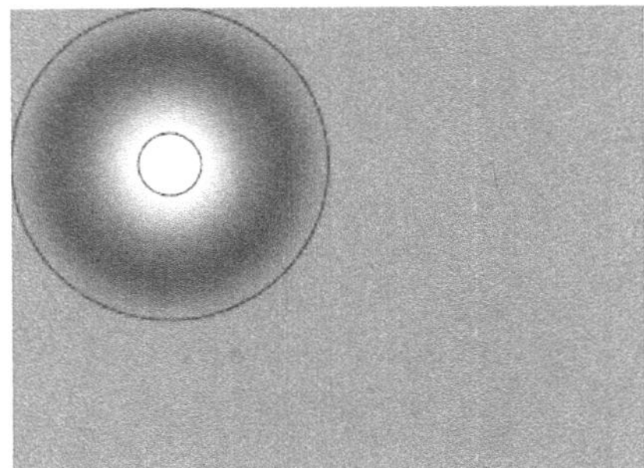

In this case the big red first circle is overwritten by the sequence of smaller circles going from red to blue then white.

A typical use of a radial fill is to suggest the lighting of a 3D curved surface. For example:

```
var path1 = new Path2D();
path1.arc(100, 100, 100, 0, 2*Math.PI);

var gradient = ctx.createRadialGradient(100,100, 100, 170, 170,10);
gradient.addColorStop(0, 'red');
gradient.addColorStop(1, 'white');
ctx.fillStyle = gradient;
ctx.fill(path1);
```

In this case the second circle is very small and positioned on the edge of the larger circle. With some experimentation you can generally create effective pseudo 3D lighting effects.

Pattern Fills

The final type of fill that you can use is a pattern or bitmap fill. This is easy to understand and easy to use. You need to create a pattern before you use it:

```
ctc.createPattern(image, repeat);
```

To fill an arbitrary object the pattern specified by the `image` is likely to need to be repeated and the `repeat` parameter is a string that determines how this is done:

- `"repeat"` (both directions)
- `"repeat-x"` (horizontal only)
- `"repeat-y"` (vertical only)
- `"no-repeat"` (neither direction)

The default is repeat.

The source of the pattern can be any of:

- `HTMLImageElement` (<img>)
- `SVGImageElement` (<image>)
- `HTMLVideoElement` (<video>)
- `HTMLCanvasElement` (<canvas>)
- `ImageBitmap`
- `OffscreenCanvas`

Some of these are obvious and some are described in later chapters. The biggest problem in using many of these sources is knowing when they are ready to be used.

For example:

```
var img = new Image();
img.src = 'url of graphics file';
var pattern = ctx.createPattern(img, 'repeat');
ctx.fillStyle = pattern;
ctx.fillRect(0, 0, 300, 300);
```

This is a very standard way of loading a bitmap without involving any markup. The `Image` object starts to download the file as soon as its `src` property is set to a URL but it does this in the background. You cannot simply continue and use the image as if it was downloaded – sometimes you might be lucky, other times strange things will happen.

The correct way to do the job is to use the onload event to wait until the file
has loaded:

```
var img = new Image();
img.src = 'url of graphics file';
img.onload = function() {
  var pattern = ctx.createPattern(img, 'repeat');
  ctx.fillStyle = pattern;
  ctx.fillRect(0, 0, 300, 300);
}
```

This is easy enough but notice that now the rest of your graphics code has to
be in the callback function and this is a nuisance. There are better ways to
organize the code using promises or using async and await, but an even
better idea is to avoid asynchronously loading bitmaps wherever possible.
For example, if we place the graphic in the page using an <img> tag with id
bitmap1 then we can use it as a pattern source:

```
window.onload=function(){
var img = document.getElementById('bitmap1');
  var pattern = ctx.createPattern(img, 'repeat');
  ctx.fillStyle = pattern;
  ctx.fillRect(0, 0, 300, 300);
  };
```

The window.onload event only fires after all of the resources have loaded. In
this case the advantage is that you would write your entire graphics program
as the load event callback function. If you don't want the image to be seen
you can hide it.

Another way of avoiding an asynchronous load is to draw the pattern using
another canvas or an Offscreencanvas (see later).

This only works if the pattern can be easily and quickly drawn:

```
var myPath = new Path2D();
myPath.moveTo(25, 0);
myPath.lineTo(50, 50);
myPath.lineTo(0, 50);
myPath.lineTo(25, 0);

var c1 = document.createElement("canvas");
c1.width = 50;
c1.height = 50;
c1.getContext("2d").stroke(myPath);

var pattern = ctx.createPattern(c1, 'repeat');
ctx.fillStyle = pattern;
ctx.fillRect(0, 0, 800, 800);
```

Notice that the second canvas object doesn't have to be added to the DOM and so doesn't show.

There are many other ways of creating bitmaps suitable for use in patterns – see Chapter 8.

Summary

- The `stroke` function simply colors the outline of the path, whereas `fill` colors all of the points in the interior of the path.

- Color can be specified by name, RGB components or HSL.

- Alpha values control the transparency of the color, with `1.0` being opaque and `0.0` being completely transparent.

- For stroke you can set the `lineWidth`, `lineCap`, `lineJoin` and `lineDash`.

- Anti-aliasing makes drawing look smoother, but it can cause unexpected results for small details. It cannot be disabled.

- The simplest way of combining old and new colors is the painter's algorithm, which allows the latest color to cover up the old.

- Determining what is a "hole" in a closed path is difficult. There are two general rules, odd-even and non-zero winding, and they are both valid ways of defining a hole.

- As well as solid color fills, you can also use linear gradient and radial gradient fills.

- Pattern fills allow you to use any bitmap as a sort of "wallpaper" for the interior of paths.

So far we have been working with the default co-ordinate system that, apart from antialiasing concerns, is a pixel co-ordinate system. Canvas provides a full transformation facility that allows you to use any co-ordinate system you want to. Alternatively you can view it as a way of drawing paths at the location and scale that you require.

Transformations

The drawing context has a transformation matrix associated with it and every pair of co-ordinates is multiplied by this matrix before drawing occurs.

When the context is created the matrix is set to the identity, which means you are drawing using the default pixel co-ordinates. However, there is a set of methods that can be used to set the transform to anything you like.

A general transformation takes the form:

$$x' = ax + cy + e$$
$$y' = bx + dy + f$$

The values of a, c, b and d specify a rotation, a scaling or a skew depending on their values. The values e and f specify a shift of the origin to the new location e, f.

This is all you need to know, but to understand the way that these transformations are presented is it worth knowing about homogeneous co-ordinates.

The transformation can be written in matrix form as:

$$p' = Ap + t$$

where in terms of the previous transformation values we have:

$$A = \begin{pmatrix} a & c \\ b & c \end{pmatrix}$$

$$p' = \begin{pmatrix} x' \\ y' \end{pmatrix} \qquad p = \begin{pmatrix} x \\ y \end{pmatrix} \qquad t = \begin{pmatrix} e \\ f \end{pmatrix}$$

Notice that the rotation/scale/skew part of the transformation can be written as a matrix multiplication, but the translation is untidy in that we have to add another vector.

The whole transformation can be written as a single matrix multiplication if we add an extra dummy dimension, set to 1, that we simply ignore when actually drawing. That is, the transformation can be written in homogeneous co-ordinates as:

$$p' = Tp + t$$

where

$$T = \begin{pmatrix} a & c & e \\ b & d & f \\ 0 & 0 & 1 \end{pmatrix}$$

and

$$p' = \begin{pmatrix} x' \\ y' \\ 1 \end{pmatrix} \qquad p = \begin{pmatrix} x \\ y \\ 1 \end{pmatrix}$$

So now you know that homogeneous co-ordinates are just a trick that let us treat translation, along with rotation, etc, as part of a matrix multiplication.

This is how the canvas transformation works - you specify a 3x3 matrix in homogeneous co-ordinates - which is used to multiple the co-ordinates you specify before any drawing operation.

Now to return to the details of the programming. We have a method:

```
setTransform(a,b,c,d,e,f)
```

which sets the transformation to the matrix specified, and a method:

```
transform(a,b,c,d,e,f)
```

which multiplies the existing transformation matrix by the one specified.

Notice that multiplying transformations together effectively applies them one after another. If you want to reset the transformation use:

```
setTransform(1,0,0,1,0,0)
```

Transformation Functions

Setting the transformation in this general way is powerful, but also a bit abstract and difficult. To make things easier we also have:

- `scale(x,y)` which applies a scaling in the x and y direction to the transformation matrix
- `rotate(angle)` which applies a rotation `angle` in the clockwise direction; the angle is measured in radians
- `translate(x,y)` which performs a translation by x,y.

Notice that each of these multiplies the existing transformation matrix and so this allows the transformations to be applied one after the other. So:

```
ctx.rotate(Math.Pi());
ctx.translate(10,10);
```

first rotates the co-ordinate system and then translates it.

If you already know how matrices and transformation matrices work, this will be seem quite straightforward. If not, there are a lot of traps waiting to trip you up. The main one, that troubles just about everyone at first, is that the order in which you do things matters. A translation followed by a rotation isn't the same thing as a rotation followed by a translation. Try it if you don't believe me.

Another is that these transformations change the co-ordinate system and don't affect anything you have already drawn. They only change what happens when you draw something after the transformation has been applied.
For example, to draw a rectangle and rotate and draw another rectangle:

```
ctx.setTransform(1,0,0,1,0,0);
ctx.fillRect (0, 0, 50, 50);
ctx.rotate(Math.PI/4);
ctx.fillRect (200, 50, 50, 50);
```

In this case there is a 45 degree rotation, PI/4 in radians, after the first rectangle has been drawn and before the second is drawn. The result is that the first rectangle stays where it was but the second is rotated:

After the rotation, everything you draw will be at 45 degrees. Notice that the rotation is about the origin, i.e. `0,0` which is the top left corner. This also means that the second rectangle is not at `200,50` in the co-ordinate system of the first rectangle.

If you want to draw the second rectangle at `200,50` in the original co-ordinate system you have to use a more complicated algorithm. First move the origin of the co-ordinate system to 200,50, rotate 45 degrees, then draw the second rectangle at 0,0.

```
ctx.setTransform(1,0,0,1,0,0);
ctx.fillRect (0, 0, 50, 50);
ctx.translate(200,50);
ctx.rotate(Math.PI/4);
ctx.fillRect (0, 0, 50, 50);
```

Notice that the second rectangle is rotated about its top left corner.

Of course as you have changed the co-ordinate system this affects anything you subsequently draw. The solution is to return the co-ordinate system back to what it was before you changed it.

In this case it is simple as we are using the default co-ordinate system and we can set the default co-ordinate system simply by setting the transformation matrix back to the identity using:

```
ctx.setTransform(1,0,0,1,0,0);
```

If you aren't using the default co-ordinate system then you can save and restore the current transform matrix using the `save` and `restore` functions, see later.

There is a `currentTransform` property which can be read and written to access the current transform matrix. The only problem is that this isn't well supported at the time of writing and is best avoided.

A Logical Approach to Transforms

Transformations are key to making drawing on Canvas easy, but if you think about things in the wrong way it is very easy to make mistakes.

There are two ways to think about transformations – active and passive – and humans tend to prefer thinking about active transformations. An active transformation is one that actually changes what you have already drawn. Unfortunately, Canvas transformations are passive and change the co-ordinate system so that what is drawn next is changed and what is already drawn is unchanged.

As already mentioned, in general we find it easier to imagine what happens with active transformations. For example, one approach to working with transformations is to draw everything centered on the origin, and then translate, scale and rotate it to its final position. This is a good approach, but if you think of it as an active transformation then it doesn't work with Canvas.

For example, to draw the rectangle:

```
ctx.fillRect (200,350,160,160);
```

rotated through 45 degrees you would first draw a unit square centered on the origin, then you would then scale it to its desired size, rotate it about the origin and finally you would move it to its correct location:

```
ctx.fillRect (-0.5, -0.5, 1, 1);
ctx.scale(160,160);
ctx.rotate(Math.PI/4);
ctx.translate(200,350);
```

These are imagined to be active transformations and of course they don't work as imagined. The reason is that we have been transforming the object: draw a square, scale the square, rotate it and move it to the desired location. However, Canvas transformations don't transform objects but the co-ordinate system. You can immediately see that this means you should draw the square last after you have performed all of the transformations.

Indeed this is the rule:

- Do everything you would have done to the geometric shape using active transformations in the reverse order when changing the co-ordinate system.

So the correct transformation sequence is:

```
ctx.translate(200,350);
ctx.rotate(Math.PI/4);
ctx.scale(160,160);
ctx.fillRect (-0.5, -0.5, 1, 1);
```

Notice that when you do a `scale` this applies to any `strokeWidth` you may set, i.e. double the scale and a `strokeWidth` of 1 becomes an effective `strokeWidth` of 2. To set it you need to use an explicit setting of `lineWidth` and you also need to remember that you are working in the current co-ordinate system. For example to set a line width of 1 pixel in the previous example after a scaling of 160 you would need to use:

```
ctx.lineWidth=1/160;
```

You can always work out the transformation sequence you need by considering the graphical object, working out the transforms needed to change it to what you want and applying them in the reverse order. This leads to the approach where every object is drawn centered on the origin at unit size and in a "normal" orientation. The object is then transformed into the size, location and orientation you need.

Some programmers take to this idea and think it is the best and only way to do logical systematic graphics, some adopt it a little bit, and others draw things where they are needed in the size and orientation needed.

Setting Your Own Co-ordinates

When you first use a canvas the co-ordinate system is in terms of the number of pixels in the Bitmap. Often, however, you want to work with a different co-ordinate system. For example, you might want to work with the origin in the middle and the x and y co-ordinate ranging from -1 to +1.

You can set any co-ordinate system you care to work with using suitable transformations. If your co-ordinate system runs from `xmin` to `xmax` and from `ymin` to `ymax` you can apply it to the canvas using:

```
ctx.scale(width/(xmax-xmin),height/(ymax-ymin))
ctx.translate(-xmin,-ymin)
```

where `width` and `height` are the size in pixels of the canvas.

Using this formulation the y co-ordinate increases down the screen, as did the original pixel co-ordinates. If you want the y co-ordinate to increase up the screen then use the transformation:

```
ctx.scale(width/(xmax-xmin),-height/(ymax-ymin))
ctx.translate(-xmin,-ymax)
```

and notice the change to `ymax` in the second line.

So, for example, if you wanted to draw a graph using co-ordinates between
`0,0` in the bottom left corner and `10,10` in the top right, i.e. y increasing up
the screen, you would use:

```
var ctx = document.body.appendChild(
                  createCanvas(500, 500)).getContext("2d");
var xmax = 10;
var xmin = 0;
var ymax = 10;
var ymin = 0;
var width = 500;
var height = 500;

ctx.beginPath();
ctx.scale(width / (xmax - xmin), -height / (ymax - ymin));
ctx.translate(-xmin, -ymax);

ctx.moveTo(0, 0);
ctx.lineTo(0, 10);
ctx.moveTo(0, 0);
ctx.lineTo(10, 0);
ctx.moveTo(0, 0);
ctx.lineTo(10, 10);
ctx.lineWidth = 0.1;
ctx.stroke();
```

This draws axes and a 45 degree line:

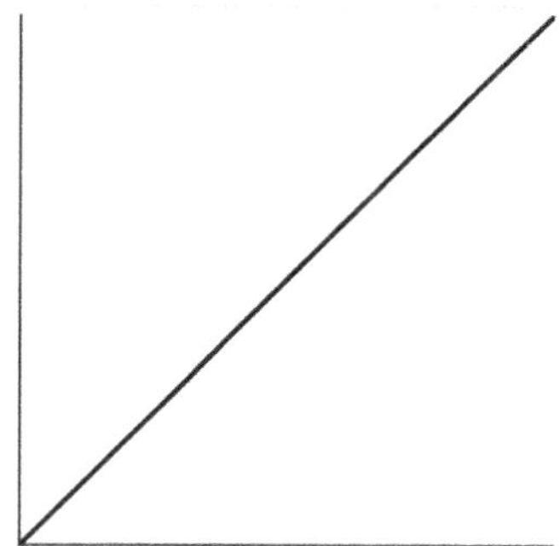

Notice the need to set the `lineWidth` to take account of the scaling. Also
notice that the vertical axis is centered on `x=0` and hence half of its thickness
is "off" the Canvas. To see this more clearly remove the lineWidth setting.

Plotting A Graph

Now let's try a change in the co-ordinate system to make plotting a graph easy.

In principle you could plot a `sin` function using:

```
ctx.beginPath();
ctx.moveTo(0,0);
for(var i=0;i<4*Math.PI;i+=0.1){
   ctx.lineTo(i,Math.sin(i));
}
ctx.stroke();
```

However, if you try it you will just see a small splodge at the top of the canvas. The reason is, of course that the x value varies from `0` to about `12` and the y value varies between `+1` and `-1`, which in pixel co-ordinates gives you the small splodge!

You can use constants to scale and shift the graph to make it fit in with the current co-ordinate system if you want to.

For example:

```
ctx.beginPath();
ctx.moveTo(0,50);
for(var i=0;i<4*Math.PI;i+=0.1){
 ctx.lineTo(i*10,10*Math.sin(i)+50);
}
ctx.stroke();
```

This produces a reasonable sine wave, but a much cleaner method of plotting graphs is to make use of the transformation to provide the co-ordinates that we would really like to use.

We would like a co-ordinate system that varies between `0` and `12` in the x direction and `+1` and `-1` in the y direction. If we assume that the canvas is 400x400 then the change in the co-ordinate system can be created using:

```
ctx.scale(400/12,400/2)
ctx.translate(0,1);
ctx.beginPath();
ctx.moveTo(0,0);
for(var i=0;i<4*Math.PI;i+=0.1){
 ctx.lineTo(i,Math.sin(i));
}
ctx.lineWidth=2/400;
ctx.stroke();
```

First we scale so that the x axis runs from `0` to `12` and the y axis from `0` to `2`. Then we translate so the y axis runs from -1 to 1.

The only complication is that that the transformation affects every measured aspect of the drawing, including line width. So we have to reduce the line width back to roughly one pixel expressed in the new co-ordinate system.

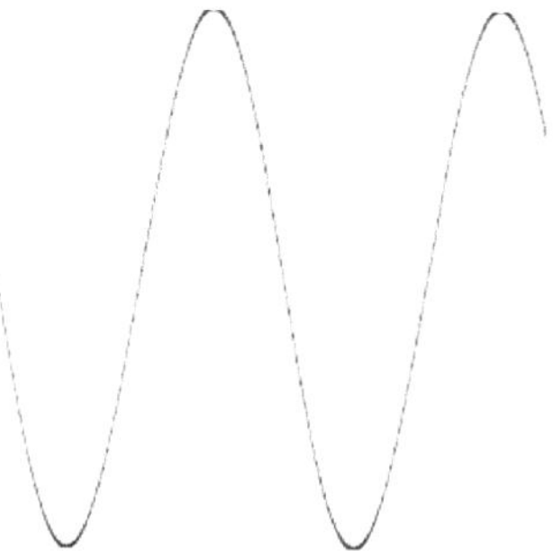

Stack of States

Typically drawing lots of shapes involves changing the transformation and attributes that are used to draw the path. After changing things you often want to restore the original canvas state. The canvas state is a set of properties that determines how graphics primitives will be drawn.

The state consists of:

- the current transformation matrix
- the current clipping region – see later
- all of the drawing attributes such as `fillStyle`, `lineWidth` and so on.

In short, it includes everything that determines what the result of a drawing operation actually produces. Notice that any drawing operation that is in progress, such as the current path or current bitmap, are not part of the state.

Why are we concerned with defining the context state?

The answer is that there is a `save` method which saves the current state to an internal stack of states and a `restore` method that sets the state to the current top of stack.

So, for example, you can set a fill color and save it on the stack of states:

```
ctx.fillStyle = "rgb(200,0,0)";
ctx.save();
ctx.fillStyle = "rgb(0,200,0)";
ctx.save();
ctx.fillStyle = "rgb(0,0,200)";
ctx.fillRect (10, 10, 55, 50);
```

At this point the current fill color is blue with green and red on the stack. Hence, we have just drawn a blue rectangle. If we now restore from the top of the stack and draw a rectangle it will be green:

```
ctx.restore();
ctx.fillRect (20, 20, 55, 50);
```

Repeat this another time and we draw a red rectangle:

```
ctx.restore();
ctx.fillRect (30, 30, 55, 50);
```

Notice that in this case we are only changing the fill color, but in practice the entire drawing state is saved and restored.

You can use the state stack to change the drawing state to draw a sub-object and then restore the state to continue with drawing the main object.

Active Transformations and State

There is another use for the stack of states - another overall approach to systematic drawing.

We have already met the idea of defining a path to draw a "standard" shape. You draw all of your paths starting at 0,0 and with a unit size. Then when you want a shape at x,y and size s you translate the co-ordinate system to x,y and scale by s. Of course, if you save the state before drawing and restore it after then nothing has changed and you are ready to draw the next standard shape.

For example, if you define a unit square:

```
var path1 = new Path2D();
path1.rect(0,0,1,1);
```

you can draw it at 100,200 and size 400 using:

```
ctx.save();
ctx.translate(100,200);
ctx.scale(400,400);
ctx.lineWidth=1/400;
ctx.stroke(path1);
ctx.restore();
```

Notice that you have to do the transformation in the opposite order to the one you might think and you do have to remember to specify the line width in the new units. Because of the `save` and `restore` you can draw the next standard shape using the same method.

This is a particularly useful approach to working with a library of complex shapes. For example, the space ship SVG string used earlier can be edited so that it is drawn starting at `0,0`:

```
path1=new Path2D( "m 0,0 c 2.891926,-25.77092 -1.958475,-65.0136
-13.037221,-73.92172 -11.072474,8.90817 -17.526591,48.1508
-14.634563,73.92172 -9.479011,8.46903 -9.015897,17.40218
-9.068381,29.71617 l 5.92022,-0.074 c 0,0 2.493141,-15.15787
5.105513,-16.98251 l 3.15542,8.06751 -1.537022,9.15649 c 13.277647,-
0.17974 7.242537,-0.17974 20.52018,0 l -1.537022,-9.15649 3.15552,-
8.06751 c 2.979241,2.08093 3.605942,17.00168 3.605942,17.00168 l
6.61799,0.0548 c -0.0526,-12.31399 1.21238,-21.24714 -8.266576,-
29.71617 z");
```

It can now be drawn at any position, any angle and any scale using:

```
ctx.save();
ctx.translate(200,200);
ctx.rotate(Math.PI/8);
ctx.scale(2,2);
ctx.lineWidth=1/2;
ctx.stroke(path1);
ctx.restore();
```

The only problem with this is defining the "center" of the shape. The center is the point of the shape that is located at `0,0` when then shape is drawn at `0,0`. Usually you want this to be at a "natural" position - the center of the rocket or the tip of the nose. The reason is that the pixel at `0,0` when the shape is drawn is the one located at `x,y` when you do a translate to `x,y` and it is the point that any rotate is taken about. It is usually easy to fix the center when you hand-construct shapes - it is more difficult when you use an automatic method such as InkScape. In these cases the easiest solution is to find an initial offset that places the center where you want it when the shape is drawn at 0, 0. For the spaceship changing the initial `m` command to `m 13.5,74.5` puts the center at the top of the nose.

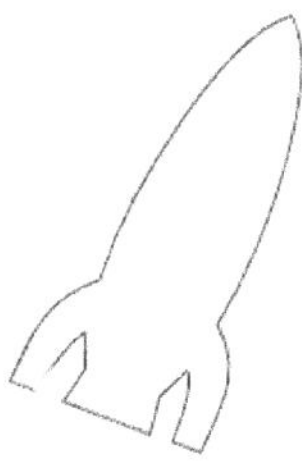

Summary

- Transformations include rotation, scaling and translation.

- You can write all three as a simple matrix if you use homogeneous co-ordinates (x,y,1)

- You can set the transform matrix directly or use one of the utility methods to set scaling, rotation and translation.

- The order in which you apply transformations makes a difference.

- You can think of transformations as actively moving something or just changing the co-ordinates. Canvas transforms change the co-ordinate system.

- If you want to think "actively" then think of the transformations you want to perform on a shape and then apply them in the reverse order before drawing the shape.

- One approach to organizing graphics is to draw everything centered on the origin and at unit scale and then use transformations to size, rotation and position where you really want to draw the shape.

- You can change the co-ordinate system in use to anything that suits the current drawing task.

- You can save the drawing state before changing the co-ordinate system so that it can be restored.

- The drawing state includes the current transformation matrix, clipping region and all drawing attributes.

Chapter 6

Drawing Text on Canvas

For a Canvas object, drawing text is just another path to render. You can select a font and then render the shapes or glyphs it defines using stroke and fill methods. Going beyond this there are a lot of ways of positioning glyphs that control the typography and this is very specialized. What is important is that as text is just another example of a path it can be used with all of the techniques we have learned so far. This is good, but Canvas text processing is very primitive in terms of typography. Finally there is the problem of Unicode. We have moved beyond the 128 or 256 characters available in ASCII - how does this work in JavaScript?

fillText and strokeText

The two fundamental text rendering methods are:

```
ctx.fillText(string,x,y,max);
```

and:

```
ctx.strokeText(string,x,y,max);
```

The first fills the text using the current `fillStyle` and the second uses the current stroke. The `x,y` value gives the starting position for the text and the final optional parameter specifies the maximum width to be used. The exact meaning of `x,y` depends on the font in use and the alignment option, see later. With a default co-ordinate system and default alignment you can think of `x,y` as being the bottom left corner of the text area. If you draw a bounding box around the first character then its bottom left corner is at `x,y`, see `textBaseline` and `textAlign` for a more accurate explanation.

If the string cannot fit into the space allocated then the font will be modified to make it fit. In some cases this will involve changing the spaces between letters, kerning, but in most cases a smaller font will be selected. The drawing of text doesn't alter the current path and it is unaffected by the current path's location.

If you try these two methods:

```
ctx.strokeText("Hello Text World",10,10);
ctx.fillText("Hello Text World",10,50);
```

you will immediately discover some of the problems. The first is that the default font is likely to be too small and the second is what is "single line spacing"?

The first problem is solved by the font property. You can specify a font using CSS font values. The basic format is:

```
[font style][font weight][font size][font face]
```

where `font style` is one of:

- normal
- italic
- oblique
- inherit

and `font weight` is one of:

- normal
- bold
- bolder
- lighter
- auto
- inherit

or a number in the range `100` to `900`.

Font size is the size in pixels, e.g. `10px`, and the font face is the name of a font as you would use in a CSS font specification e.g. `arial`, `serif` etc..

For example:

```
ctx.font="normal normal 20px arial";
```

sets the font to `arial 20px` with no effects.

There is no automatic facility for multi-line text. If you want to create multi-line text you have to implement line spacing by adjusting the y co-ordinate. The question is by how much? When you specify the size of the font as say `20px` this means that the height of a line of text is 20 pixels but the whole of the space allotted might be used by some characters. For example, if you print Hello World twice at `40px` and move the y co-ordinate on by `40px` it looks like single spacing:

But if you change the message to Hello Texty Worldy then it doesn't look quite as good:

Hello Texty Worldy

You can see that the y almost touches the top of the T. In some fonts with a

Hello Texty Worldy

longer descender the two would touch. The size of the font is the smallest spacing that qualifies as single-line spacing. Most word processors use 115% of the size of the font as single spacing.

Double line spacing is generally 200% of the text height, but many word processors use 190% or less.

Typographic Positioning - textBaseline and textAlign

The meaning of the x,y in the positioning of text is more complicated than you might think. If you accept the defaults then it more or less corresponds to the bottom left corner of the text's bounding box.

You can change the horizontal positioning relative to the x value specified by setting `textAlign` property to one of:

`start or left` The text is drawn just after the x position.

`center` The center of the text is located at the x position.

`end or right` The end of the text is located the x position.

You can use these values to left or right justify or center text. For example:

```
ctx.font="normal normal 20px arial";
ctx.textAlign="right";
ctx.fillText("line of text followed by",200,60);
ctx.fillText("A shorter line of text",200,60+20*115/100);
```

gives:

line of text followed by
A shorter line of text

The `textBaseline` property determines how y alters the vertical position of the text relative to the horizontal line, the baseline. It can be set to one of:

- `alphabetic`   Bottom of vertically oriented glyphs (default)
- `ideographic`   Bottom of horizontally oriented glyphs
- `top`   Text is aligned based on the top of the tallest glyph
- `bottom`   Text is aligned based on bottom of the glyph
- `middle`   Text is aligned according to the middle of the text
- `hanging`   Used by Tibetan and other indic scripts

You can see the essential details in this chart from the WHATWG specification:

Notice that the bounding box is the maximum area a font can use and not all glyphs fill it. In some fonts the majority of glyphs use a much smaller area of the total allowed to them. The key measurement is the em square. This is a square with sides equal to the current point size of the font.

When you render text onto the canvas you simply specify x,y and perhaps a maximum width. The x value gives the horizontal alignment and the y value sets the baseline - so what is the bounding box?

The answer is that the bounding box depends on the font in use and you can use the `measureText()` method to return a `TextMetrics` object which contains all of the information on the layout of a particular string in the current font as read only properties. The only problem at the moment is that this is only fully supported on Safari and on Chrome but only if you enable Experimental Web Platform Features using chrome://flags. All browsers support the `TextMetrics` object and at least the `width` property:

- `width`

calculated width of the text. This is not the width of the bounding box but the number of pixels needed to the end of the text. That is, it is the y distance in pixels you need to move to continue the text in the same font.

- `actualBoundingBoxLeft`   `actualBoundingBoxRight`

distance from x,y to the left and right edge of the bounding box. Notice that these depend on the alignment used.

- `fontBoundingBoxAscent`   `fontBoundingBoxDescent`
  `actualBoundingBoxAscent`   `actualBoundingBoxDescent`

distance from x,y to the top and bottom of the bounding rectangle. The actual version of the properties gives you the top and bottom of the bounding rectangle for the actual text used in the call and the other two properties give the value for the font. This means the "actual" versions give a bounding box for the current text and the other two give a bounding box that includes any text in the font.

- `emHeightAscent`   `emHeightDescent`

the distance from x,y to the top and bottom of the em square in the line box, in pixels. This gives you the font's "point" size measured in pixels.

- `hangingBaseline`   `alphabeticBaseline`   `ideographicBaseline`

the distance from x,y given baseline in pixels.

For example, suppose you want the actual bounding box for a specific piece of text:

```
ctx.font="normal normal 40px arial";
text="Hello Text World";
metric=ctx.measureText(text);
x=200;y=60;
boxL=x-metric.actualBoundingBoxLeft;
boxR=x+metric.actualBoundingBoxRight;
boxT=y-metric.actualBoundingBoxAscent;
boxB=y+metric.actualBoundingBoxDescent;
ctx.strokeRect(boxL,boxT,boxR-boxL,boxB-boxT);
ctx.fillText(text,x,y);
```

Where `boxL,boxT` is the top left corner of the bounding box and `boxR,boxB` is the bottom right corner. This produces a tight bounding box for the text you specify:

If you change the program to read:

```
boxL=x-metric.actualBoundingBoxLeft;
boxR=x+metric.actualBoundingBoxRight;
boxT=y-metric.fontBoundingBoxAscent;
boxB=y+metric.fontBoundingBoxDescent;
```

then you will get a bounding box that will contain any text from the font:

That is, there are characters in the font that will use the apparently extra space in the bounding box.

Note these programs currently only work on Chrome or Safari.

It is likely that support for typographic metrics will improve and it is worth checking the current state before making use of any of these properties. There are font libraries that can extract typographic metrics from font files and this might be the only way to perform accurate layout until browsers implement the full `textMetric` object.

There is also the `direction` property which can be set to one of:

- `ltr`   left to right
- `rtl`   right to left
- `inherit`   default.

SVG Text on Canvas

This is an advanced topic that uses techniques from later in the book.

Canvas text is fine for basic tasks but it lacks the typographical control needed for more advanced tasks. SVG text, on the other hand, has all of the characteristics of CSS text and is much more sophisticated. For example, you can adjust the individual positions of characters, change letter spacing, change word spacing, select kerning and so on. To find out how to do these things, all you need to do is to look up the CSS attributes needed to style text.

This is one function that will render SVG text:

```
async function text(ctx,x,y, text, style) {
    var svg = '<svg xmlns="http://www.w3.org/2000/svg"
                                height="80" width="800">';
    svg += '<text x="0" y="0" dominant-baseline="text-before-edge" ';
    svg += style + '>' + text + '</text>'+ '</svg>';
    svg = btoa(svg);
    var img = new Image();
    img.src = 'data:image/svg+xml;base64,' + svg;
    await imgLoaded(img);
    ctx.drawImage(img, x, y);
}
```

We also need:

```
function imgLoaded(img) {
    return new Promise(
                    resolve => {
                      img.onload =  () => {
                          resolve(img);
                      };
                    }
                );
}
```

Notice that we are using promises and so it is assumed that ECMA 2015 is available. Also notice that the text that you draw has to fit into an 80x800 area - you can increase the size if this is too small.

Using the function is easy:

```
text(ctx, x, y, text, style)
```

This renders the string in `text` on the canvas context `ctx` at position `x,y` using the style specified in `style`. The only problem is in specifying the SVG style in a string with single and double quotes.

For example:

```
text(ctx,100,100,"Hello SVG Text!",
                'font-family="symbol" font-size="20pt"');
```

produces:

$$Η ε λ λ ο\ \ Σ ς Γ\ \ Τ ε ξ τ!$$

The typographic controls are another issue. For example, you can use `x="0"` `y="0"` to set the position of the text to `0,0`, but you can also supply a list of values that will be used to position each letter in the string. If you just want to add an increment then you can also use `dx` and `dy` and again specify a list. For example:

```
text(ctx, 50,50,"H2O is water", 'dy="0,8,-8"');
```

produces:

$$H_2O\ is\ water$$

You can also specify a rotation for each character using `rotate=` and a list of angles in degrees:

```
text(ctx,100,100,"Hello SVG Text!",'font-family="serif"
          font-size="20pt" rotate="90,45,60,33,22,34,55"');
```

The final angle applies to the remaining characters:

You can adjust the letter spacing:

```
text(ctx,10,100,"Hello SVG Text!",'font-family="serif"
                  font-size="20pt" letter-spacing="4"');
```

This produces:

$$Hello\ SVG\ Text!$$

You can also adjust word spacing, kerning, and even word wrap for multline text. If you need to change the format in part of a string then use the `<tspan>` tag. For text to a path use `<textpath>`, but you will also need to set an SVG path before rendering. Look up SVG text or CSS text styling.

Character Sets

At its most basic, data on the Internet consists of groups of 8-bits known at an "octet", but usually just called a "byte". Obviously to represent character data we need a mapping between numeric values and characters. One of the first standards for this was, and is, ASCII. This defines 127 alphanumeric characters: A-Z, a-z, 0-9, command characters such as carriage return and backspace, and assorted special characters. Of course, using 8 bits you can represent 256 characters, but this isn't enough to represent all of the characters used by even a small selection of the written languages of the world.

The first solution to this problem was to simply reuse the same 256 numeric codes and associate them with different sets of characters. The most commonly used on the Internet is ISO 8859-n where n is between 1 and 16. Each value of n maps a different set of characters onto the 0 to 255 values that a byte can represent. For example, ISO 8859-1 is Latin-1 Western European and, if selected, provides characters for most Western European languages. ISO-8859-2 is Latin-2 Central European and provides characters for Bosnian, Polish, Croatian and so on.

Notice that we now have a situation where a single character code can correspond to different characters depending on which ISO-8859 character set is selected. This is a potential problem if a server sends data using one ISO-8859 character set and the browser displays it using another. The data hasn't changed, but what is displayed on each system is different. To stop this from happening, servers send a header stating the character set in use. For example:

```
Content-Type: text/html; charset=ISO-8859-1
```

sets the character set to Latin 1. The problem with this is that the server can't adjust its headers for an individual page. Setting the HTTP header for an entire site is reasonable, but you still might want to send a page in another character set.

To allow this you can use the <meta> tag:

```
<meta http-equiv="Content-Type" content="text/html;
                                    charset=ISO-8859-1">
```

This has to be the first tag in the <head> section because the page cannot be rendered until the browser knows the `charset` is in use.

You can also set the character set of a script using:

```
<script src="./myProgram.js" charset="ISO-8859-1">
```

Notice that adding any of these character set specifications only tells the browser what encoding is in use, it doesn't actually enforce the encoding or convert anything from one encoding to another.

What matters is what encoding the file is stored using. For example, to use ISO-8859-2 when you save a file when using an editor such as Notepad++, select encoding ANSI and character set Eastern European. The encoding used for the file determines how all of the characters it contains are represented, and this includes string literals used in JavaScript or PHP programs.

The advice is that if you are creating a library to be used by others then limit your code to the ASCII character set, which is the same in any encoding. If you can't do this the best thing to do is to use UTF-8, i.e. `charset = UTF-8`, which is what all modern browser use and what all encodings are converted into on load.

Unicode

Most of what we have just looked at is legacy because the proper way to do character representation today is to use Unicode. You will still encounter websites using ISO character sets and need to understand how they work, but by comparison Unicode is more logical and complete. Unicode is just a list of characters indexed by a 32-bit value called the character's code point. There are enough characters in Unicode to represent every language in use and some that aren't.

Unicode defines the characters, but it doesn't say how the code point should be represented. The simplest is to use a 32-bit index for every character. This is UTF-32 and it is simple, but very inefficient. It is roughly four times bigger than ASCII. In practice we use more efficient encodings.

UTF-8

There are a number of encodings of Unicode, but the most important for the web is UTF-8. There are 1,112,064 characters in UTF-8 and clearly these cannot all be represented by a value in a single byte as the 256 characters of ASCII could. Instead UTF-8 is a variable length code that uses up to four bytes to represent a character. The number of bytes are used to code a character is indicated by the most significant bits of the first byte.

```
0xxxxxxx    one byte
110xxxxx    two bytes
1110xxxx    three bytes
11110xxx    four bytes
```

All subsequent bytes have their most significant two bits set to 10. This means that you can always tell a follow-on byte from a first byte. The bits in the table shown as x carry the information about which character is represented. To get the character code you simply extract the bits and concatenate them to get a 7, 11, 16 or 21-bit character code. Notice that, unlike the ISO schemes, there is only one character assigned to a character code. This means that if the server sends UTF-8 and the browser interprets the data as UTF-8 then there is no ambiguity.

The first 128 characters of UTF-8 are the same as ASCII, so if you use a value less than 128 stored in a single byte then you have backward compatible ASCII text. That is, Unicode characters U+0000 to U+007F can be represented in a single byte. Going beyond this needs two, three and four bytes. Almost all the Latin alphabets plus Greek, Cyrillic, Coptic, Armenian, Hebrew, Arabic, Syrian, Thaana and N'Ko can be represented with just two bytes.

Modern browsers work in UTF-8 internally and any other encoding is converted to UTF-8 when the page or file is read in. This means that web pages and scripts have to be created using UTF-8 encoded files - i.e. the editor must be set to create and work with UTF-8 files.

If you want to include a UTF-8 character in HTML that is outside the usual range, i.e. one you cannot type using the default keyboard, then you can enter it using:

`&#decimal;`

or:

`&#xhex;`

where `decimal` and `hex` are the character codes in decimal and hex. For example:

`∑`

will display a mathematical summation sign, i.e. a Greek sigma.

Σ

If you don't see this symbol when a page with this character code is loaded into a browser then the character set is something other than UTF-8.

You also have to be careful about text that is processed by the server. For example, text stored in a database needs to be in the same representation that the server is going to use. Similarly, you have to pay attention to text processed by server-side languages like PHP.

The most important single idea is:
The browser always works with UTF-8 encoded data and, if it can, it will convert any other encoding as the web page is read in.
To do this it has to know what the encoding is and it has to "know" how to convert it.

UTF-16 in JavaScript

Now we come to a confusing twist in the story. JavaScript has Unicode
support and all JavaScript strings are UTF-16 coded – this has some
unexpected results for any programmer under the impression that they can
assume that one character is one byte. While you can mostly ignore the
encoding used, the fact that web pages and script files use UTF-8 and
JavaScript uses UTF-16 can cause problems. The important point to note is
that when JavaScript interacts with a web page characters are converted
from UTF-8 to UTF-16 and vice versa.

As you can guess, UTF-16 is another variable length way of coding Unicode,
but as the basic unit is 16 bits we only need to allow for the possibility of an
additional two-byte word. For any Unicode character in the range U+0000 to
U+FFFF, i.e. 16 bits, you simply set the single 16-bit word to the code. So how
do we detect that two 16-bit words, called a surrogate pair, are needed? The
answer is that the range U+D800 to U+DFFF is reserved and doesn't represent
any valid character, i.e. they never occur in a valid string. These reserved
codes are used to signal a two-word coding.

If you have a Unicode character that has a code larger than U+FFFF then you
have to convert it into a surrogate pair using the following steps:

1. Subtract 0x010000 from it to give a 20-bit number in the range
    0x000000 to 0x0FFFFF.

2. The top 10 bits are added to 0xD800 to give the first 16-bit surrogate
    in the range 0xD800 to 0xDBFF.

3. The low 10 bits are added to 0xDC00 to give the second 16-bit
    surrogate in the same range.

Reconstructing the character code is just the same process in reverse.

If you find a 16-bit value in the range x0800 to xDFFF then it and the next
16-bit value are a surrogate pair. Take 0xD800 from the first and 0xDC00 from
the second. Put the two together to make a 20-bit value and add 0x0100000.
The only problem is that different machines use different byte orderings -
little endian and big endian. To tell which sort of machine you are working
with, a Byte Order mark or BOM can be included in a string U+FEFF. If this is
read as FFEF the machine doing the decoding has a different byte order to the
machine that did the coding.

The most important thing to know is that JavaScript only uses a single 16-bit
value to represent a character. This means it doesn't naturally work with the
full range of Unicode characters as there are no surrogate pairs.

The BMP - Basic Multilingual Plane

A JavaScript string usually uses nothing but characters that can be represented in a single 16-bit word in UTF-16. As long as you can restrict yourself to the Basic Multilingual Plane (BMP), as this set is referred to, everything works simply. If you can't, then things become much harder.

You can enter a Unicode character using an escape sequence:

```
\xHH
```

for characters that have codes up to xFF, i.e. 0 to 255, and:

```
\uHHHH
```

for characters that have codes up to xFFFF, where H is a hex digit.

For example:

```
var a = "Hello World\u00A9";
console.log(a);
```

adds a copyright symbol to the end of Hello World. This is simple enough, but if you now try:

```
console.log(a.length);
```

you will find that it correctly displays 12, because the length property counts the number of 16-bit characters in a string.

What about the Unicode characters that need two bytes? How can you enter them?

The answer is that in ECMAScript 2015 and later you can enter a 32-bit character code:

```
\u{HHHHHHHH}
```

Alternatively you could use the new string functions also introduced in ECMAScript 2015, `fromCharCode` and `fromCodePoint` do the same job of converting a character code to a string. However, `fromCharCode` only works with 16-bit values and not surrogate pairs, while `fromCodePoint` will return a surrogate pair if the code is greater then 0xFFFF. The only problem is that `fromCodePoint` was introduced with ECMAScript 2015 and isn't supported in older browsers, although a polyfill is available. The functions `charCodeAt` and `codePointAt` will return the character code at a specified position in a string. The `charCodeAt` function, which also isn't supported by older browsers, works in 16-bit values and is blind to surrogate pairs, whereas `codePointAt` will return a value greater than 0xFFFF if the position is the start of a surrogate pair. Notice, however, that the position is still in terms of 16-bit values and nct characters.

For example:

```
var s1="\u{1F638}";
```

or:

```
var s1=String.fromCodePoint(0x1F638);
```

stores the surrogate pair \uD83D\uDE38 in s1 which is the "grinning cat face with smiling eyes" emoji:

Notice that you specify the code point and JavaScript converts this into two 16-bit values - the surrogate pair.

If you cannot assume ECMAScript 2015 then you have to enter the surrogate pair as two characters.

You can easily write a function that will return a UTF-16 encoding of a Unicode character code:

```
function codeToUTF16(code) {
 if (code <= 0xFFFF) return "\\u" + code.toString(16).toUpperCase();
 code = code - 0x10000;
 var sLead = 0xD800 | (code >> 10);
 var sTrail = 0xDC00 | (code & 0x3FF);
 return "\\u" + sLead.toString(16).toUpperCase() +
         "\\u" + sTrail.toString(16).toUpperCase();
}
```

For example:

```
console.log(codeToUTF16(0x1F638));
```

produces:

```
\uD83D\uDE38
```

which is the "grinning cat face with smiling eyes" again.

Notice JavaScript sends the UTF-16 to the browser unmodified – it is the browser that converts it to equivalent UTF-8 and then displays it.

JavaScript Problems

As long as you restrict yourself to the BMP everything works an a fairly simple way. If you move outside of the BMP to make use of emojis say then things are more complicated. Most of the JavaScript functions only work when you use characters from the BMP and there is a one-to-one correspondence between 16-bit values and characters. JavaScript may display surrogate pairs correctly, but in general it doesn't process them correctly. For example, length gives you the wrong number of characters if there are surrogate pairs. Functions like charAt(n) will return the wrong character if n is beyond a surrogate pair and it might not even return a valid character if it selects the second value of the pair. In general, you just have to think that all JavaScript functions work with 16-bit characters and if you use a surrogate pair then these are treated as two characters and one of these might even be invalid.

There is one final problem that you need to be aware of. In Unicode a single code always produces the same glyph or character, but there may be many characters that look identical. In technical terms, you can create the same glyph in different ways. Unicode supports combining codes which put together multiple characters into a single character. This means that you can often obtain a character with an accent either by selecting a character with an accent or selecting a character without an accent and combining it with the appropriate accent character. The end result is that two Unicode strings can look identical and yet be represented by different codes. This means the two strings won't be treated as being equal and they might not even have the same length. The solution to this problem is to normalize the strings so that characters are always produced in the same way. This is not an easy topic to deal with in general as there are so many possible ways of approaching it.

For example there are two ways of specifying an accented e:

```
var s1 = '\u00E9';
var s2 = 'e\u0301';
ctx.font="normal normal 40px arial";
ctx.fillText(s1+" "+s2,10,60);
```

both of which produce apparently the same character:

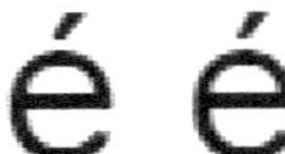

However, the characters are created in two different ways and they will test
as non-equal. That is `s1!==s2` is true.

ECMA 2015 introduced the normalize method and:

```
s1.normalize() ===s2.normalize();
```

is true and both are equal to `\u00E9`. You can also specify the particular type
of normalization you require, but this is beyond the scope of this introduction
to working with Unicode text.

Summary

- Canvas text is just another example of a path to be filled or stroked using `fillText` or `strokeText`. Drawing text does not interact with or modify the current path.

- You can set the font used via the CSS font values and the font property.

- Line spacing has to be set manually as there is no concept of multiline text in Canvas text.

- There is limited typographic control in Canvas text and the degree to which `TextMetrics` is supported is limited.

- An alternative to using Canvas text is to use SVG text which has full typographic control.

- Old ISO character sets are converted to Unicode UTF-8 by the browser.

- JavaScript works with UTF-16 restricted to a single word which means you can only work directly with the Basic Multilingual Plan (BMP).

- Unicode characters can be entered as literals using escape sequences.

- The new Unicode functions help, but there are still some problems to overcome. In particular if you go beyond the BMP then JavaScript string functions will give you the wrong results as they don't handle characters that correspond to two 16-bit words.

- There is also the problem that a Unicode glyph has more than one way to specify it. The new normalize function can help with testing for equality in such cases.

Chapter 7

Clipping, Compositing & Effects

There are ways that you can control how what you draw is combined with what is already drawn on the canvas. You can use a path, not as something to render on the canvas, but as a clipping path which determines what is rendered when you draw other paths. This leads us to consider how what you draw is composited with what is already there. At its very simplest, compositing is just the way color values are logically combined to create new values, but Canvas takes this idea a lot further. Finally there are some special effects which have to be covered somewhere and this is as good a place as any!

Clipping

You have already been relying on clipping without even realizing it. When you set up a canvas and draw on it, anything that goes outside of the canvas rectangle isn't drawn. Notice that while some graphics systems treat drawing outside of the rendering window as an error, Canvas clips the graphic to the rendering window.

You can generalize this idea by defining a clipping path. This can be any path you have created and once the clipping path is set anything you draw is only rendered inside the path.

To set a path as the current clipping path use:

```
ctx.clip(path,fillrule);
```

where `path` is any path and `fillrule` is optional.

For example,, using the star path introduced earlier we can clip text to its
interior:

```
var myPath = new Path2D();
myPath.moveTo(50, 50);
myPath.lineTo(100, 100);
myPath.lineTo(0, 100);
myPath.lineTo(50, 50);
myPath.moveTo(50, 110);
myPath.lineTo(0, 60);
myPath.lineTo(100, 60);
myPath.lineTo(50, 110);
ctx.stroke(myPath);
ctx.clip(myPath);
ctx.font="normal normal 20px arial";
ctx.fillText("Hello Text World",10,80);
```

Notice that the path has been rendered before being used as a clipping path
so that it can be seen. The text would be clipped as shown, even without
rendering the star.

Clipping to the inside of the clipping path depends on what you consider to
be "inside" and `fillrule` works in the same way as described in Chapter 4 in
connection with `fillStyle`. You can set it to "nonzero" which is the default
or "evenodd" for the odd-even winding rule. If you change the example to
read:

```
ctx.clip(myPath, "evenodd");
```

then only the points of the star are considered to be inside.

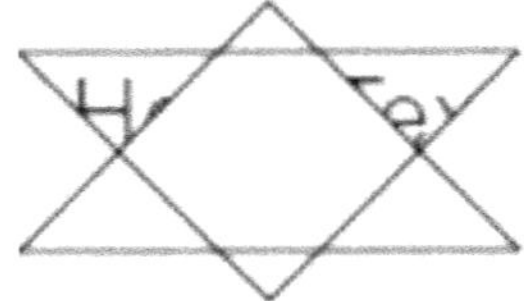

Notice that there is a lot of overlap between `fillStyle` and `clip`. You can often produce the same effect as clipping by filling the shape with whatever would be clipped. The exception is for anything that cannot be simply used as a fill. This is why text is used in the example.

Of course, a clipping path doesn't change what has already been drawn and you can change the clipping path as you draw to produce interesting effects. You can only use a real path as a clipping path - shapes you draw directly to the canvas using `strokeRect` don't work. You can use the default path and then you simply leave out any parameters to the clip function. Any open paths are automatically closed.

Another interesting problem in using `clip` is clearing the clip path you have set. If you set a clip path then this is a permanent change to the canvas state. If you use another `clip` to set another path this is not what happens. Instead, the new clipping region is the intersection of the current clipping area and the new. This means you cannot reset a clipping path by simply specifying a new clipping path.

A the time of writing the only way to rest a clipping path is to use the `save` method before setting the clipping path and then `restore` when you want to remove it. Of course, this saves and restores the entire canvas state, but as long as you are aware of it this is generally not a problem. There is a `resetClip` function in the standard, but it is not well supported.

Compositing

Compositing is the grand terms for how you combine the new pixel value with the existing pixel value. Traditionally compositing rules were simple logical operations, but Canvas has a great many options which attempt to provide additional creative effects. It is difficult to give guidance on how to make use of these. In many cases you simply have to try it out and see if the result is pleasing.

All rendering operations use the same global compositing rule set by:

```
ctx.globalCompositeOperation=type;
```

where *type* is one of the many compositing operations.

Compositing mainly works by using the transparency values of the pixels to control how they are combined, i.e. the Alpha channel is used to determine how pixels from the source and destination are combined. The theory of all this and the names used for compositing operations was worked out in 1984 by Thomas Porter and Tom Duff and presented in their seminal paper titled *"Compositing Digital Images"*. Canvas implements some of the Porter-Duff methods. As these are based on the use of the Alpha channel, they are also known as "alpha compositing modes".

Alpha Compositing Modes

After listing the pairs of options that determine how the source and destination images are displayed, there's a program that produces the illustrations shown.

over

The first pair of options simply determine which image appears in front:

- **`source-over`**   The source image is displayed over, i.e in front of, the destination image.

- **`destination-over`** The destination image over is displayed over, i.e in front of, the source image.

The default composition is `source-over` and we generally use it without giving it any thought - the pixel values of the source simply replace the corresponding pixels already in the canvas. The `destination-over` option is almost as simple, but the source pixel values only replace pixels that haven't already been drawn. This has the effect of making anything you are drawing appear behind anything that is already there.

The blue rectangle is drawn first and, on the left, the red is drawn with `source-over` and on the right with `destination-over`:

The question is what distinguishes a drawn pixel from one that is considered to be not drawn? You could phrase this question as what is a foreground pixel and what is a background pixel. The rule is that any pixel that is set to 100% transparency is a background pixel and any other transparency is a foreground pixel. When you create a canvas all of the pixels are set to transparent black i.e. `rgba(0,0,0,0)`. Similarly when you use `clearRect` the area is set to transparent black.

The way that destination-over works is that each destination pixel is tested for 100% transparency and only if this is the case is the source pixel value used to overwrite it.

This deals with the situation when pixels are either transparent or opaque, i.e. Alpha is either 0.0 or 1.0. How do we composite pixels that have intermediate transparency? The answer is best summed up in the equations used to compute the composite.

For source-over the new pixel values are computed using:

$$A_n = A_s + (1-A_s)*A_d$$
$$C_n = C_s + (1-A_s)*C_d$$

where subscript n is new, s is source and d is destination and A is for Alpha and C is for any of the three colors red, green or blue. You can see that if A_d is 0 and A_s is 1 the resulting Alpha is A_s and the color is C_s i.e if the destination is fully transparent then the source replaces the pixel value. For intermediate Alpha values the colors and Alpha are blended as a weighted average using A_s.

For destination-over the new pixel values are computed using:

$$A_n = A_d + (1-A_d)*A_s$$
$$C_n = C_d + (1-A_d)*C_s$$

This behaves in the same way but with the roles of A_s and A_d reversed.

You can see the effect of overlapping the same blue and red rectangles but with Alpha set to 0.5 for source-over (left) and destination-over (right):

In both cases Alpha is set to 0.5 but they differ in which color dominates in the overlap.

atop

The pair of `atop` modes are very similar to their `over` counterparts, but they "clip" the source or destination.

- ◆ **`source-atop`**   The part of the source image that is outside the destination image is not shown, i.e. the destination acts as a clipping region.

- ◆ **`destination-atop`** The part of the destination image that is outside the source image is not shown, i.e. the source acts as a clipping region.

The same two rectangles are shown using `source-atop` on the left and `destination-atop` on the right. You can see that the red rectangle has been clipped to the blue and vice versa. Notice that in the second case everything on the canvas outside of the red rectangle is erased.

Again, to find out what happens in the case of intermediate transparency, it is best to see what the equations are.

For `source-atop` we have:

$$A_n = A_d$$
$$C_n = A_d * C_s + (1 - A_s) * C_d$$

You can see that the Alpha is always just the destination Alpha which means only the current foreground pixels are changed by the source and the change is just a weighted average of the colors.

For `destination-atop` we have:

$$A_n = A_s$$
$$C_n = (1 - A_d) * C_s + A_s * C_d$$

and only the foreground pixels in the source are modified.

You can see the effect of overlapping the same blue and red rectangles but with Alpha set to 0.5 for `source-atop` (left) and `destination-atop` (right):

in

This pair of modes clips the images, clearing the canvas.

- **source-in** Only the part of the source image that is inside the destination image is shown.
- **destination-in** Only the part of the destination image that is inside the source image is shown.

The same two rectangles drawn before are shown using `source-in` on the left and `destination-in` on the right. You can see that the red rectangle has been clipped to the blue and vice versa.

Notice that this clears the entire area of the canvas outside of the source or destination.

Again to find out what happens in the case of intermediate transparency it is best to see what the equations are.

For `source-in` we have:

$$A_n = A_s * A_d$$
$$C_n = A_d * C_s$$

You can see that the Alpha is always just product and so if either is zero the new pixel is also zero. The color value is multiplied by the destination Alpha so it only shows within foreground pixels.

For `destination-in` we have:

$$A_n = A_s * A_d$$
$$C_n = A_s * C_d$$

and only the pixels in the destination that are within the destination and the source are left.

You can see the effect of overlapping the same blue and red rectangles but with Alpha set to `0.5` for `source-in` (left) and `destination-in` (right):

out

This pair of modes displays only the parts of the image outside the overlap.

- **`source-out`**   Only the part of the source image that is outside the destination image is shown.

- **`Destination-out`** Only the part of the destination image that is outside the source image is shown.

The same two rectangles drawn before are shown using `source-out` on the left and `destination-out` on the right. You can see that the red rectangle has been clipped to what is outside of the blue and vice versa.

Again to find out what happens in the case of intermediate transparency it is best to see what the equations are.

For `source-out` we have:

$$A_n = (1-A_d)*A_s$$
$$C_n = (1-A_d)*C_s$$

You can see that the Alpha is a product and so if the destination is 1 or source is 0 the pixel is not rendered. The color value is multiplied by one minus destination Alpha so it only shows within background pixels.

For `destination-out` we have:

$$A_n = (1-A_s)*A_d$$
$$C_n = (1-A_s)*C_d$$

and only the pixels in the destination that are outside the source are left.

You can see the effect of overlapping the same blue and red rectangles but with Alpha set to `0.5` for `source-out` (left) and `destination-out` (right):

A Demonstration Program

It is slightly harder to create the dual source and destination illustrations shown above than you might realize. The problem is that while you can display both left and right rectangle pairs by changing the composite mode between the two, some compositing modes wipe the canvas outside of the source or destination. We have to isolate the two pairs of rectangles from one another. The solution is to use a clip path to restrict where the compositing mode is applied, i.e. apply clipping to compositing.

The program is:

```
ctx.fillStyle = "rgba(0,0,255,0.5";
ctx.fillRect(100,  50,  100,  50);
ctx.fillRect(300,  50,  100,  50);
var myPath = new Path2D();
myPath.rect(75,25,200,125);
ctx.save();
ctx.clip(myPath );

ctx.globalCompositeOperation="source-out";
ctx.fillStyle = "rgba(255,0,0,0.5";
ctx.fillRect(150,  75,  100,  50);

ctx.restore();
myPath = new Path2D();
myPath.rect(275,25,200,125);
ctx.clip(myPath);

ctx.globalCompositeOperation="destination-out";
ctx.fillStyle = "rgba(255,0,0,0.5";
ctx.fillRect(350,  75,  100,  50);
```

Notice the use of save and restore to allow two rectangular clipping paths to be used. You can change the CompositeOperation and fillStyle parameters to see the effects of different configurations.

More Compositing Modes

There are three other compositing modes that can be used to good effect:.

- ◆ **lighter**   Displays the sum of the source image and the destination image but only where they overlap.

Notice that this sum is not the maximum of the overall brightness, but of each of the color channels in turn. In this case the resulting color is `255,0,255` because in the overlap we have `0,0,255` and `255,0,0`.

The equations governing the mode are:

$$A_n = \max(0, \min(A_s + A_d, 1))$$
$$C_n = \max(0, \min(C_s + C_d, 255))$$

These look complicated but they are simply the sums restricted to be within range.

- ◆ **copy**   Displays the source image and erases the destination image.

Notice that the destination image has been cleared by the background pixels in the source.

The equations governing the mode are:

$$A_n = A_s$$
$$C_n = C_s$$

◆ **xor** The source and destination pixels are cleared where foreground source and destination pixels overlap.

You can see that this does correspond to a logical XOR in the sense that two foreground pixels make a background pixel, i.e. `1 xor 1 = 0`

The equations governing the mode are:

$$A_n = (1-A_d)*A_s + (1-A_s)*A_d$$
$$C_n = (1-A_d)*C_s + (1-A_s)*C_d$$

For shapes with intermediate transparency the operation doesn't look so much like XOR. For example, if both rectangles have an Alpha of `0.5` the transparency of all the pixels is `0.5` and the color is an average of the two colors:

Blending

As well as the Porter-Duff compositing operations, you can also specify blends. A blend is a mixing of color between the source and destination pixels, but modulated by the destination alpha. If $B(C_s,C_d)$ is the blend function the final color is:

$$C_n = (1-A_d)*C_s + (1-A_d)* B(C_s,C_d)$$

That is, the new color is a weighted average of the source color and the blended color. The blend function is always adjusted to make sure that it stays within the legal range for a color.

Blends are difficult to work with because even when you know what they do it is hard to guess what outcome their application will produce. They tend only to be effective on complex colors and in this sense they are more like special effects to be applied to photos.

Blend modes

You can use a variety of blend modes with the blending function $B(Cs,Cd)$.

- **normal** This is the default blend which specifies no blending and simply selects the source color:
  $$B(C_s,C_d)= C_s$$

- **multiply** The source color is multiplied by the destination color. The resultant color is always at least as dark as either the source or destination color. Multiplying any color with black results in black. Multiplying any color with white preserves the original color:
  $$B(C_s,C_d)= C_s* C_d=Multiply(C_s, C_d)$$

- **screen** Multiplies the complements of the destination and source color values, then complements the result. The effect is supposed to be like projecting multiple images onto a screen:

```
B(C_s,C_d)= 1- [(1-C_s)*(1-C_d)]
    =   C_s + C_d -   (C_s * C_d) = Screen(C_s,C_d)
```

- **hard-light** A combination of Multiply and Screen based on the source color. It is supposed to look like a spotlight on the destination:

```
if(C_s <0.5)
   B(C_s,C_d)= Multiply(2*C_s,C_d)
else
   B(C_s,C_d)=Screen(2*C_s-1,C_d) = HardLight(C_s,C_d)
```

- **soft-light** Darkens or lightens the color depending on the source color. The effect is intended to be like to shining a diffused spotlight:

```
if(C_s <0.5)
    B(C_s,C_d)=   C_d -   (1-2C_s) * C_d  *(1-C_d)
else
    B(C_s,C_d)=   C_d -   (2C_s-1) * (D(C_d)   -C_d)
where D(C_d)  is given by:
if(C_d <0.25)
    D(C_d)=   ((16C_d - 12)* C_d +4)   *C_d
else
    D(C_d)= sqrt(C_d)
```

- **overlay** This is the "inverse "of the hard-light blend:

```
B(C_s,C_d)= HardLight(C_d,C_s)
```

◆ **lighten** Selects the lighter of the source and destination colors. The destination is replaced with the source where the source is lighter; otherwise, it is left unchanged:

$$B(C_s, C_d) = \max(C_s, C_d)$$

Notice that this is not the maximum of the overall brightness but of each of the color channels in turn. In this case the resulting color is 255,0,255 because in the overlap we have 0,0,255 and 255,0,0.

◆ **darken** This is similar to `lighten` but it takes the minimum. The destination is replaced with the source where the source is darker; otherwise, it is left unchanged:

$$B(C_s, C_d) = \min(C_s, C_d)$$

Notice that is is not the minimum of the overall brightness but of each color component. As in the overlap we have we have 0,0,255 and 255,0,0 the minimum of each color channel is 0,0,0.

- **color-dodge** Brightens the destination color to reflect the source color:

```
if(C_d==0)
    B(C_s,C_d)= 0
else if(C_s==1)
  B(C_s,C_d)=1
else
  B(C_s,C_d)=min(1, C_d/(1-C_s))
```

- **color-burn** This darkens the destination color to reflect the source color:

```
if(C_d==1)
    B(C_s,C_d)= 1
else if(C_s==0)
  B(C_s,C_d)=0
else
  B(C_s,C_d)=min(1, (1-C_s)/C_d)
```

- **difference** Subtracts the darker of the two constituent colors from the lighter color. Painting with white inverts the backdrop color; painting with black produces no change:

$$B(C_s,C_d)=|C_s-C_d|$$

- **exclusion** Like difference but lower in contrast:

$$B(C_s,C_d)=C_d + C_s - 2C_d * C_s$$

HLS Blend Modes

There are some color blends that cannot be achieved in RGB color space. In this case the colors are first converted to HLS and then a blend function is defined and finally the colors are converted back to RGB.

- **Hue**   Converts the color to the hue of the source and saturation and luminosity of the destination:
  $$H_n = H_s, \qquad L_n = L_d, \qquad S_n = S_d$$

- **Luminosity**   Converts the color to the luminosity of the source hue and saturation of the destination:
  $$H_n = H_d, \qquad L_n = L_s, \qquad S_n = S_d$$

- **Saturation**   Converts the color to the saturation of the source and hue and luminosity of the destination:
  $$H_n = H_d, \qquad L_n = L_d, \qquad S_n = S_s$$

- **color** Converts the color to the saturation and hue of the source and luminosity of the destination:
  $$H_n = H_s, \qquad L_n = L_d, \qquad S_n = S_s$$

This can be used to apply color while preserving the brightness. For example you could use it to color a gray scale photo.

Shadows

Canvas shadows are a special effect that could be considered to be a blend. There are four graphics context properties that control the shadow:

```
shadowColor=color
shadowOffsetX=value;
shadowOffsetY=value;
shadowBlur = value;
```

The first of these should be set to a non-transparent color for the shadow to show, the offsets are in the current co-ordinate system and the blur is a number from zero for no blur to any large number.

For example:

```
ctx.fillStyle = "red";
ctx.shadowColor="rgba(0,0,0,1)";
ctx.shadowOffsetX=10;
ctx.shadowOffsetY=10;
ctx.shadowBlur=15;
ctx.fillRect(150, 75, 100, 50);
```

The general idea is that the color of the shadow is the light that is
illuminating the object and the offset gives the direction that the lighting
effect seems to be coming from. If you make the offset too large or the blur too
great then the result isn't as effective. If you use an offset of zero then you can
use shadow to give the object a glow.

For example:

```
ctx.fillStyle = "red";
ctx.shadowColor="green";
ctx.shadowOffsetX=0;
```

```
ctx.shadowOffsetY=0;
ctx.shadowBlur=15;
ctx.fillRect(150, 75, 100, 50);
```

Notice that the shadow applies to everything you draw until you set its color
back to `rgba(0,0,0,0)`.

Summary

- Paths can be used to clip whatever you are drawing.

- If you specify another clipping path it is added, as the intersection, to the current path. To remove a clipping path use `save` and `restore`.

- Compositing controls the way new colors are added to the existing colors in an image.

- There are a large number of compositing rules that you can select using `globalCompositeOperation`.

- Most of the Porter-Duff alpha compositing rules are supported.

- Blending involves mixing colors taking into account the alpha value of the source and destination.

- You can set a drop shadow on any object and specify its offset, color and blur.

- A shadow with zero offset can be used to add a "glow" to an object.

Part II Working with Bitmaps

In this part of the book we look at the activity that Canvas was made for - working with bitmaps.

Chapter 8

Generating Bitmaps

Bitmaps, gifs, jpegs and so on are common in almost all web pages. With Canvas you now work with bitmaps at the pixel level. It's not difficult, but you need to organize things to make it really easy and a good understanding helps.

Our first challenge is to find out how to get bitmaps into the system so that they can be used by JavaScript, and Canvas in particular.

The Image Object

The most basic way of getting an image into a web page is the `img` tag:

```
<img src=url width="100" height="200">
```

This loads the bitmap specified by the *url* into the web page and displays it at 100 by 200 pixels irrespective of its actual size.

If you want to work with an `img` tag in JavaScript then you need to work with the `HTMLImageElement` DOM object. Assuming the `img` tag is:

```
<img id="myImage" src=url width="100" height="200">
```

then you can get a reference to the `HTMLImageElement` using:

```
var img1=document.getElementById("myImage");
```

Now you can access the properties including `height`, `width` and `naturalHeight`, `naturalWidth` which give you the actual size of the bitmap.

You can use an `HTMLImageElement` that has been created in this way as the source of a bitmap to use with Canvas, but the problem is that the tag will be loaded along with the page and displayed.

If you want to load a bitmap into an `HTMLImageElement` using JavaScript then you have to use the well known idiom of creating the element and then setting its `src` property.

129

For example:

```
var img1=document.createElement("img");
```

creates an HTMLImageElement. You can start it loading a bitmap using:

```
img1.src=url;
```

If you just do this the bitmap will be loaded, but not displayed as the new HTMLImageElement isn't part of the DOM. To make it visible you have to add it to the DOM using one of the many methods provided for doing this. For example:

```
document.body.appendChild(img1);
```

Where the bitmap appears depends on where it is added to the DOM. How big the image is displayed depends on what you set the height and width properties to. If you don't set them then the image is displayed at its full size, i.e. naturalHeight, naturalWidth.

There is a slightly simpler way of doing the same job. The JavaScript Image object is in fact a wrapper for the HTMLImageElement DOM object and:

```
var img1 = new Image(w,h);
```

is exactly equivalent to:

```
var img1=document.createElement("img");
img1.width=w;
img1.height=h;
```

If you leave out w and h then the natural size of the bitmap is used. If you leave out h then the height is scaled correctly for the given w. So to load an image into an HTML page you might use something like:

```
var img1 = new Image(200);
img1.src = "jeep.jpg";
document.body.appendChild(img1);
```

Notice that if you don't want the image to show in the web page you can simply not add it to the DOM.

This works, but if you want to go on to process the image using JavaScript you cannot simply continue writing instructions. The image takes time to load and you cannot process it before it is finished loading. For example, suppose you wanted to scale the loaded image to 1/10th its natural size. If you try:

```
var img1 = new Image();
img1.src = "jeep.jpg";

img1.width = img1.naturalWidth / 10;
img1.height = img1.naturalHeight / 10;
document.body.appendChild(img1);
```

you will find that it doesn't work.

Asynchronous Loading

The reason is that you are trying to use properties of the image that are only available after the image has loaded. When you first encounter this sort of behavior, especially if you are used to other languages, the tendency is to think that the quick fix is to put in a delay to give the image time to load. For JavaScript this doesn't work because any delay that you put in, by whatever method, freezes the UI and many other actions. That is, if you wait for the image load with a delay, the image stops loading until the delay is complete.

For example, a delay function is easy to create:

```
function delay(ms) {
    var curTicks = Date.now();
    var endTicks = curTicks + ms;
    while (curTicks < endTicks) {
        curTicks = Date.now();
    }
}
```

This keeps the processor busy while waiting for the specified number of milliseconds to pass. If you put a call to `delay` in the image load to create a delay of 10 seconds:

```
var img1 = new Image();
img1.src = "jeep.jpg";
delay(10000);
img1.width = img1.naturalWidth / 10;
img1.height = img1.naturalHeight / 10;
document.body.appendChild(img1);
```

you will most likely discover that the image hasn't loaded after the delay. Even if it has, the browser UI will have frozen for the full 10 seconds, which is unacceptable.

The traditional correct solution is to define a load event handler:

```
var img1 = new Image();
img1.src = "jeep.jpg";

img1.addEventListener("load",
            function () {
                img1.width = img1.naturalWidth / 10;
                img1.height = img1.naturalHeight / 10;
                document.body.appendChild(img1);
            });
```

Now everything works but you have the complication of an event handler. This is more complicated and subtle than it looks. For example, the event will occur long after the main program has completed and yet the event handler makes reference to `img1`, which is a variable that shouldn't exist after the main program ends. The only reason the event function can make use of it is due to closure. For an explanation, see my book ***JavaScript Async: Events, Callbacks, Promises and Async Await*** *(ISBN: 978-1871962567)*.

Setting an event handler in this way is the most basic way of dealing with the problem of waiting for the image to load. A more modern way is to make use of a `Promise` object. To do this we have to write a function which wraps the `onload` event:

```
function imgLoaded(img) {
  return new Promise(
            function (resolve,reject) {
                img.addEventListener("load", function () {
                                        resolve(img);
                                    });
            }
        );
}
```

This immediately returns a `Promise` object which calls the `resolve` function when the image is loaded. Using this you would write the previous example as:

```
var img1 = new Image();
img1.src = "jeep.jpg";
imgLoaded(img1).then(function (img) {
                        img.width = img.naturalWidth / 10;
                        img.height = img.naturalHeight / 10;
                        document.body.appendChild(img);
                    });
```

Notice that now the code to be executed when the image is loaded is in the then function of the promise. Also notice that we are using the parameter returned by the promise i.e. `img` rather than `img1`. The advantage of this approach is that you can chain multiple promises when loading multiple images and arrange to use the `reject` function to handle errors.

Promises are an improvement on event handling and callbacks but the very best way of implementing this is to use `async/await` and as these are now implemented by every browser that implements promises there is no reason not to use it. The only problem is that you cannot `await` a function from the main program and this means it is better to write a function that loads the image and awaits it:

```
async function getImage(url) {
    var img = new Image();
    img.src = url;
    await imgLoaded(img);
    img.width = img.naturalWidth / 10;
    img.height = img.naturalHeight / 10;
    document.body.appendChild(img);
}
```

Now the `await` causes the function to return to the main program. It is restarted at the instruction after the `await` as soon as the image is loaded.

If you can use `async` and `await`, this is the best way to work. It preserves the look of the code that you would write if the image was loaded instantly and it throws an exception if there is an error. This means you can put the await in a `try-catch` and handle errors in the usual way.

Drawing an Image

The first of the Canvas bitmap operations that we need to look at is the `drawImage` method, which draws a bitmap onto a canvas. What is interesting about this method is not so much that it provides a link between a bitmap and the canvas object, but the range of bitmap sources that can be used.

The source for a bitmap can either be a bitmap object, another canvas object or a video object. Notice that if you are using a canvas object as the source of the bitmap you have to have actually drawn something on it first and you have to use the canvas object not the drawing context - see later for an example. If you use a video object then the current frame is rendered to the canvas.

To start with the simplest example, you can take any standard `Image` object and draw it to the canvas. You can derive your image object from the DOM or create it directly within JavaScript. For example, suppose the page contains an image in `img` then you can then display it on the canvas, with the 2D drawing context stored in `ctx` using:

```
ctx.drawImage(img,10, 10);
```

The `drawImage` method takes a number of different parameters, but:

```
drawImage(image,x,y)
```

simply draws as much of the image as can fit on the canvas with its top left corner at x,y:

The complete program is:

```
async function getImage(url) {
    var img = new Image();
    img.src = url;
    await imgLoaded(img);
    var ctx = document.body.appendChild(createCanvas(600, 600)).
                                        getContext("2d");
    ctx.drawImage(img,10, 10);
}
```

```
var img1 = getImage("jeep.jpg")
```

and makes use of `imgLoaded` given in the previous section.

If you want to scale the image then use the alternative form of the `drawImage` method:

```
drawImage(image,x,y,w,h);
```

where w and h specify the width and height that the image is scaled to.

For example:

```
ctx.drawImage(img,10,10,300,300);
```

The problem here is that you might well distort the bitmap by scaling it unequally in the x and y directions. The solution is to use the object's `img.width` and `img.height` properties:

```
ctx.drawImage(img,10,10,img.width/4,img.height/4);
```

Notice that if you don't specify a width and height when you create the image then these are set to the `naturalWidth` and `naturalHeight` properties.

The final form of the `drawImage` method gives you complete control over the way the image is drawn:

```
drawImage(image,sx,sy,sw,sh,dx,dy,dw,dh)
```

This looks complicated, but it simply specifies the location of a source and a destination rectangle. The source rectangle has its top left corner at `sx,sy` and is `sw` wide and `sh` high. The destination rectangle has its top left corner at `dx,dy` and is `dw` wide and `dh` high. The `drawImage` copies pixels in the source rectangle to the destination rectangle, performing any scaling that is needed. For example, to display the area of the bitmap cropped and scaled to show the jeep you would use:

```
ctx.drawImage(img,900,600,img.width/1.5,img.height/1.5,
                        0,0,img.width/8,img.height/8);
```

Notice that both the source and destination rectangles are scaled versions of the full image size. If you want to avoid distortion, this is the usual method.

Finally you can use all three versions of the `drawImage` method with another canvas object as the source of the bitmap. For example:

```
ctx2.drawImage(ctx.canvas,0,0);
```

will draw the contents of `canvas` onto the drawing context `ctx2` of another canvas object.

You can also draw a canvas object onto itself. For example:

```
ctx.drawImage(ctx.canvas,0,0.200,200);
```

will copy the contents of the canvas object back onto itself in a 200 by 200 rectangle if `ctx` is the drawing context of the canvas object. Notice that the source bitmap is copied before it is drawn back to the canvas so there are no strange interactions between source and destination.

So to summarize:
There are three `drawImage` methods:

- `drawImage(image,dx,dy)`
- `drawImage(image,dx,dy,dw,dh)`
- `drawImage(image,sx,sy,sw,sh,dx,dy,dw,dh)`

where `image` is either a canvas, video or an image object derived either from the DOM or constructed in JavaScript, and `sx,sy,sw,sh` define the source rectangle and `dx,dy,dw,dh` define the destination rectangle.

ImageBitmap

There is a replacement for using an `Image` object as the source of bitmap data – the `ImageBitmap`. It is intended to be faster to draw than alternatives, but at the time of writing it hasn't full support on modern browsers – Edge and Safari don't support it at all. In time, it should become the preferred way of sourcing bitmap data in the `drawImage` method.

You can create `ImageBitmap` using either form of the object factory:

```
createImageBitmap(image, options);
createImageBitmap(image, x, y, w, h, options);
```

where `image` can be an image object, SVG, video, canvas, `Blob`, `ImageData`, `ImageBitmap`, or `OffscreenCanvas` object. The `x`, `y`, `w` and `h` parameters give the location of the rectangle in the source used to initialize the ImageBitmap. The `options` parameter, which can be omitted, has a great many settings which optimize the `ImageBitmap`:

◆	`imageOrientation`	Vertical orientation - `none` (default) or `flipY`
◆	`premultiplyAlpha`	Color channels should be premultiplied by alpha `none`, `premultiply`, or `default`
◆	`colorSpaceConversion`	Image should be decoded using color space conversion - `none` or `default`
◆	`resizeWidth`	Use output width
◆	`resizeHeight`	Use output height
◆	`resizeQuality`	`pixelated`, `low` (default), `medium`, or `high`.

Once you have your `ImageBitmap` it can be used in `drawImage` in exactly the same way as an `Image` object or any of the bitmap sources.
Notice that `createImageBitmap` returns a `Promise` that resolves to the `ImageBitmap`.

Animation

One of the main uses of Canvas is to create simple animations. The principle of animation is well known. You show an image for a short time, change the image, show the new image and so on. How fast should you show new images? The answer is that one new image every 1/25th of a second generally creates the impression of movement, but in most cases programs try to show a new image every time the display frame is updated by the hardware. This the fastest rate possible and usually produces smooth animation.

JavaScript has a method that will call a function as soon as possible after each frame refresh. The `requestAnimationFrame` method will call a function that you supply so that it has the most time possible to update the graphics before the next paint update to generate the frame. The function is:

```
var id = requestAnimationFrame(animate);
```

The id returned can be used to cancel an animation using:

```
cancelAnimationFrame(id);
```

The function, called `animate` in this example, is passed a single parameter which is the time, usually in milliseconds, at the start of the frame as measured from the load of the web page.

The `requestAnimationFrame` method is simple enough to understand, but it does have some subtle points. The first is that the `animate` function has to end with a call to `requestAnimationFrame` if it wants to be called for each frame. That is, `requestAnimationFrame` runs the function just once at the start of the next frame. The amount of time that the function has to run is as much of the time between frames as the JavaScript engine can give it. After a frame finishes, the engine deals with all events and outstanding tasks and then calls the `requestAnimationFrame` function, i.e. `animate` in our example.

The function can run for as long as it likes, but if it runs for longer than the time to the next frame it misses the update and any changes are visible in the next frame after it finishes. If there are multiple `requestAnimationFrame` functions pending then they all get the same time stamp, which is just an indicator of the frame that they are supposed to be preparing for. As you might expect, if any of the functions take longer than a frame time then the next frame is skipped.

What all of this means is that it is advisable to keep your
`requestAnimationFrame` functions down to one per application and keep its
processing time short.

How short is short?

The simple answer is less than 16 ms.

If you try the following program:

```
time=[];
count=20;
function animate(t){
    count--;
    time.push(t);
    if(count==0){
        for(i=0;i<19;i++){
            console.log(time[i+1]-time[i]);
        }
            return;
    }
    requestAnimationFrame(animate);
}
requestAnimationFrame(animate);
```

you will be able to see a sample of interframe times for the particular browser
you are targeting.

For Chrome, at the time of writing, the results were mostly 16.66
milliseconds, which is close to the time between frames for 60 fps. However,
occasionally you will see values of 50 ms and even 500 ms. These are caused
by the browser having to do something else other than service your request.
There is nothing you can do about these glitches and in the main they go
undetected by users.

Draw or BitBlt?

There are two ways you can achieve a changing image between frames. You
can draw your image using paths and so on or you can BitBlt a bitmap to the
canvas. BitBlt, pronounced bit-blit, is short for bit-block operation and is
often shortened to blit. This is essentially a low-level copy of a group of bits
stored in memory to another area of memory and, as we have just discovered,
we can do this with `drawImage`.

To compare the two methods let's animate a simple rotating square first using
drawing methods and then by blitting.

To draw a rotating square all we need is to adjust the co-ordinate system so
that we are rotating about the center of the square, see Chapter 5.

```
var inc = 0.1;
var ctx = document.body.appendChild(createCanvas(600, 600)).
                                        getContext("2d");
var path = new Path2D();
path.rect(-25, -25, 50, 50);
ctx.translate(100, 100);
requestAnimationFrame(animate);
```

The `animate` function simply clears the canvas, rotates the co-ordinate system
and draws the path:

```
function animate(t) {
  ctx.clearRect(-100, -100, ctx.canvas.width, ctx.canvas.height);
  ctx.rotate(inc);
  ctx.fill(path);
  requestAnimationFrame(animate);
}
```

If you try the program you will see a smoothly rotating square. There are
some minor problems with this approach - mainly having to remember what
the current co-ordinate system is. Generally this can be avoided by using `save`
and `restore`.

The same animation achieved by blitting needs a single sprite animation
image. A sprite animation image is a single bitmap with a shape, the sprite,
drawn in different positions for the animation. In this case 16 sub-images are
sufficient:

How this bitmap is made isn't really relevant. You could use a bitmap editor
or you could write a program to generate it. The basic idea is load the bitmap
and use `requestAnimationFrame` to show each cell of the animation in turn:

```
async function getImage(url) {
 function animate(t) {
     var cellx = 76;
     var celly = 76;
     var cellno = 16;
     ctx.clearRect(100, 100, cellx, celly);
     ctx.drawImage(img, cellx * i, 0, cellx, celly,
                                100, 100, cellx, celly);
     i++;
     i = i % cellno;
     requestAnimationFrame(animate);
 }
 var img = new Image();
 img.src = url;
 await imgLoaded(img);
 var i = 0;
 requestAnimationFrame(animate);
}
```

In this case the `getImage` function is now acting more like an asynchronous main program - which is what often happens. The `animate` function is defined within it so that it can access the local variables of `getImage`. The `getImage` function collects the sprite images and then calls `requestAnimationFrame` to start the animation. The variable i sets which cell of the bitmap is displayed.

If you try the program you will find that you get a smooth animation, although not quite as smooth as the first version. To get an even smoother animation would require more cells.

The key difference between the two approaches is that the drawing method takes as long to complete as it takes to render the paths involved. The BitBlt method always takes the same time, no matter how complex the sprite. The drawing method does have the advantage of being dynamically changeable, whereas in most cases blitting is restricted to the sprites that you have already created.

The Problem of Speed

In both of the examples given above the amount of rotation is fixed at each update, which is fine as long as each update takes the same amount of time. If the update rate changes then you need to modify the amount of rotation to keep the speed constant. To do this you have to take into account the time since the last frame. Essentially you have to use a velocity variable and multiply by the time since the last frame to discover how far the object has moved. For example, to make the rotating square take account of frame rate, the `animate` function has to be modified to:

```
var pt = 0;
var inc = 0.1/16;
function animate(t) {
  if (pt === 0) {
    pt = t;
    requestAnimationFrame(animate);
    return
  }
ctx.clearRect(-100, -100, ctx.canvas.width, ctx.canvas.height);
var dt=t-pt;
pt=t;
ctx.rotate(inc*dt);
ctx.fill(path);
requestAnimationFrame(animate);
}
```

You can see now that `inc` is the amount that the square rotates in one millisecond. Notice that `pt` has to be a global variable to retain its value between function calls, although there are other ways of achieving this.

When it comes to varying frame rates, due to the browser having to attend to other matters such as garbage collection or updating other graphical elements, there are two approaches. Firstly, you can simply show the same movement per frame. In this case when a frame pauses your animation pauses. Alternatively, you can use the time between frames to alter the amount of distance moved. In this case when a frame pauses, your animation seems to jump forward to the correct position. Neither effect is particularly good from the user's point of view.

Position, Speed & Acceleration

In many cases it is good to think of what you are animating as having a position, a speed and an acceleration. This is ideal for implementation as an object - usually called a sprite. There are many different ways of organizing this idea, but the basics are to create an object with a position, velocity and acceleration property. After this things vary, but the object usually has an `update` method which modifies its position based on its velocity and its velocity based on its acceleration.

The big problem is trading elegant design for efficiency. Let's start off with good design and see how much it costs in terms of performance. The simplest test of animation is bouncing a ball around the screen - it is the hello world of animation. In this case we are going to create a ball sprite and use this to animate any number of bouncing balls.

First we need some objects to hold position, velocity and acceleration.

```
function Pos(x, y) {
  this.x = x;
  this.y = y;
}
function Vel(x, y) {
  this.x = x;
  this.y = y;
}
function Acc(x, y) {
  this.x = x;
  this.y = y;
}
```

Now we can create the `Ball` constructor:

```
function Ball(pos, vel, acc, r) {
  this.pos = pos;
  this.vel = vel;
  this.acc = acc;
```

The r variable isn't being stored as a property, but the methods of the object can access it via closure.

The first method, and the most complicated is the `update` method:

```
this.update = function () {
this.pos.x += this.vel.x;
this.pos.y += this.vel.y;
this.vel.x += this.acc.x;
this.vel.y += this.acc.y;
```

As the ball is going to bounce when it hits the edges of the canvas we can include this in the `update` method:

```
 if (this.pos.x + r > ctx.canvas.width) {
     this.pos.x = ctx.canvas.width - r;
     this.vel.x = -this.vel.x;
 }
 if (this.pos.y + r > ctx.canvas.height) {
     this.pos.y = ctx.canvas.height - r;
     this.vel.y = -this.vel.y;
 }
 if (this.pos.x - r < 0) {
     this.pos.x = r;
     this.vel.x = -this.vel.x;
 }
 if (this.pos.y - r < 0) {
     this.pos.y = r;
     this.vel.y = -this.vel.y;
 }
};
```

We also need a `render` method which will draw the ball at its current location:

```
 this.render = function () {
             var path = new Path2D();
             path.arc(this.pos.x, this.pos.y, r, 0, 2 * Math.PI);
             ctx.fill(path);
         };
}
```

This uses a path to draw a filled circle. Later we will modify the program to use a bitmap.

Having defined the ball sprite we still need to animate it. There could be many sprites involved in the animation and so we need a general `Animation` object that will look after all of them. There usually only needs to be one animation object so it can be constructed as a singleton:

```
Animation = {};
Animation.spriteList = [];
```

The `spriteList` contains all of the sprites to be animated.

We need two methods to implement the animation - `clearCanvas`:

```
Animation.clearCanvas = function () {
                    ctx.clearRect(0, 0, ctx.canvas.width,
                                        ctx.canvas.height);
                };
```

and `run`:

```
Animation.run = function (t) {
              Animation.frameRate(t);
            Animation.clearCanvas(t);
            for (var i = 0;i<Animation.spriteList.length;i++){
                Animation.spriteList[i].update();
                Animation.spriteList[i].render();
            }
            requestAnimationFrame(Animation.run);
        };
```

Notice that every sprite has to have an `update` and a `render` method. As we want to see how fast all of this works, there is also a `frameRate` method which updates an input tag with id fps:

```
Animation.frameRate = function (t) {
                    if (typeof t !== "undefined") {
                      Animation.frameRate.temp = 0.8 *
                        Animation.frameRate.temp + 0.2 *
                          (t - Animation.frameRate.tp);
                      Animation.frameRate.tp = t;
                    }
                    Animation.frameRate.count++;
                    if (Animation.frameRate.count === 120) {
                      fps.value=(1000/Animation.frameRate.temp)
                                            .toFixed(2);
                      Animation.frameRate.temp = 0;
                      Animation.frameRate.count = 0;
                    }
                };
Animation.frameRate.count = 0;
Animation.frameRate.tp = 0;
Animation.frameRate.temp = 0;
```

The frame rate is calculated by taking the difference in the time each frame starts. This is used to form a running weighted average in `temp`. Every 120 frames the form is updated to show the new `frameRate`.

Now all we need is the main program to use the ball object:

```
var ctx = document.body.appendChild(createCanvas(600,
600)).getContext("2d");
var noBalls = 3;
var balls = [];
for (i = 0; i < noBalls; i++) {
  balls[i] = new Ball(new Pos(Math.floor(Math.random() * 250),
                         Math.floor(Math.random() * 250)),
                      new Vel(Math.floor(Math.random() * 10) - 5,
                         Math.floor(Math.random() * 10) - 5),
                      new Acc(0, 0.1), 20);
}
Animation.spriteList = balls;
Animation.run();
```

A `for` loop is used to create an array of ball instances with random starting points and velocities. All of the balls have an acceleration of `0,0.1` which makes them appear to fall and bounce.

Listing - Ball 1

The complete program can also be found and tried on the I/O Press website: www.iopress.info.

```
<!DOCTYPE html>
<html>
  <head>
    <title>JavaScript Graphics</title>
    <meta charset="UTF-8">
    <meta name="viewport" content="width=device-width,
                                    initial-scale=1.0">
  </head>
  <body>
    <input id="fps">
    <script>
      function createCanvas(h, w) {
            var c = document.createElement("canvas");
            c.width = w;
            c.height = h;
            return c;
      }
```

```javascript
function Pos(x, y) {
    this.x = x;
    this.y = y;
}

function Vel(x, y) {
    this.x = x;
    this.y = y;
}

function Acc(x, y) {
    this.x = x;
    this.y = y;
}

function Ball(pos, vel, acc, r) {
    this.pos = pos;
    this.vel = vel;
    this.acc = acc;

    this.update = function () {
        this.pos.x += this.vel.x;
        this.pos.y += this.vel.y;
        this.vel.x += this.acc.x;
        this.vel.y += this.acc.y;

        if (this.pos.x + r > ctx.canvas.width) {
            this.pos.x = ctx.canvas.width - r;
            this.vel.x = -this.vel.x;
        }
        if (this.pos.y + r > ctx.canvas.height) {
            this.pos.y = ctx.canvas.height - r;
            this.vel.y = -this.vel.y;
        }
        if (this.pos.x - r < 0) {
            this.pos.x = r;
            this.vel.x = -this.vel.x;
        }
        if (this.pos.y - r < 0) {
            this.pos.y = r;
            this.vel.y = -this.vel.y;
        }
    };
    this.render = function () {
        var path = new Path2D();
        path.arc(this.pos.x, this.pos.y, r, 0, 2 * Math.PI);
        ctx.fill(path);
    };
}
```

```javascript
Animation = {};
Animation.spriteList = [];

Animation.clearCanvas = function () {
     ctx.clearRect(0, 0, ctx.canvas.width,ctx.canvas.height);
    };

Animation.run = function (t) {
     Animation.frameRate(t);
     Animation.clearCanvas(t);
     for (var i = 0;i < Animation.spriteList.length; i++) {
         Animation.spriteList[i].update();
         Animation.spriteList[i].render();
     }
     requestAnimationFrame(Animation.run);
    };

Animation.frameRate = function (t) {
    if (typeof t !== "undefined") {
     Animation.frameRate.temp = 0.8 * Animation.frameRate.temp +
                              0.2 * (t - Animation.frameRate.tp);
     Animation.frameRate.tp = t;
    }
    Animation.frameRate.count++;
    if (Animation.frameRate.count === 120) {
     fps.value = (1000 / Animation.frameRate.temp).toFixed(2);
     Animation.frameRate.temp = 0;
     Animation.frameRate.count = 0;
    }
   };
```

```
Animation.frameRate.count = 0;
Animation.frameRate.tp = 0;
      Animation.frameRate.temp = 0;
            var ctx = document.body.appendChild(createCanvas(600,
600)).getContext("2d");
            var noBalls = 3;
            var balls = [];
      for (i = 0; i < noBalls; i++) {
         balls[i] = new Ball(
                      new Pos(Math.floor(Math.random() * 250),
                         Math.floor(Math.random() * 250)),
                      new Vel(Math.floor(Math.random() * 10) - 5,
                         Math.floor(Math.random() * 10) - 5),
                      new Acc(0, 0.1), 20);
      }
      Animation.spriteList = balls;
      Animation.run();
   </script>
  </body>
</html>
```

Using BitBlt

You can change `noBalls` to see how many you can animate with acceptable
performance. This is subjective, but a frame rate of close to 60 fps and not too
many pauses gives around 400 on the latest Chrome and 250 on Firefox.

What if the render method used a BitBlt?

The advantage of blitting is that the ball can now be as complex as you need,
it can even have internal animation, but all for the same overall effort. To
change the render method to use a bitmap, we first have to create the bitmap,
which has to be done before the call to `createCanvas`:

```
var ctx2 = createCanvas(40, 40).getContext("2d");
var path = new Path2D();
var r = 20;
path.arc(20, 20, r, 0, 2 * Math.PI);
ctx2.fill(path);
```

The new render method is just:

```
this.render = function () {
            ctx.drawImage(ctx2.canvas,this.pos.x-r,this.pos.y-r);
         };
```

With these changes the performance improves to 600 fps on Chrome and 800
on Firefox and still produces a good result with 1000 balls.

You can see that using a bitmap to render a sprite is a good idea. But how
much are we losing using this elegant object-oriented approach?

Raw Animation

Implementing the same overall algorithm, but using a blit for the render and using arrays to store the position, velocity and acceleration and performing the update in a single `requestAnimationFrame` call is easy to implement:

```javascript
function createCanvas(h, w) {
 var c = document.createElement("canvas");
 c.width = w;
 c.height = h;
 return c;
}

var tp = 0;
fps.value = "0.0";
var count = 0;
var temp = 0;

function animate(t) {
  if (typeof t !== "undefined") {
      temp = 0.8 * temp + 0.2 * (t - tp);
      tp = t;
  }
  count++;
  if (count === 120) {
  fps.value = (1000 / temp).toFixed(2);
  temp = 0;
  count = 0;
}

ctx.clearRect(0, 0, ctx.canvas.width, ctx.canvas.height);
for (i = 0; i < noBalls; i++) {
  posX[i] += velX[i];
  posY[i] += velY[i];
  velX[i] += accX[i];
  velY[i] += accY[i];
  if (posX[i] + r > ctx.canvas.width) {
     posX[i] = ctx.canvas.width - r;
     velX[i] = -velX[i];
  }
  if (posY[i] + r > ctx.canvas.width) {
     posY[i] = ctx.canvas.height - r;
     velY[i] = -velY[i];
  }

  if (posX[i] - r < 0) {
     posX[i] = r;
     velX[i] = -velX[i];
  }
```

```javascript
  if (posY[i] - r < 0) {
      posY[i] = r;
      velY[i] = -velY[i];
  }
  ctx.drawImage(ctx2.canvas, posX[i] - r, posY[i] - r);
 }
 requestAnimationFrame(animate);
}

posX = [];
posY = [];
velX = [];
velY = [];
accX = [];
accY = [];

var ctx = document.body.appendChild(createCanvas(600, 600)).
                                        getContext("2d");
var ctx2 = createCanvas(40, 40).getContext("2d");
var path = new Path2D();
var r = 20;
path.arc(20, 20, r, 0, 2 * Math.PI);
ctx2.fill(path);
var noBalls = 1000;

for (i = 0; i < noBalls; i++) {
    posX[i] = Math.floor(Math.random() * 250);
    posY[i] = Math.floor(Math.random() * 250);
    velX[i] = Math.floor(Math.random() * 10) - 5;
    velY[i] = Math.floor(Math.random() * 10) - 5;
    accX[i] = 0;
    accY[i] = 0.1;
}
animate();
```

Using this approach, Chrome managed around 1000 balls and Firefox 2500 balls at 60 fps.

From this you can conclude that an elegant design loses you about 1/3 of the power you could have, but differences between browsers makes this a difficult thing to quantify.

It is important to notice that when you move to a mobile device things slow down a lot. On a mid-range Android Phone the object-oriented version can manage 100 balls at 60fps and the primitive version can manage 200. You have to decide on your target device and test to see what you can achieve. Notice that bouncing 100 balls at the same time is often more than enough for simple animation. If you need more then you will have to use more sophisticated techniques, but at the end the limit is the time it takes to move that many pixels.

For example, removing the update from the primitive version, i.e. just leaving the BitBlt operation, increases the number of balls on the Android phone from 200 to around 300. That is, position computation takes around 1/3 of the time taken to transfer the bits.

Summary

- The fundamental way of getting bitmaps into a web page is to use the `<img>` tag or the `Image` object.

- Loading an image is always asynchronous. There is no way to pause and wait for an image to load, no matter how hard you try.

- The only way to handle asynchronous image loading is to use the `onload` event handler.

- A more modern approach is to wrap the event handler in a function that returns a `Promise`. The function can then be used with `async/await` to make the asynchronous operation look perfectly like a synchronous load.

- Once you have an image loaded, you can use the `drawImage` method to draw the pixels to a canvas.

- `ImageBitmap` is the new and faster way to source a bitmap for a canvas.

- Animation can be achieved by repeated drawing of the animated object or by drawing a bitmap into a new location – BitBlt. In most cases blitting is faster.

- You can arrange to take into account the time between frames to determine how far an object should have moved.

- Animation is often best organized around the idea of a sprite, a shape with position, velocity and acceleration.

- Sprites are perfect for implementation using object-oriented methods. Doing this loses about 1/3 of the speed you can achieve using a non-object-oriented, direct implementation.

Chapter 9

Web Workers & OffscreenCanvas

Even if you can make your animation run fast enough, you still have the problem of the pauses that occur whenever the UI thread has to deal with something else. There are situations when your animation can freeze for a considerable time. The solution is to move the animation from the UI thread to a different thread.

Until recently there was no way that a JavaScript programmer could take advantage of the OS to schedule threads or multiple cores to implement true parallelism, but now we have web workers which implement background processing on a non-UI thread. The only problem is that a web worker cannot access the DOM and the canvas object is part of the DOM. To make it possible to implement graphics processing off the UI thread, the `OffscreenCanvas` object was introduced. It is still reasonably new and at the time of writing Chrome is the only browser to fully support it. While supported in Firefox, it is disabled by default and you need to set a flag to enable it, and even then it only supports the WebGL graphics context.

It is worth making clear that while `OffscreenCanvas` has been introduced as something to make animation smoother, almost any intensive graphics operation is better implemented as a web worker. Indeed any intensive operation of any kind is best implemented in this way.

Before we look at how to use `OffscreenCanvas` we need to find out the basics of using a web worker.

Basic Web Worker

The good news is that web workers are very easy to use. What is slightly difficult to get to grips with is working out what you are not allowed to do and achieving simple communication between the threads. Ideally you should wrap any web worker task you create as a `Promise` to make the code easier to use, but for the moment simpler is better.

There really is only one key object when using web workers, the Worker object, which automatically starts a new thread and begins executing JavaScript code as soon as it is created.

The basic action is that the worker loads the JavaScript file that you specify in its constructor and starts the script executing on a new thread. It is possible to avoid using a separate file to store the code, but it is messy and best avoided. The reason the code is in a separate file is to keep the execution contexts separated on the threads. That is, the program that starts on the new worker thread has no shared variables with the code that creates it.

So, for example, if you have a program stored in `myScript.js` the instruction to run it is:

```
var worker=new Worker("myScript.js");
```

Although this is simple, there is a subtlety that you need to get clear if you are to avoid making silly mistakes.

When you create a `Worker` object two things happen.

1. The code stored in `myScript.js`, or whatever file you specify, is loaded and set running using a new OS level thread.

2. A `Worker` object is created on the UI thread and this is the object that your "standard" JavaScript code running on the UI thread can use to communicate with the new worker thread.

If you think that this is obvious and doesn't need to be said, so much the better.

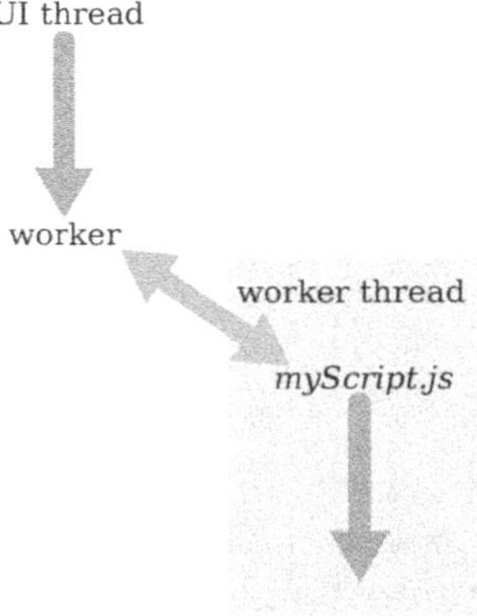

In the example given above `worker` is an object that exists on the UI thread and "`myScript.js`" loaded and running in isolation from the UI thread and the program that worker belongs to. Of course, the `Worker` object provides methods that allow communication between the two programs and this is something we have to find out how to use.

If you need to load a library into the worker thread's code you can use the `importScripts` function. You simply supply the URLs of the scripts to load as parameters. The scripts are downloaded in any order, but executed in the order you specify. The `importScripts` function is synchronous and blocks until all of the libraries have been downloaded. You can try to load standard libraries into a worker thread but, as the DOM is unavailable, they might not work. For example jQuery certainly doesn't work as it needs the DOM to function.

The Trouble With Threads

If you have experience of writing multi-threaded programs, and all of the problems that this creates, this is where you might be getting worried. In general, multi-threaded programs are difficult to get right.

Starting a new thread so easily seems to be a simple way to do something dangerous. However, web workers have been implemented in a way that restricts the way that you use them to make them safe. At first these restrictions might seem tough to live with, but after a while you realize that they are perfectly reasonable and don't really stop you from doing anything.

- The main simplification about threading with web workers is that the new thread cannot share anything with the UI thread.

The new thread cannot access any objects that the UI Thread can. This means it cannot interact with any global objects and it cannot interact with the DOM or the user interface in any way. As the canvas is a DOM object, it is out of bounds. The good news is that there is a new object, the `OffscreenCanvas` object. This is not part of the DOM so web workers can access it and it is very easy to transfer its contents to a canvas object which is part of the DOM. However, it is important to know that the worker thread is isolated from the UI thread and cannot access any objects that are created by the UI thread and vice versa. The new thread runs in a little world of its own, but don't panic as it can communicate with the UI thread in a very simple way.

This inability to share objects may seem a little restrictive, but it is a restriction that is necessary to make sure that the two threads you now have don't try to access the same object at the same time. If this was allowed to happen you would need to introduce a lot of complicated machinery – locks, semaphores and so on – to make sure that the access was orderly and didn't give rise to any very difficult to find bugs such as race conditions, deadlock and so on.

The problem is that if you have multiple threads accessing the same data you can't be sure of the order that things are happening in. Suppose one thread is in the middle of updating a shared object and a second thread deletes it in the middle of the update. This would at best lead to a program that didn't do what the user expected and at worst would generate a runtime error. The only way to stop this from happening is to use mechanisms that restrict access to shared objects so that only one thread can be working with it at any given time. This is potentially very complex and it is very difficult to prove that you have things correct. The alternative to managing shared objects in this way is to ban shared objects. In this case there is absolutely no danger of a simultaneous access to any object, but it makes interaction impossible.

In other words, the web worker has big restrictions so that you can use it without complication and without any danger. For most purposes, however, it is sufficient and hence very effective.

- Web workers do have access to all of the global core JavaScript objects that you might expect, but they are not shared.

They can also access some functions that are normally associated with the DOM, including `XMLHttpRequest()` and `setInterval`.

The rule is that if the object is unique to the UI thread, or could be shared in any way with the UI thread, then you cannot get access to it and this is a condition that is obviously satisfied for all of the core JavaScript objects and the few DOM derived objects that are allowed.

To make up for this restriction there are two new objects that the web worker can access - `WorkerNavigator` and `WorkerLocation`. The navigator provides basic information about the app's context - the browser in use, `appName`, `appVersion` and so on. The location object provides details of where the app is in terms of the current URL.

If these two objects don't provide enough information you can easily arrange to pass the worker thread additional data of your choosing.

Basic Communication Methods

So if the web worker is isolated from the UI thread, how do the two communicate? The answer is that they both use events and a method that causes events on the other thread.

UI Thread to Worker Thread

Let's start with the UI thread sending a message to the worker thread. The `Worker` object that is created on the UI thread has a `postMessage` method which triggers a message event on the worker thread. Notice that this is where the thread crossover occurs. The `Worker` object is running on the UI thread, but the event occurs in the code running on the worker thread, which has an event queue all of its own – it is a complete event-driven program.

For example:

```
var worker=new Worker("myScript.js");
worker.postMessage({mydata:"some data"});
```

The `postMessage` method triggers a message event in the web worker code and sends it an event object that includes the data object as its data property. That is, `event.data` has a `mydata` property equal to `"some data"`.

To get the message sent to the worker you have to set up an event handler and retrieve the event object's data property. For example:

```
this.addEventListener("message", function (event) {
```

In the web worker code the global context is provided by `this` or `self` and gives access to all of the methods and objects documented. To get the message you would use:

```
var data = event.data.mydata;
```

Of course, as you are passing an object to the event handler you could package as many data items as you needed to.

It is important to be very clear what is going on here. The `postMessage` method call is on the UI thread, but the event handler is on the worker thread. It is also important to realize that the data that is passed between the two threads isn't shared. A copy is made using the structured clone algorithm and it is this copy that the worker receives. You can use a wide range of types of data to pass to the worker, but if it is big the time taken to copy could be significant. If this is the case. you need to use a transferable object, which is shared rather than copied. As you can guess, an `OffscreenCanvas` is too big to move between threads in this way and it is a transferable object, as explained later.

Worker Thread to UI Thread

Passing data from the worker thread to the UI thread works in exactly the same way – only the other way round. You use the `postMessage` method of the `DedicatedWorkerGlobalScope` object in the Worker thread and attach an event handler for the message event in the UI thread.

The `DedicatedWorkerGlobalScope` object can be accessed using `this` or `self`. For example, in the web worker code:

```
this.postMessage({mydata:"some data"});
```

or:

```
self.postMessage({mydata:"some data"});
```

Notice that in this case you can use `this` or `self` to call `postMessage` because you are running inside the web worker. Use `self` when `this` is set to something else other than the web worker, i.e. when you are programming within another object.

A message event is triggered in the UI thread and you can define a handler and retrieve the data using:

```
worker.addEventListener("message",
 function (e) {
   var somedata= e.data.mydata;
 });
```

Once again you have to be very clear that you understand what is running where. In this case the `postMessage` method is running on the Worker thread and the event handler is `running` on the UI thread.

This is about all there is to using web workers. There are some details about error handling and terminating the thread before it is complete, but these are just details. The general idea is that you use the message event to communicate between the two threads.

There is one subtle point that is worth keeping in mind. The events that you trigger in passing data between the two threads will happen in the order that you trigger them, but they may not be handled promptly.

For example, if you start your worker thread doing an intensive calculation then triggering a "*how are you doing*" message event from the UI thread might not work as you expect. It could be that the worker thread is so occupied with its task that events are ignored until it reaches the end. The same happens with messages passed from the worker thread, but in this case the UI thread is generally not so focused on one task and so events usually get processed.

The rule is that UI thread events are generally handled promptly because that's the way we tend to build UI code, but worker thread events aren't because that's the way we tend to build worker code. That is, events going from the worker thread to the UI get processed as part of keeping the UI responsive. Events going the other way, i.e. from the UI thread to the web worker, are not so reliable. If you want to drive the worker thread using events from the UI thread you basically have to design it to be event-driven. This means writing the worker thread as an event handler that responds to the messages that the UI thread sends, and this means that your code has to give up the worker thread every so often to allow it to process events. For a general worker thread this can be difficult because you have to essentially pause the calculation it is performing and allow the thread to service the event queue. For a graphics worker thread this is much easier because generally when a frame is complete the thread is released.

To sum up:

- Communication between the UI and worker thread is via events fired by one thread and received by the other.
- Each thread only processes events when not occupied with running code.
- This means that events may not be dealt with promptly.
- Data can be transferred between threads using the event object that is made available to the event handler.
- Data is not shared – a copy is made for the receiving thread.
- The UI thread is generally set up to respond to events promptly, but the worker thread isn't.
- A graphics-oriented worker thread is the exception to the rule as it generally gives up its thread with each call to `requestAnimationFrame`.

Transferable Objects

The way that worker threads avoid many of the problems of multi-threading is by limiting the way threads can interact. They can only communicate by sending messages and any data that is included in the message isn't shared, but copied. This means that each thread is always working on its own data and no object can be used by more than one thread at a time.

Copying data is safe, but if the data is large it can be slow. An alternative is to use transferable objects. These are not copied, but even so only one thread can access them at any given time. The idea is that the object belongs to just one thread and only that thread can access the object. Ownership of the thread can be passed to another thread by the object being included in a message sent from the current owner to another thread.

Transferable objects are only supported in the latest browsers. The mechanism only applies to four types of object - `ArrayBuffer`, `MessagePort`, `ImageBitMap` and `OffscreenCanvas`. This makes sense because these are all potentially large objects which are best not passed by copy.

To send a transferable object you simply follow the usual data object in `postMessage` by an array of transferable objects.

The way that transferable objects work is simple, but it can be confusing. As usual, you pass data using the message object which becomes the data property of the event object passed to the event handler. The data that you want to transfer has to be included either as the message object or a property of the message object.

To be passed by transfer rather than clone, the object also has to be listed in the transfer array. So, for example:

```
postMessage(object,[object]);
```

will transfer *object* and the event handler will receive the object as `event.data`.

Alternatively, you could use:

```
postMessage({mydata: object},[object]);
```

which will also transfer *object*, but the event handler will receive it as `event.data.mydata`. Obviously, you could pass additional properties and if these were not included in the transfer list they would be passed by cloning.

Once an object has been transferred it is no longer usable in the original thread. For example in the case of an `ArrayBuffer` its size is reduced to zero in the original thread. Notice that once transferred its ownership cannot be simply transferred back because the reference that is passed is in `event.data` or `event.data.myobject` and not the original reference. That is, it is not a simple turning off and on of the original reference.

You can arrange for this to happen, however. We need a very simple example and to do this we need to work with an `ArrayBuffer`. An `ArrayBuffer` is a raw collection of bytes and you cannot access it directly. It has to be converted into a typed array before you can access its data, see Chapter 11 for details. However, we can simply create a raw buffer and pass it back and forth between the main thread and the worker thread as an example without worrying about what data it contains:

```
var worker = new Worker("transfer.js");
var arrayBuf = new ArrayBuffer(8);
console.log("UI before transfer " + arrayBuf.byteLength);
worker.postMessage(arrayBuf, [arrayBuf]);
console.log("UI after transfer" + arrayBuf.byteLength);
```

This simply creates an eight byte `ArrayBuffer` and transfers it to the worker thread. When the program is run you see:

```
UI before transfer 8
UI after transfer 0
```

indicating that the `ArrayBuffer` is no longer available in the UI thread.

In the Worker thread we can use the `ArrayBuffer` in the standard way:

```
this.addEventListener("message",
      function(event){
       console.log("Worker got data! " + event.data.byteLength);
      });
```

You will see the message:

```
Worker got data! 8
```

indicating that the `ArrayBuffer` is now available in the worker thread.

The web worker can pass the `ArrayBuffer` back to the UI thread:

```
this.addEventListener("message",function(event){
    console.log("Worker got data! " + event.data.byteLength);
    postMessage(event.data,[event.data]);
    console.log("Worker sent data! " + event.data.byteLength);
});
```

After the data has been transferred back to the UI thread you will once again see that the length of the `ArrayBuffer` is 0.

In the UI thread the data can be retrieved in the usual way:

```
worker.addEventListener("message",
    function (event) {
    console.log("UI after return " + event.data.byteLength);
    console.log("UI after return original " + arrayBuf.byteLength);
    });
```

In this case you will see that the `event.data` is an `ArrayBuffer` of eight bytes and the original `arrayBuf` is still 0, that is the original transferred data is not restored.

You can, of course, restore the reference to the original data:

```
worker.addEventListener("message",
    function (event) {
      console.log("UI after return " + event.data.byteLength);
      arrayBuf=event.data;
      console.log("UI after return original " + arrayBuf.byteLength);
    });
```

Now it looks as if the original data has been handed back by the worker thread.

The big problem with transferring data is that the thread that owned it originally doesn't get the use of it, not even a copy, while the other thread is using it. This doesn't matter as long as the initial owner is generating the data for the first time. For example, if a worker thread is downloading a resource it can transfer it to the UI thread to be used with no problems. Compare this to a Worker thread that is modifying, rather than originating, the data. If the UI thread passes the worker thread a bitmap or an `OffscreenCanvas` to process, what does the UI thread show while the worker has ownership?

OffscreenCanvas

An `OffscreenCanvas` is a canvas object that isn't part of the screen display. It is simply an area of memory that you can draw into using all of the familiar methods. The fact that it isn't part of the display, and isn't part of the DOM, means that it can be used from the UI thread and from a worker thread. When used from the UI thread it behaves a lot like a canvas object that you haven't added to the DOM, but it also has some additional methods.

You create an `OffscreenCanvas` object using:

```
var offCanvas=new OffscreenCanvas(width,height);
```

Notice that as this is not part of the DOM it doesn't have a style width and height like a canvas object. It does have `width` and `height` properties, however. It also has a `getContext` method that you can use to draw on it and a pair of new methods:

- ◆ `convertToBlob()` converts the image to a binary blob using the format of any of the supported graphics file types – jpg, png. For lossy compression you can also specify a quality parameter.

- ◆ `transferToImageBitmap()` returns an `ImageBitmap` object based on the current contents of the `OffscreenCanvas`.

OffscreenCanvas in the UI Thread

As already mentioned, you can use an `OffscreenCanvas` wherever you would otherwise use a canvas object not added to the DOM and, as long as you are only targeting browsers that support `OffscreenCanvas`, it is sensible to use it instead. However, at the time of writing only Chrome supports it in the 2d context.

For example, the bitmap for the ball in the example at the end of the previous chapter can be created using, in the main program;

```
var ctx2 = new OffscreenCanvas(40, 40).getContext("2d");
var path = new Path2D();
var r = 20;
path.arc(20, 20, r, 0, 2 * Math.PI);
ctx2.fill(path);
```

And to make this visible you simply use, in render:

```
ctx.drawImage(ctx2.canvas, this.pos.x - r, this.pos.y — r);
```

which is exactly how you would do it with a standard canvas object.

You can see the complete modified program at www.iopress.info.

Alternatively you could create an `ImageBitmap` and use it in place of the canvas:

```
var ballImage=ctx2.canvas.transferToImageBitmap();
```

You would then render the ball using:

```
ctx.drawImage(ballImage, this.pos.x - r, this.pos.y – r);
```

which is in principle faster.

OffscreenCanvas in the Worker Thread

As another example of using `OffscreenCanvas`, we can modify the ball drawing in the ball bounce example so that the ball image is drawn in a worker thread. This isn't a useful thing to do as the ball image is drawn just once and there is no advantage in handing it off to a worker thread, but it is a simple example of how an `OffscreenCanvas` can create some graphics on a worker thread and pass it back to the UI thread.

First we need the `Worker`:

```
var worker=new Worker("animate.js");
```

The file `animate.js` will contain all of the code needed to create the ball image:

```
var ctx2 = new OffscreenCanvas(40, 40).getContext("2d");
var path = new Path2D();
var r = 20;
path.arc(20, 20, r, 0, 2 * Math.PI);
ctx2.fill(path);
var ballImage = ctx2.canvas.transferToImageBitmap();
```

Now we have the ball image and we need to send it back to the UI thread. As an `ImageBitmap` is a transferable, we can use:

```
this.postMessage({ballImage:ballImage},[ballImage]);
close();
```

The call to `close` disposes of the worker thread. If you use `return` or just allow the code to run out, the worker thread continues to live and will process any events that the UI thread sends to it.

The UI thread now has to set up an event handler to receive the bitmap:

```
worker.addEventListener("message", function (e) {
  ballImage = e.data.ballImage; }
);
```

Of course, we now have to postpone any animation in the UI thread until the `ballImage` is returned by the worker thread. There are many ways of doing this. For example, you can write the call to initiate animation into the event handler:

```
var worker = new Worker("animate.js");
var ctx = document.body.appendChild(createCanvas(600, 600)).
                                            getContext("2d");
var ballImage;
worker.addEventListener("message",
                        function (e) {
                            ballImage = e.data.ballImage;
                            Animation.run();
                        });
var noBalls = 2;
var balls = [];
for (i = 0; i < noBalls; i++) {
        balls[i] = new Ball(new Pos(Math.floor(Math.random()*250),
                                Math.floor(Math.random()*250)),
                        new Vel(Math.floor(Math.random()*10)-5,
                                Math.floor(Math.random()*10)-5),
                        new Acc(0, .2), 20);
}
Animation.spriteList = balls;
```

Notice that the call to `Animation.run` is now in the event handler. Also notice that you can be sure that the main program finishes before the event handler fires because events can only be processed when the UI thread is freed at the end of the main program. JavaScript is asynchronous but most JavaScript code isn't interruptable, i.e. once a block of code is started it generally runs to completion.

In practice you wouldn't simply create the ball image in the worker thread. Once you have established a worker thread you could use it to do all of the graphics, leaving the UI thread to service the user's clicks and so on.

A Worker Animation Example

Now that we have the basics of how we can implement graphics using a
worker thread it is time to see a bigger example. In general all you have to do
is move the graphics and animation code into the Worker. For example, the
ball bounce example can be written as a web worker, animate.js, as:

```
function Pos(x, y) {
    this.x = x;
    this.y = y;
}
function Vel(x, y) {
    this.x = x;
    this.y = y;
}
function Acc(x, y) {
    this.x = x;
    this.y = y;
}
function Ball(pos, vel, acc, r) {
    this.pos = pos;
    this.vel = vel;
    this.acc = acc;
    this.update = function () {
        this.pos.x += this.vel.x + this.acc.x / 2;
        this.pos.y += this.vel.y + this.acc.y / 2;
        this.vel.x += this.acc.x;
        this.vel.y += this.acc.y;
        if (this.pos.x + r > ctx.canvas.width) {
            this.pos.x = ctx.canvas.width - r;
            this.vel.x = -this.vel.x;
        }
        if (this.pos.y + r > ctx.canvas.height) {
            this.pos.y = ctx.canvas.height - r;
            this.vel.y = -this.vel.y;
        }
        if (this.pos.x - r < 0) {
            this.pos.x = r;
            this.vel.x = -this.vel.x;
        }
        if (this.pos.y - r < 0) {
            this.pos.y = r;
            this.vel.y = -this.vel.y;
        }
    };
    this.render = function () {
        ctx.drawImage(ballImage, this.pos.x - r, this.pos.y - r);
    };
}
```

```javascript
Animation = {};
Animation.spriteList = [];

Animation.clearCanvas = function () {
    ctx.clearRect(0, 0, ctx.canvas.width, ctx.canvas.height);
};

Animation.frameRate = function (t) {
    if (typeof t !== "undefined") {
        Animation.frameRate.temp = 0.8 * Animation.frameRate.temp +
                                   0.2 * (t - Animation.frameRate.tp);
        Animation.frameRate.tp = t;
    }
    Animation.frameRate.count++;
    if (Animation.frameRate.count === 120) {
        Animation.fps = (1000 /Animation.frameRate.temp).toFixed(2);
        Animation.frameRate.temp = 0;
        Animation.frameRate.count = 0;
    }
};
Animation.frameRate.count = 0;
Animation.frameRate.tp = 0;
Animation.frameRate.temp = 0;
Animation.fps = 0;

Animation.run = function (t) {
    Animation.frameRate(t);
    Animation.clearCanvas();
    for (var i = 0; i < Animation.spriteList.length; i++) {
        var ball1 = Animation.spriteList[i];
        ball1.update();
        ball1.render();
    }

    var frame = ctx.canvas.transferToImageBitmap();
    self.postMessage({frame: frame, fps: Animation.fps}, [frame]);
    requestAnimationFrame(Animation.run);
};
```

There are no changes to the `Ball` class and the `Animation` singleton only has
small changes in the `frameRate` and run methods. Now that it cannot access
the DOM to display its result, `frameRate` is instead stored in `Animation.fps`.
While run is the same as before, now the final few lines create an update for
the UI thread. You can see that the `postMessage` function call sends a frame
bitmap by transferring it to the UI thread and the fps value by copying. Notice
that it is perfectly OK for the worker to call `requestAnimationFrame`, which
ensures that it doesn't try to update the UI faster than the frame rate.

The web worker main program simply has to set things up and then call the run method:

```
var ctx = new OffscreenCanvas(600, 600).getContext("2d");
var ctx2 = new OffscreenCanvas(40, 40).getContext("2d");
var path = new Path2D();
var r = 20;
path.arc(20, 20, r, 0, 2 * Math.PI);
ctx2.fill(path);
var ballImage = ctx2.canvas.transferToImageBitmap();

var noBalls = 80;
var balls = [];
for (i = 0; i < noBalls; i++) {
    balls[i] = new Ball(new Pos(Math.floor(Math.random() * 250),
                                Math.floor(Math.random() * 250)),
                         new Vel(Math.floor(Math.random() * 10) − 5,
                                 Math.floor(Math.random() * 10) − 5),
                         new Acc(0, .2), 20);
}
Animation.spriteList = balls;
Animation.run();
```

The UI thread is now very simple:

```
var worker = new Worker("animate.js");
var ctx = document.body.appendChild(createCanvas(600,
600)).getContext("2d");

worker.addEventListener("message",
                        function (e) {
                            ctx.drawImage(e.data.frame,0,0);
                            fps.value =e.data.fps;
                        });
```

You can see that all the UI thread has to do is respond to the event sent by the worker. It draws the image to the canvas and updates the text box.

If you try this out you will discover that it doesn't quite work. The reason is that when you clear the `OffscreenCanvas` all of the pixels are set to transparent black, i.e. background pixels. When you draw the bitmap onto the canvas only the foreground pixels change the canvas. What this means is that you don't get a clearing of the canvas at each frame. There are a number of different ways around the problem. If you are using `drawImage` then the simplest is to change the composition rule to:

```
ctx.globalCompositeOperation="copy";
```

With this change the `OffscreenCanvas` replaces all of the pixels in the DOM canvas.

You can see the complete modified program at www.iopress.info.

This raises the question of why the `OffscreenCanvas` cannot be used to replace the current bitmap displayed by the canvas without the need to use compositing. The latest part of the standard provides a new graphics context for the canvas and a new method that allows the bitmap being displayed to be swapped to another. To use this you have to change the UI graphics context to:

```
var ctx = document.body.appendChild(createCanvas(600, 600)).
                                  getContext("bitmaprenderer");
```

Currently only Chrome supports the "bitmaprenderer" context. With this change we can now transfer the bitmap without compositing and at maximum speed:

```
worker.addEventListener("message",
                    function (e) {
                        ctx.transferFromImageBitmap(e.data.frame);
                        fps.value =e.data.fps;
                    });
```

TransferControlToOffScreen

There is another way to organize things that makes animation very simple. As the use of an `OffscreenCanvas` to update a DOM canvas is so common, there is a way to link an `OffscreenCanvas` and a DOM canvas so that updates to the `OffscreenCanvas` are automatically transferred to the DOM canvas. Simply create a DOM canvas and use the `transferControlToOffScreen` method to return an `OffscreenCanvas` that is linked to it. You can pass this `OffscreenCanvas` to a web worker and it can draw on it. Every time the browser does a repaint the `OffscreenCanvas` is automatically used to update the DOM canvas. The only downside is that you cannot make use of the DOM canvas directly – it is essentially just a "front" for the object doing all the work, the `OffscreenCanvas`. This is potentially the fastest way to use an `OffscreenCanvas` to display changes at the highest frame rate.

So how would we change the previous bouncing ball program to make use of this?

You can see the complete modified program at www.iopress.info.

The main program in the UI thread is just:

```
var worker = new Worker("animate.js");
var offCanvas = document.body.appendChild(createCanvas(600, 600)).
                            transferControlToOffscreen();

worker.postMessage({canvas: offCanvas}, [offCanvas]);
```

That is all you need as the worker thread does everything else. It needs an event handler to accept the message that gives it the `OffscreenCanvas` and make use of it:

```
var ctx;
var ballImage;
this.addEventListener("message", function (e) {
     ctx = e.data.canvas.getContext("2d");
     var ctx2 = new OffscreenCanvas(40, 40).getContext("2d");
     var path = new Path2D();
     var r = 20;
     path.arc(20, 20, r, 0, 2 * Math.PI);
     ctx2.fill(path);
     ballImage = ctx2.canvas.transferToImageBitmap();
     var noBalls = 80;
     var balls = [];
     for (i = 0; i < noBalls; i++) {
      balls[i] = new Ball(new Pos(Math.floor(Math.random()*250),
                                  Math.floor(Math.random()*250)),
                           new Vel(Math.floor(Math.random()*10)-5,
                                   Math.floor(Math.random()*10)-5),
                           new Acc(0, .2), 20);
     }
     Animation.spriteList = balls;
     Animation.run();
  });
```

Notice that this means the whole of the web worker's main program is now in the event handler. The worker can't start doing anything until it has the `OffscreenCanvas` provided by the GUI thread and, once it has it, it can get on with the animation as before. The only changes needed are to keep `ctx` and `ballImage` global so that other methods can access them.

The `Animation.run` method is now reduced to:

```
Animation.run = function (t) {
    Animation.frameRate(t);
    Animation.clearCanvas();
    for (var i = 0; i < Animation.spriteList.length; i++) {
        var ball1 = Animation.spriteList[i];
        ball1.update();
        ball1.render();
    }
    requestAnimationFrame(Animation.run);
  };
```

Notice that now there is no need to post any data back to the UI. All that has to be done is to wait for the next animation frame. The update to the UI thread is performed at the next page render.

If you try this out you will find that there is no longer any frame rate feedback because the web worker is no longer sending any data to the UI thread. This is easy to fix by making the `frameRate` method post the data back to the UI thread:

```
Animation.frameRate = function (t) {
    if (typeof t !== "undefined") {
        Animation.frameRate.temp = 0.8 * Animation.frameRate.temp +
                                   0.2 * (t - Animation.frameRate.tp);
        Animation.frameRate.tp = t;
    }
    Animation.frameRate.count++;
    if (Animation.frameRate.count === 120) {
        Animation.fps = (1000 /Animation.frameRate.temp).toFixed(2);
        Animation.frameRate.temp = 0;
        Animation.frameRate.count = 0;
        self.postMessage({fps: Animation.fps});
    }
};
Animation.frameRate.count = 0;
Animation.frameRate.tp = 0;
Animation.frameRate.temp = 0;
Animation.fps = 0;
```

The UI thread simply needs an event handler to show the frame rate data:

```
worker.addEventListener("message",
                        function (e) {
                            fps.value = e.data.fps;
                        });
```

With this change it all works as before. The advantage is that the browser is responsible for optimizing the update of the display and this should minimize any inefficient moving of data between bitmaps.

Summary

- A web worker can run JavaScript code using a separate thread from the UI thread.

- The web worker's code is isolated from any code running in the UI thread and in any other thread. It is also unable to access the DOM and other objects that are freely available to the UI thread.

- Communication between the UI thread and the worker thread is via events and event handlers.

- Data cannot be simply shared between the threads. Instead you can send a copy of the data as part of the event or you can transfer ownership of a limited number of objects using the transferable object protocol.

- The `OffscreenCanvas` object has all of the functionality of a canvas object but it is not part of the DOM and can be used by the UI thread or a Worker thread.

- `OffscreenCanvas` is a transferable object and this allows the Worker thread to update a canvas object in the UI thread.

- This connection between a canvas in the UI thread and an `OffscreenCanvas` in the Worker thread is so common that the `transferControlToOffscreen` method will connect the UI thread to an `OffscreenCanvas`. The UI thread will be automatically updated to show the current content of the `OffscreenCanvas`.

Chapter 10

Bit Manipulation In JavaScript

If you are going to work with bitmaps at the most basic level you have to know how to test and modify bit patterns. The reason is that each pixel is stored using a set of bits to record each of the color channels. You need to know how to manipulate bits. Bit manipulation in JavaScript is complicated by the way it attempts to be type free, but it can be done. One of the consequences of this type free approach is that numbers are always stored as 64-bit floating point values - i.e. double precision floating point.

Yes - that's correct, JavaScript doesn't have an integer type that you can make use of. When needed JavaScript will perform an internal conversion to a 32-bit value but you can't gain access directly to this integer and it is converted back to floating point format as soon as it is possible.

So JavaScript is different when it comes to bit manipulation but it is not that difficult. Let's see how it all works.

The Bitwise Operators

JavaScript has a number of operators designed to allow you to perform bit manipulation. There are four bitwise operators:

AND	&
OR	|
XOR (exclusive or)	^
Not	~

As you would expect, the NOT operator has the highest priority.

Notice that there are also corresponding logical operators &&, || and ! that only work with Boolean values and not bit patterns.

If you are more familiar with other languages you might well confuse ^ with raise to a power.

The bitwise operators work with numeric data which is converted from floating point to a 32-bit integer, operated on and then converted back to floating point. As a floating double can store a 32-bit integer without loss of precision everything works transparently as long as you stay within the 32-bit limit.

For example:

```
var a = 0xF0;
var b = 0xFF;
var c = ~a & b;
alert(c);
```

This first works out the bitwise NOT of `a`, i.e. `0F`. This is then bitwise ANDed with `b`, i.e. `0F & FF`, which is `F`. You should see the result `15` in decimal displayed. Bit manipulation is usually easiest to try out using hexadecimal notation with the results returned in decimal, `0xF` is `15,` or in binary, `0xF` is `1111`. There is no way of entering binary directly in JavaScript but you can use hex and octal and there is the `paresInt` function which will convert from a range of bases.

So what happens if you go over the 32-bit limit?

In fact, strange things start to happen before you reach the 32-bit limit because the 32-bit value is signed and this means that if the highest bit is `1` the returned value is negative.

For example:

```
var a = 0xFFFFFFF;
var b = 0xFFFFFFF
var c = a & b;
alert(c.toString(16));
```

displays `0xFFFFFFF`, which is what you would expect. Notice that `toString(16)` converts the floating point number to a hex string.

Now try adding one more `F` to both values i.e. a full 32-bit value all set to `1`. The result displays as `-1` which might not be what you expect but it is perfectly correct.

The result of ANDing two full 32-bit values both set to `1` is a 32-bit value with all bits set to one but as the 32-bit value is interpreted as a signed value when converted to floating point this displays as `-1` using two's complement.

You don't have to worry about this too much as the bit pattern corresponding to `-1` is 32 bits all set to `1,` so everything should carry on working if you use the value for further bit manipulation. That is, although it looks wrong it still works as far as bit manipulation is concerned.

Now consider what happens if you add one more `F` to the values. In this case the values are 36 bits, all set to `1` and the result should also be 36 bits, all set to `1`. But no, both the `a` and `b` values are converted to 32-bit values, the two values are ANDed together and give a 32-bit result, i.e. `-1` as before. You can't do bit manipulation with more than 32 bits.

Beyond 32 Bits

So what exactly happens if you try to work with bitwise operators on values that aren't representable as 32-bit integers? To do this the JavaScript interpreter calls the internal `ToInt32` function, which you can't use in your programs. This performs an "intelligent" conversion to a 32-bit integer with the following restrictions:

- It truncates all fractional parts.
- If the value is larger than what a 32-bit integer can store then the result is 32 bits all set to 1, i.e. `-1` in two's complement.
- If the value is a fraction smaller than 1 then the result is `0`.
- If the value is infinity (plus or minus) or NaN, (Not a Number) then the result is `0`.

You will also be pleased to learn that, as true evaluates to 1 and false to 0, you can use the bitwise logical operators on Boolean values as long as you remember that true is 1 and false 0. For example:

```
var c = 0xF & (1===1);
```

is 1 as (1===1) evaluates to `0x01`. However, notice that due to JavaScript's use of the idea of truthy or falsey, values that are considered to be true can be any non-zero value.

The only real problem with JavaScript's bitwise operators is that, due to the restriction to 32 bits, they are not especially fast because of the need to be converted from floating point double precision to 32-bit integer and then back again.

Masks

So what do you use the bitwise logical operators for?

You often encounter the problem of setting or clearing particular bits in a value. The value is usually stored in a variable that is usually regarded as a status variable or flag. You can set and unset bits in a flag using another value usually called a mask that defines the bits to be changed. For example, if you only want to change the first (least significant) bit then the mask would be `0x01`. If you wanted to change the first and second bits the mask would be `0x03` and so on.

To work out the correct hexadecimal value needed for any particular mask, you can use the `parseInt` function with a radix of 2. For example:

```
a=parseInt("1",2);
```

sets a to 0x01 and:

```
a=parseInt("11",2);
```

sets a to 0x03 and so on.

In general, just write down a string of 0s and 1s with a **1** in the positions you want to change and use `parseInt` to convert it to a mask value.

Now that you have a mask what do you do with it?

Suppose the mask contains a value that in binary has a **1** at each bit location you want to change. Then:

```
flag | mask;
```

returns a bit pattern with the bits that the mask specifies set to **1**. Notice that the bits that the mask doesn't specify are left at their original values. This is often expressed as the mask sets the bits it specifies.

For example:

```
var mask=parseInt("11",2);
var flag = 0xFFF0;
var result = flag | mask;
```

sets result to 0xFFF3, i.e. it sets the first (least significant) two bits.

If you use:

```
flag & ~mask;
```

then the bits specified in the mask are set to **0** - or unset if you prefer. Notice that you have to apply a NOT operator to the mask.

For example:

```
var mask=parseInt("11",2);
var flag = 0xFFFF;
var result = flag & ~mask;
```

sets result to 0xFFFC, i.e. it unsets the first two bits.

As well as setting and unsetting particular bits, you might also want to "flip" specified bits, i.e. negate them so that if the bit was a **1** it is changed to a **0** and vice versa. You can do this using the XOR operator, so:

```
flag ^ mask
```

flips the bits specified by the mask.

For example:

```
var mask=parseInt("11",2);
var flag = 0xFFFF;
var result = flag ^ mask;
alert(result.toString(16));
```

sets result to 0xFFFC because it changes the lower two bits from 1s to 0s. Again, bits not specified by the mask are unaffected.

Of course, in each case you don't have to use a variable to specify the mask, you could just use a numeric literal.

For example, instead of:

```
var flag = 0xFFFF;
var result = flag ^ mask;
```

you can write:

```
var result = flag ^ 0xFFFF;
```

Also if you want to update the flag rather than derive a new result, you can use &=, |= and ^= to perform the update directly.

For example, instead of:

```
flag = flag | mask;
```

you can use:

```
flag |= mask;
```

Using Masks

What sorts of things do you use masking operations for?

Often a low level API will require that particular bits in a status word are set or unset to make it operate in a particular way. However, this is unusual in JavaScript because it generally doesn't access lower level APIs. However, new developments like Canvas, WebGL and so on are changing this.

One of the best known uses of bit manipulation predates HTML5 - extracting the color codes from an RGB color value. For example:

```
var RGBcolor=0x010203;
var B=RGBcolor & 0x0000FF;
var G=RGBcolor & 0x00FF00;
var R=RGBcolor & 0xFF0000;
```

This takes an RGB value and splits it up into its components using appropriate masks.

The result is that you end up with 0x010000 stored in R, 0x000200 in G and 0x000003 in B. Notice that while the value of B is correct, R and G are incorrect and the bits need shifting to the right. This brings us to the use of the shift operators.

Shifting values

As well as the basic logical operators, JavaScript also provides three shift operators which move the pattern of bits to the left or the right.

The << operator shifts the pattern of bits to the left, shifting in 0 into the low order.

So for example:

```
var data=0x0F;
var result=data << 4;
```

shifts the bit pattern in data four places to the left and so result contains 0xF0.

Similarly the >> operator shifts to the right and shifts in a bit that is the same as the old topmost bit into the high order bit F. For example:

```
var data=0x0F;
var result=data >>3;
```

shifts the bit pattern in data three places to the right and so result contains 1, i.e. 1111 -> 0001. In this case the topmost bit, in the 32-bit value, is a 0 and so 0 is shifted in from the left. Now consider:

```
var data=0x80000000;
var result=data >>3;
```

In this case the high order bit of the 32-bit value is set and so shifting it right three times gives the result 0xF0000000, i.e the topmost bit is a 1, so 1s have been shifted in, which is -268435456 when converted to floating-point decimal using two's complement.

Notice that shifting one place to the left is the same as multiplying the value by two, and shifting one place to the right is almost the same as integer division by two. For example:

```
var data=1;
var result=data <<1;
```

stores 2 in result and:

```
var data=8;
var result=data >>1;
```

stores 4 in result.

What this means is that you can use either right and left shifts or multiplication and division by two to do the same job. Usually the shift operators are to be preferred because they are faster, but this isn't as clear cut with JavaScript because of the converting from floating point to integer.

There is another problem with using multiplication and division as replacements for shift in JavaScript. Division doesn't convert to 32-bit integers, it does full floating-point division, and so the results can be different. For example, 1>>1 is 0 but 1/2 is 0.5. There are other problems when it comes to negative numbers but more of this later.

The third shift operator, >>>, is an unsigned right shift operator and it is the same as the >> operator, but it always shifts in a 0 to the high order bit. For positive 32-bit integers the effect of >>> and >> is the same because in this case the initial topmost bit is 0 and so both shift in a 0. However, they behave very differently on negative values. For example:

```
var data=-1;
var result=data >>1;
```

stores -1 in result. The reason is that the initial bit pattern is all 1s, i.e. 32 bits all set to 1, and so shifting one place to the right shifts in another 1 as the high order bit.

Compare this to:

```
var data=-1;
var result=data >>>1;
```

In this case a 0 is shifted into the high order bit and the value stored in result gives zero followed by thirty-one 1s, which is a positive value equal to 2147483647.

Which sort of shift should you use?

The answer is that it depends on what you are trying to do. If you are simply shifting bit patterns then using >>> is usually what you need because you don't want to treat the value as signed. If you are treating the number as signed then you need to use >>. That is, shifting using >> preserves the sign of the value, whereas >>> doesn't. For example:

```
var data=-200;
var result=data >>1;
```

stores -100 in data, but:

```
var data=-200;
var result=data >>>1;
```

stores 2147483548 in result.

Notice that >> gives the result that you get if you use division, but >>> doesn't. For this reason >> is usually called an arithmetic shift right and >>> is called a logical shift right. For example, consider the problem of separating out the RGB values given earlier:

```
var RGBcolor=0x010203;
var B=RGBcolor & 0x0000FF;
var G=RGBcolor & 0x00FF00;
var R=RGBcolor & 0xFF0000;
```

To shift the bits into the correct locations you would use:

```
var RGBcolor=0x010203;
var B=RGBcolor & 0x0000FF;
var G=RGBcolor & 0x00FF00;
var R=RGBcolor & 0xFF0000;
G=G >>> 8;
R=R >>>16;
```

and now R is 1, G is 2, and B is 3, as required.

Of course, this isn't a good way to write the code because of the repeated conversion to 32-bit integers. Much better is:

```
var RGBcolor=0x010203;
var B=RGBcolor & 0x0000FF;
var G=(RGBcolor & 0x00FF00) >>> 8;
var R=(RGBcolor & 0xFF0000) >>>16;
```

Also notice that you can write <<=, >>= and >>>= to shift the value of a variable "in place". For example:

```
value>>=9;
```

shifts the bit pattern in value 9 places to the right and stores the result in value, i.e. it shifts value 9 places to the right.

Testing a bit

One common requirement is to test if a particular bit is set or unset. Actually it is just as easy to test for any number of bits set or unset because the job is done using a mask. As before, if you create a mask with bits set corresponding to the bits you want to test then:

```
(value & mask)===0
```

is true if and only if all of the bits mask specifies are 0. If all of the bits mask specifies are set to 1 then it returns mask. That is:

```
(value & mask) === mask
```

is true if all the bits mask specifies are set to 1.

Similarly:

```
(~value & mask)===0
```

is true if and only if all of the bits mask specifies are **1**. Again, if the bits mask specifies are set to 0 then the result is mask. This means you can use:

```
(~value & mask) === mask
```

to test for all the bits mask specifies being 0.

Which form you use to test bits is up to you and the particular situation.

Usually you only want to test for a single bit and this make the mask particularly simple. For example, if you test for the fifth bit to be a 0 using:

```
var value=0x1F;
var mask=0x10;
var result=value & mask;
```

then in this case the result is non-zero, **16** to be precise and the fifth bit is not 0. Perhaps confusingly the result is 0 if and only if the fifth bit is 0.

Testing for a **1** can be even more confusing at first. For example:

```
var value=0x1F;
var mask=0x10;
var result=~value & mask;
```

The mask tests the fifth bit in the value which is a **1** and so it is 0 in the negation. This gives a result of 0 and we conclude that that the fifth bit was set to **1**. Again the result is 0 if an only if the fifth bit is a **1**.

If you want a simple true or false result then you can avoid using the equality operator === by using !, the logical NOT operator. For example:

```
!(~value & mask)
```

is true if and only if all of the bits in value specified by the mask are **1** and false otherwise.

Similarly:

```
!(value & mask)
```

is true if and only if all of the bits in the value specified by the mask are 0 and false otherwise.

In this form you can use the bit tests directly in an if statement without having to worry about using falsey and truthy values or testing for equality to zero or the mask.

One very common error is to test the value and mask computed within an `if` statement without taking account of operator priorities. For example:

```
if( value & mask === mask){...}
```

seems to be testing if all of the bits specified by the mask are set. It isn't. As === has a higher priority than &, what you are actually working out is:

```
if( value & (mask === mask)){...}
```

which isn't quite what is required.

The correct expression is:

```
if( (value & mask) === mask){...}
```

or you could use

```
if( !(~value & mask)){...}
```

It can be very easy to make mistakes with bitwise logical operations when testing for bits set or unset – always check that you have the correct expression.

Summary

- As well as the usual logical operators, &&, ||, and !, there are also three bitwise operators, &, | and ~. These operate on each bit in a 32-bit word.

- If you try to work with values outside of the range of 32-bits then you might get results you don't expect.

- Setting and unsetting bits is best thought of in terms of using a mask to specify which bits to change.

- You can use `parseInt` to convert binary to a 32-bit value.

- Masking is a common operating when trying to extract color values and other data from bitmaps.

- The shift operators, >>, << and >>>, also allow you to move bits to a new location before further use.

- The >> operator is an arithmetic shift right and it maintains the sign of the value shifted. The >>> is a logical shift right and it always shifts a 0 into the high order bit and doesn't maintain the sign of the value.

- You can use a mask to test if the specified bits are set or unset. There are a number of ways of doing this and it can be confusing. When testing bits it is very easy to make a mistake – always check your results.

Chapter 11

Typed Arrays

JavaScript's typed arrays provide a way to work with binary data and to work with structures that would otherwise be very difficult. In this chapter we look at the basic idea of using typed arrays - views, `BufferArray` and block operations. This leads on to features such as blobs and dataURLs all of which are often useful when working with bitmaps and are covered in the next chapter.

JavaScript is a lightly typed language, and this is how most users like it, but there are times when you need to work with data that has specific representations. For example, you might need to read in and work with a byte array. Here it isn't only the case that each array element should behave like a byte data type, i.e. be limited to `0` to `255`, but it is also important that it is stored using a single byte of memory and the array should be a contiguous area of memory treated as a sequence of bytes. In such a situation it isn't clear that is really is a case of data typing, but more a way of getting back to the underlying representation of the data.

To make the point clearer - anything you can store in a typed array can be stored in a standard JavaScript `Array` object. In this sense you get nothing new apart from the guarantee of a particular layout in memory and the representation used.

Typed arrays were introduced in JavaScript to allow it to work with OpenGL as part of the implementation of WebGL. While previously you could arrange to convert a JavaScript Array into whatever the API needed, a byte array say, this proved to be too slow. Typed arrays enable the data to be constructed in JavaScript in a format that can be consumed without conversion by the API, so improving performance.

Since their introduction, typed arrays have become a way of working with external frameworks of all kinds and a way of accessing binary data directly. Before typed arrays the standard way of working with binary data was to store it as a string and convert each character to and from its representation as an integer. Typed arrays make binary data much easier to work with.

There is also the issue of efficiency. Typed arrays allow the JavaScript engine to perform some optimizations, but these depend on the engine and are a matter of some ongoing debate. Here we focus on the way typed arrays allow us to work with binary data rather than matters of efficiency.

Basic Typed Arrays

The way that typed arrays work is very simple and very powerful and very similar to the way that arrays work in C.

Creating a typed array is just a matter of using the array's constructor. For example:

```
var bytes=new Uint8Array(10);
bytes[0]=0xFF;
bytes[9]=0xFF;
console.log(bytes[0]);
```

creates an array of 10 unsigned 8-bit types. Notice that once created you can use the array as normal, but it doesn't have all of the methods that the `Array` object does. In this case the array elements are single bytes representing 0 to 255. All typed arrays are initialized to 0 when created.

Notice that the array is allocated enough memory to hold all of the elements when it is first constructed. For example:

```
var Ints=new Uint16Array(10);
```

creates an array of 16-bit unsigned integers and hence allocates 20 bytes of memory to store the entire array.

There are types for one-, two- and four-byte integer values, both signed and unsigned, and a four- and eight-byte float and using any of the typed arrays follows the same pattern:

Type	Size	Description	Equivalent C type
`Int8Array`	1	8-bit two's complement signed integer	`signed char`
`Uint8Array`	1	8-bit unsigned integer	`unsigned char`
`Uint8ClampedArray`	1	8-bit unsigned integer	`unsigned char`
`Int16Array`	2	16-bit two's complement signed integer	`short`
`Uint16Array`	2	16-bit unsigned integer	`unsigned short`
`Int32Array`	4	32-bit two's complement signed integer	`int`
`Uint32Array`	4	32-bit unsigned integer	`unsigned int`
`Float32Array`	4	32-bit IEEE floating point number	`float`
`Float64Array`	8	64-bit IEEE floating point number	`double`

The only type that might need further explanation is the `Uint8ClampedArray`. A byte variable has a very small range 0 to 255 and usually overflow is a problem. There are generally two ways to deal with this, either rollover to 0 after 255, or to use saturation arithmetic which clamps the value to 255. In other words, `Uint8ClampedArray` doesn't allow a value bigger than 255 and:

```
clamped[0]=255+1
```
is 255.

If you need to support a wide range of browsers, note that IE10 doesn't support clamped arrays. Notice also that for the unclamped array types the alternative strategy is taken and the value rolls over. For example:

```
bytes[0]=255+1;
```

is 0. It also rolls over if you try to assign a value that is too large. So rollover is the rule for all typed arrays except for clamped.

Operators

If you create an array of a given type then the data stored is of that type. However, the arithmetic and other operators that you might apply to an array element perform the usual JavaScript operations after type conversion. This is very reasonable, but it can also be confusing. For example, what would you expect the result of:

```
bytes[0]=0xFF;
console.log(~bytes[0]);
```

to be?

The "~" is a bitwise NOT, see the previous chapter, and so the byte `11111111` should be converted into `00000000` and the result should be 0. However, it is actually -256. How can this be? The answer is that all JavaScript bitwise operations work with a 32-bit integer and so the value that the NOT operates on is:

```
00000000000000000000000011111111 i.e. 0x000000FF
```

and when you apply the bitwise NOT you get:

```
11111111111111111111111100000000 i.e. 0xFFFFFF00
```

which treated as a 32-bit signed integer is -256. The result isn't truncated back to 8-bits before being printed, thus the output is -256. Notice that the final value is actually treated as a full floating-point value.

In this case the high order bits are lost if you assign the operation back to an array element of type `Uint8Array`. That is:

```
bytes[0]=0xFF;
bytes[0]=~bytes[0]
console.log(bytes[0]);
```

does give the expected result of `0`, but only because the 32-bit result is truncated to 8-bits by the type conversion.

The same is true of arithmetic when the value stored in the array will be converted into a 64-bit float. Notice that none of the integer or floating-point array types will lose precision in this conversion. What non-JavaScript frameworks do when you pass a typed array is another matter and you just have to investigate on a case-by-case basis.

The ArrayBuffer

In many cases you can simply use typed arrays as described above, but sometimes you need to do more sophisticated things. Every typed array makes use of an `ArrayBuffer` object to store its data. This is simply the block of memory that the typed array allocates to store its data and it doesn't have methods that allow you to access the data. To access the data you need a typed array which provides a view into the `ArrayBuffer` object.

The reason for this two-level approach is so that you can acquire data and only later determine how you want to treat it. It is even possible to use multiple views with a single `ArrayBuffer`, so providing for alternative interpretations of the data. Some API calls return an `ArrayBuffer`, leaving it up to you how to set up a view to process the data.

Think of the `ArrayBuffer` as just being the data storage and the view as being how to interpret the data.

When you create a typed array an `ArrayBuffer` object is automatically created big enough to store the array. You can retrieve a reference to the `ArrayBuffer` via the `buffer` property. For example:

```
var buffer=bytes.buffer;
```

To associate a new view with an existing `ArrayBuffer` all you have to do is specify it within the constructor. For example:

```
var buffer= bytes.buffer;
var uint16=new Uint16Array(buffer);
console.log(uint16.length);
```

In this case a 10-byte `buffer` is now viewed via `uint16` as five 16-bit unsigned integers. You can see the advantages of this approach in that you can get to the individual high and low bytes of the 16-bit integer via the `bytes` array and the entire 16-bit integer via the `uint16` array. This saves a lot of additional work that would be necessary if you needed to combine the high and low bytes as a special operation.

If you want to do a lot of this sort of view swapping then you can create an instance of the `ArrayBuffer` directly. For example:

```
var buffer= new ArrayBuffer(10);
```

creates a buffer with ten bytes initialized to 0 and:

```
var bytes=new Uint8Array(buffer);
```

creates an array of unsigned 8-bit integers using it. You can also set another view into the same buffer using something like:

```
var uint16=new Uint16Array(buffer);
```

Notice that arrays that share the same `ArrayBuffer` really do share the same data. In our example if you store something in `uint16[0]` then you have modified what is stored in `bytes[0]` and `bytes[1]` which share the same location in the buffer.

You can also specify an offset and a length for a view which determines exactly which part of the `ArrayBuffer` it uses.

For example:

```
var uint16=new Uint16Array(buffer,5,2);
```

specifies that the view starts in the `ArrayBuffer` at the sixth byte and creates just two 16-byte integers. In this case `uint16[0]` is the same storage location as `bytes[5]` and `bytes[6]` and `uint16[1]` is `bytes[7]` and `bytes[8]`.

You can see that things could become very complicated with views sharing overlapping and non-overlapping portions of the `ArrayBuffer`, but in general things are usually kept simple.

Block Copy

One of the very standard operations that you have to perform with binary data is moving it from one place to another. The direct, and not very efficient, way of doing this is to simply write a suitable `for` loop that transfers the data one element at a time.

A better method is to use the typed array's `set` method which will transfer the contents of one array or part of an array to another:

```
array1.set(array2)
```

This copies all of the contents of `array2` into `array1` and:

```
array1.set(array2,offset)
```

copies all of `array2` into `array1` starting at `array1[offset]`

If for any reason the copy operation results in an attempt to access beyond the end of `array1` then an exception is thrown.

You can even use `set` to move data within a single `ArrayBuffer`. For example, if we set the first `50` bytes of an array to `255` and then define a view of these first `50` bytes, we can use this to move all `50` to the top of the array:

```
var bytes=new Uint8Array(100);
for(var i=0;i<50;i++){
   bytes[i]=0xFF;
};
var buffer= bytes.buffer;
var start=new Uint8Array(buffer,0,50);
bytes.set(start,50);
```

In fact, we can make this example even simpler by using the `subarray` method which constructs a new view on the same `buffer`. That is:

```
var array2=array1.subarray(start,length);
```

returns a view, `array2`, into the same `ArrayBuffer` as `array1` uses. The new view starts with `array1[start]` and has `length` elements.

So we could write the previous example as:

```
var start=bytes.subarray(0,50); bytes.set(start,50);
```

or, if you prefer one-liners, as:

```
bytes.set(bytes.subarray(0,50),50);
```

Structures and Arrays

First some data basics. The array and the structure, also called a struct or a record, are the most basic of all data structures, but the differences between a structure and an array are subtle.

- In an array every element is of the same type but in a struct each element can be a different type.

This is a basic definition, but it isn't always sufficient because as a consequence of being a weakly typed language, a JavaScript array can store different data types in each of its elements. However, in weakly typed languages stipulating that elements of a structure are of different types isn't saying very much.

Typed arrays are a much better example of a traditional array - every element is of a specified type - byte or unsigned integer or whatever. In this sense the JavaScript typed array is much more like a traditional array than the `Array` object.

The key idea is that an array consists of elements that can be treated in the same way, i.e. if you can do something to `a[23]` you can do it to `a[13]` or any element of the array - they are functionally the same. In a struct the elements can be different and you certainly can't rely on the idea of processing them in the same way.

This is the reason that arrays are accessed using an index e.g. `a[10]`, `a[11]` and so on and a struct is accessed using a field or property e.g. `s.address`, `s.telephone` etc. The index means you can write a loop that steps though each element and performs the same action. A loop should have no value for a struct, but of course JavaScript, and many other languages, allow you to write a `for each` loop which can process a struct sequentially.

Binary Representations

In many cases binary data is just the representation of an array with the same data type repeating over and over again. For example, an image file could be just an array of pixel data with color value following color value. This case is handled well by the typed array.

However, even data that is mainly in this format often has a header which contains a variety of different data types providing different information - i.e. it starts with a structure.

For example most, if not all, graphics files have a header that tells you the size of the image, the resolution, the color space and so on. By the very varied nature of the data that you find in headers different data types are generally used. This makes the header a structure rather than an array.

The problem that we are trying to solve is:

suppose you have a binary buffer, i.e. an `ArrayBuffer`, of bytes and the first two bytes gives you the number of elements in total and the next byte gives the number of rows in an image. At the moment you would have to set up two views to read the data in a simple and natural manner - one Int16 array to read the first element and one Int8 array to read the third byte.

If this was repeated with lots of arbitrary data types packed one after another then things are going to get out of hand very quickly - we need another solution. Typed arrays are for situations when all of the data in the binary buffer is of the same type.

DataView

The solution to accessing different data types in the same `ArrayBuffer` is the `DataView` object, which is just another view that can be associated with an `ArrayBuffer`. You can associate it either with the complete buffer or any portion. For example:

```
var datav=new DataView(buffer);
```

associates the `DataView` with the complete buffer.

You can use the optional offset and length parameters to pick out a sub-buffer if you want to. For example:

```
var datav=new DataView(buffer,99,10)
```

associates the view with the buffer starting at byte 99 and finishing 10 bytes further on. Notice that the units are bytes because no single data type is associated with a `DataView`.

Once you have the `DataView` object, how do you use it to get the various parts of the buffer? The answer is by using get/set methods that will retrieve or store data of various types with the location in the buffer specified by an offset.

There is a get/set method for each of:

- `Int8`   (1 byte)
- `Uint8`   (1 byte)
- `Int16`   (2 bytes)
- `Uint16`   (2 bytes)
- `Int32`   (4 bytes)
- `Uint32`   (4 bytes)
- `Float32`   (4 bytes)
- `Float64`   (8 bytes)

Each of the methods works in roughly the same way. For example:

```
var ubyte=datav.getUint8(9);
```

retrieves an unsigned byte from the buffer at the 10th byte (remember numbering starts from zero). Similarly to put a single unsigned byte back in the array you would use:

```
datav.setUint8(0xFF,9);
```

which stores 255 in the tenth byte of the `ArrayBuffer`.

You can see that by using different gets and sets you can read the same bytes as a patchwork quilt of different data types from the same `ArrayBuffer`.

Byte Order - the Endian Problem

Now we have the ability to read any group of bytes in the `ArrayBuffer` in any of the available formats, but we have one last problem. When you store a multi-byte data type in a byte array there are two ways of doing it.

Consider for a moment a 16-bit, i.e. two-byte, integer. The 16-bit integer is composed of two groups of eight bits - the low order bits and the high order bits. Different systems opt to store these bits either with the high order bits first, i.e. big-endian, or with the low order bits first, i.e. little-endian.

To be more precise:

- Big-endian order stores low order bytes at lower addresses/index positions
- Little-endian order stores low order bytes at higher addresses/index positions.

If you find this confusing, follow the next example. Suppose we have a `UInt8Array`, i.e essentially a byte array, and we want to use the first two bytes to store a 16-bit integer, i.e. a `Uint16`. To store the value 255 in the 16-bit integer all you need to know is that its binary representation in 16-bits is:

```
0000000011111111
```

To work with this as two bytes it has to be split into two groups of eight bits:

```
00000000  11111111
```

The zeros to the left are the high order byte and the ones to the right are the low order byte. In hex these are `0x0` and `0xFF`.

Now let's store these in the byte array:

```
var bytes=new Uint8Array(10);
bytes[0]=0xFF;
bytes[1]=0x00;
```

You may already have noticed that we have exercised a choice without really thinking about it. Why should we store the low byte in `bytes[0]` and not in `bytes[1]`? If you now try to use the two bytes as if it was a 16-bit integer you are in for a surprise:

```
var buffer= bytes.buffer;
var datav=new DataView(buffer);
var uint=datav.getUint16(0);
console.log(uint);
```

Notice all we have done is to associate a `DataView` with the `DataArray` and read the two bytes as if they were an unsigned 16-bit integer. The result isn't 255 but 65280.

The reason is of course that the default for the `DataView` object is to work with big-endian data. That is, it assumes that the high order byte is stored first, i.e at the lower array index. There is an optional parameter that you can specify for all of the get/set methods to specify if the byte order is big-endian or little-endian. If you set the parameter to false, or leave it out, you get big-endian. If you set it to true you get little-endian. So, to make our example work, we could set the endian parameter to true as in:

```
var uint=datav.getUint16(0,true);
```

and following this you will see 255 as the value of `uint`.

The alternative would be to store the bytes in big-endian order:

```
bytes[0]=0x00;
bytes[1]=0xFF;
```

and then the standard `DataView` methods work by default.

Of course, in "real life" you generally don't get to choose the byte order. When you read a file or handle a stream of data then the outside world has already fixed the byte order in use. In practice, you will find that processors such as the Intel 86x range use little-endian order. However, most network protocols use big-endian order and this means that the most significant bytes are sent and received first. You also need to find out what endian convention is used for files - and it can differ according to the format.

One last problem. What order do typed arrays use? There is no parameter, optional or otherwise, that allows you to set the byte order in a multi-byte typed array. What the standard says is that such arrays are to use the natural order for the hardware - which means on most systems they will use little-endian. If you are running the examples on an x86 machine then you can check this using:

```
var bytes=new Uint8Array(10);
bytes[0]=0xFF;
bytes[1]=0x00;
var buffer= bytes.buffer;
var uints=new Uint16Array(buffer);
var uint=uints[0];
```

Following this unit will have 255 stored in it. Notice that the bytes are stored in little-endian format.

To test if the machine your code is running on is big or little-endian use:

```
function littleEndian() {
  var bytes = new Uint8Array(2);
  bytes[0] = 0xFF;
  var uint = new Uint16Array(bytes,buffer)[0];
  return uint ===255;
}
```

This simply stores 255 into the low byte of the Uint8 array and then reads it back in the default order used by Uint16. If the result is 255 then the machine is using little-endian order.

Notice that in many cases you don't need to deal with the byte order problem because the machine will produce data in its own default byte order and the typed arrays work with that byte order. However, for data that is read into a program, either as a file or as a download, you do have to worry about byte order and the only way to deal with it is to use a DataView object.

Unpacking the Data

The standard technique is to use a DataView to unpack any values that form a structure into a suitable JavaScript object and any array data into a JavaScript typed array or an Array object. For example, if the ArrayBuffer contains a byte count and a 16-bit size value in big-endian order you might use something like:

```
header={};
header.count=datav.getUint8(0);
header.size=datav.getUint16(1);
```

From this point on you can forget endian issues and just use header and its properties.

If you have a big-endian array of two-byte integers and want to work with it on a little-endian machine you can use the equivalent idea for an array:

```
for (var i = 0; i < len; i++) {
  data[i]=datav.getUint16(i*2);
}
```

Notice that data could be an `Array` object or a typed array - it all depends on what you are going to do with the data. Also notice the need to step through the `ArrayBuffer` in units of the data type being read. That is, we are reading two-byte integers so the offset is i*2.

You can see these techniques in action at the end of Chapter 13.

Summary

- A type array is similar to a standard JavaScript `Array` object, but all of its elements are of a single simple type and it lacks some of the methods of `Array`.

- The behavior of all of the array data types is to roll over to zero, but `Uint8ClampedArray` saturates when you try to make it go beyond its maximum.

- The `ArrayBuffer` is used by all typed arrays to store their data. It is simply a block of memory a given number of bytes in size.

- You can use the `set` method to copy the contents of one typed array to another.

- You can use a `DataView` object to assign custom views to an `ArrayBuffer`. views can overlap and divide up a buffer in complicated ways.

- Multi-byte values raise the issue of whether you store the most significant byte at high address value, big-endian, or at the low address value, little-endian.

Chapter 12

Files, Blobs, URLs & Fetch

When working with bitmaps and many other similar resources there is a common problem of how do we actually load or save the resource? In simple cases the standard method is to use a URL within an HTML tag. For example, setting the `src` property of an `img` tag to a URL causes the browser to request the file, the server to send it and the browser to display it. If you want to do the same in JavaScript, so that you can process the file before it is displayed, then you need to know how to work with files and their precursor, the blob. If you want to create files within JavaScript you also need to know how to create URLs that reference data within the program.

This chapter looks at the problem of working with files, specifically image files from JavaScript. Although the emphasis is on image files, the ideas are general and are applicable to any type of file with slight modifications.

The Blob

The most basic type of file in JavaScript is the "blob". Its name, which derives from "binary large object", correctly suggests a collection of bits with no predefined structure. However, it is important to realize and keep in mind that a blob, despite its name, is just a file. To be more accurate, a blob is more a file-like reference to some data which is stored elsewhere. To get at the data you have to read it, which is what the `FileReader` object, see later, is for.

To create a blob you use the constructor:

```
var myBlob=new Blob([data],options);
```

The first parameter is an array of data sources for the blob. These can include strings, `ArrayBuffer`, `ArrayBufferView` and other blobs. They are each treated as binary and combined to make the final blob. After you have created the blob the data sources remain unaltered.

The second parameter, `options` is optional and can have the properties:

- `type` – a MIME type for the content
- `endings` – specifies how to deal with \n character in strings.
  The default `transparent` is to write them out unchanged but `native` will convert them to whatever the local file system uses.

199

What can you do with a blob? The answer is not much as it has just one method:

```
slice(start,end, type)
```

This creates a new blob by extracting the bytes from `start` to `end` and assigns the specified `type`. All parameters are optional and negative index values start from the end of the blob. The new blob has only two properties:

- `size` – size of the blob in bytes
- `type` – the MIME type of the blob.

Given these limited resources there isn't much you can do with a blob. What makes it useful is the URL object and its `createObjectURL` static method. This can be used to create a URL that references a blob, file or media source. Once you have a URL it can be used anywhere a "normal" URL can be used. Of course, the blob has to be correctly formatted for the type of file that the MIME type suggests it is and that the target expects.

There is one potential problem with an object URL. When you create an object URL referencing an object, that object is never garbage collected or disposed of, even when it goes out of scope and should be destroyed. Creating an object URL and not disposing of it using the `revokeObjectURL` static method when you have finished using it, will result in a memory leak. For example:

```
var myBlob=new Blob(["<p>Hello World</p>"],{type : 'text/html'});
var myURL=URL.createObjectURL(myBlob);
myIframe.src=myURL;
URL.revokeObjectURL(myURL);
```

Assuming that there is an `<iframe>` with id `myIframe` on the page this will display the HTML in the string which is exactly what would happen if the URL references a file with the same content. This isn't particularly useful because iframes have an `srcdoc` property which can be set to a string but it illustrates the general idea.

A more realistic example is to use the `canvas.toBlob` method which will convert the contents of the canvas to a blob in the desired format:

```
canvas.toBlob(callback, type, quality);
```

The `callback` is a function that is used to receive the blob once it has been constructed. The optional second parameter sets the MIME type of the blob, `png` by default. Most browsers only support `png` and `jpg`. The optional final parameter sets the quality, `0.0` to `1.0`, for formats that use lossy compression.

For example:

```
var ctx = document.body.appendChild(createCanvas(600, 600)).
                                        getContext("2d");
var myPath = new Path2D();
myPath.moveTo(50, 50);
myPath.lineTo(100, 100);
myPath.lineTo(0, 100);
myPath.lineTo(50, 50);
myPath.moveTo(50, 110);
myPath.lineTo(0, 60);
myPath.lineTo(100, 60);
myPath.lineTo(50, 110);
ctx.stroke(myPath);

ctx.canvas.toBlob(doBlob);
```

The doBlob function is:

```
function doBlob(myBlob){
    var url=URL.createObjectURL(myBlob);
    myImg.src=url;
}
```

This draws the star in the example given in Chapter 3, converts it to a blob and display it in an <img> tag with id myImg. The format for the blob is the default png. Remember to revoke the URL object after the image has loaded.

You can create other formats using the appropriate MIME types but the only formats you can reasonably rely on are png and jpeg. Chrome also support webp. If the browser doesn't support a MIME type you ask for, it simply creates a png format blob.

If you try to create a jpeg you might be surprised to find that all you seem to have is a black image:

```
ctx.canvas.toBlob(doBlob,"image/jpeg",0.8);
```

The reason is simply that jpeg doesn't support transparency and so the background pixels that are black transparent show as black. One solution is to clear the canvas to white opaque:

```
ctx.fillStyle = '#fff';
ctx.fillRect(0, 0, ctx.canvas.width, ctx.canvas.height);
```

Instead of using a callback you can convert the `toBlob` method into a function that returns a `Promise`:

```
function canvasToBlob(ctx, type) {
    return new Promise(function (resolve, reject) {
                        ctx.canvas.toBlob(function (blob) {
                                resolve(blob);
                            }, type);
                    });
}
```

This is a function that you can use with `await` to simplify your code. For example:

```
var blob=await canvasToBlob(ctx, "image/png");
```

but, of course, this only works in a function as you cannot use `await` in the main program.

The File

A JavaScript `File` is just a `Blob` with a few additional read only properties to indicate the file's characteristics:

- `File.lastModified`
  Returns the last modified time of the file, in milliseconds since the UNIX epoch (January 1st, 1970 at Midnight). Defaults to a value of `Date.now()`

- `File.lastModifiedDate`
  Returns the last modified date of the file referenced by the file object

- `File.name`
  Returns the name of the file referenced by the file object.

Being a `Blob`, a `File` also has size and type. There is a `File` constructor, but it essentially the same as the `Blob` constructor:

```
var myBlob=new File([data],name, options);
```

where `data` is an array of strings, `ArrayBuffer`, `ArrayBufferView` and blobs, `name` is the name of the file and the `options` object has the same two properties as a blob, `size` and `type` The only method a `File` object has is also inherited from `Blob`, i.e. `slice`.

You might think that `File` isn't much of an improvement on `Blob`, but other APIs return `File` objects from both the client and the server and in this case the extra information mirrors the physical files properties. Similarly, when you use a `File` object to create a physical file, its properties are used to set the physical file's properties.

Notice that anywhere you can use a `Blob` you can use a `File` and in many cases vice versa. Also notice that like a `Blob` a `File` cannot be constructed to get its data from an external source – using the constructor a `Blob` and a `File` can only be created using an existing string, `ArrayBuffer`, `ArrayBufferView` or blob, i.e. data already internal to the program. However, you can create a `File` object which gets its data from a local file using the `<input>` tag:

```
<input type="file" id="files">
```

This displays a standard file input button and, if the user clicks it, a file picker dialog box appears:

Choose file | No file chosen

There are ways of hiding this default UI and substituting your own, and you can use drag-and-drop, but the basic mechanism of working with the file remains the same.

If the user clicks on the file picker they can pick a single file. If you add the attribute `multiple` to the tag then the user can select multiple files:

```
<input type="file" multiple id="files">
```

You can retrieve the list of file names using the input object's `files` property. Of course, there is no point examining this before the user has selected a file so you have to define an event handler for the input's `change` event. For example:

```
files.addEventListener("change", handleFiles, false);

function handleFiles(e){
    var file=this.files[0];
    console.log(file.size);
}
```

will report the size of the file that the user selects.

At this point the usual question is, *"can I read any file on the user's machine?"*

The answer should be obvious – for security reasons only files that the user selects can be read by your program. If you find a way to read any file, and some have, you will have created malware and your application is likely to attract some unwanted attention. The only files on the local machine your program can read are ones that the user selects.

FileReader

At the moment we have the `File` object, but don't have access to its data. All we have is its name and some information about it. If you want to get the data you have to use a `FileReader` to actually read the data into the program. You create a `FileReader` object using a constructor:

```
var fileReader=new FileReader();
```

Once you have a `FileReader` you can use one of its methods to get the data in the format you desire:

```
readAsArrayBuffer(file)
readAsDataURL(file)
readAsText(file)
```

The `DataURL` format will be explained later and the rest should be obvious. The `file` parameter specifies the file object to read. This is an **asynchronous** operation and when it is complete the load event is triggered and the data are available as `e.target.result` or equivalently as the result property of the `FileReader`.

Of course, the result is in the specified format and appropriate object. If things go wrong then the `error` event is raised. You can also call the `abort` method and this stops the reading of the file and raises `onabort` when it is completed. The `readyState` property also indicates the progress of the reading:

- 0   EMPTY   Reader has been created. None of the read methods called yet.
- 1   LOADING   A read method has been called.
- 2   DONE   The operation is complete.

You can also use a `FileReader` to read a blob. In this case it is mostly a matter of converting the `Blob` or `File` to another data type.

Reading a Local File

If the File object is derived from the user selecting a file on the local machine then you really are reading in data that wasn't part of your program. For example:

```
files.addEventListener("change", handleFiles, false);

function handleFiles(e) {
    var file = this.files[0];
    var fileReader = new FileReader();
    fileReader.addEventListener("load", fileRead, false);
    fileReader.readAsText(file);

}

function fileRead(e) {
   console.log(e.target.result);
}
```

lists the contents of any text file the user cares to select on the `console`.

While this approach works it uses two event handlers. A more modern way of doing the job is to create functions which wrap each of the tasks of getting the `File` object and reading the `File` object.

The `getFile` function returns a `File` object when the user selects a file. To be more accurate it returns a `Promise` that resolves when the user selects a file:

```
function getFile() {
  return new Promise(function (resolve, reject) {
      files.addEventListener("change", function (e) {
                                  var file = e.target.files[0];
                                  resolve(file);
                              });
      });
}
```

The `readFile` function returns a `Promise` that resolves to the contents of the `File` object passed to it:

```
function readFile(file) {
  return new Promise(function (resolve, reject) {
                var fileReader = new FileReader();
                fileReader.addEventListener("load", function (e) {
                            resolve(e.target.result);
                }, false);
                fileReader.readAsText(file);
          });

}
```

Notice how in both cases the event handlers call the promise's `resolve` method with the result of the task.

Now we have these two "modernized" functions we can either write code that makes use of their promises or, even more modern and much better, use async and await:

```
async function displayFile() {
  var file = await getFile();
  var result = await readFile(file);
  console.log(result);
}
```

Now to get the contents of a user selected file we simply call `displayFile`. Notice that you have to call `getFile` and `readFile` from within a function as `await` doesn't work in the main program.

Wrapping old legacy calls and event handlers in a `Promise` function is the best way to organize things. You can also add calls to the promise's `reject` function if there is an error and handle the errors in the `displayFile` function using `try catch`.

As a final example, let's get a graphics file from the local machine and display it, ready to be manipulated, in a canvas object. In this case we need a modified version of the reading function:

```
function readGraphic(file) {
        return new Promise(function (resolve, reject) {
                var fileReader = new FileReader();
                fileReader.addEventListener("load",
                    function (e) {
                        resolve(e.target.result);
                    }, false);
                fileReader.readAsDataURL(file);
            });
}
```

We could read the file as an array or string of values, but then we would have to process the file according to its type and extract the raw image data. This can be done – see the example of reading a PCX file in the next chapter – but it is usually unnecessary. Instead we read the file as a data URL because we can use this to get an `Image` object to read and decode the file for us. For the moment you can think of a data URL as being a URL that encodes the associated data so that it can be read like a file.

Now that we have the data URL we can use it to load an `Image` object and
then draw this to the canvas:

```
async function displayGraphic(ctx) {
   var file = await getFile();
   var url = await readGraphic(file);
   var img = new Image();
   img.src = url;
   await imgLoaded(img);
   ctx.drawImage(img, 0, 0);
}
```

The `imgLoaded` function was given in an earlier chapter:

```
function imgLoaded(img) {
      return new Promise(
                 function (resolve, reject) {
                    img.addEventListener("load", function () {
                                resolve(img);
                    });
                 })
}
```

In fact, there is a more direct way of doing the same job without using
`FileReader`. A `File` object can be directly converted to an object URL and this
can be assigned to an `Image` object which will do the download and the
conversion to a bitmap in one step. To use this method we need to modify
`readGraphic` to return an `Image` object:

```
async function readGraphic(file) {
        return new Promise(
                  function (resolve, reject) {
                      var url = URL.createObjectURL(file);
                      var img = new Image();
                      img.addEventListener("load", function (e) {
                               resolve(img);
                               URL.revokeObjectURL(url);
                      }, false);
                      img.src = url;

                  });
}
```

Using this `displayGraphic` is just:

```
async function displayGraphic(ctx) {
        var file = await getFile();
        var img = await readGraphic(file);
        ctx.drawImage(img, 0, 0);
}
```

This is not only simple, it is also faster as constructing a data URL can be slow.

The general point is that an `Image` object already knows how to load and decode many different types of graphics files and, unless you need access to the raw file data, it is better to use it to load graphics in preference to `FileReader`.

Writing a Local File

It is usually said that you cannot write a file to the user's local file system. The reason is that if you could it would be a very big security problem. The truth of the situation is very similar to the case of reading a file from the local file system. You can write to the local file system, but the user is made aware of the operation and has to click an OK button to allow it to happen.

There is no "packaged" way to write a file. The basic method is to create a DOM `HTMLAnchorElement`, associated with <a>, set its `href` attribute to the URL of the file you want to save and its download attribute to the name of the file you want to save. You can then use its `click` method to simulate a user click on the link. Notice that, in Chrome, you don't have to add the link object to the DOM and the user doesn't have to see it. Firefox and some other browsers will only let you use the `click` method if the link is added to the DOM. However, it is easy to hide it by setting its display style to "none".

When you call its `click` method, a file save dialog box opens and the user has to click the Save button to "download" the file. This ensures that you cannot sneak a file save past the user without them knowing about it.

For example, to save the current contents of a canvas to the local file system you would use:

```
async function saveCanvas(ctx) {
    var blob = await canvasToBlob(ctx, "image/png");
    var a = document.createElement('a');
    a.download = 'download.png';
    a.style.display = "none";
    document.body.appendChild(a);
    var url=URL.createObjectURL(blob);
    a.href = url;
    a.click();
    URL.revokeObjectURL(url);
}
```

where the `carvasToBlob` function was listed earlier in the chapter:

```
function canvasToBlob(ctx, type) {
        return new Promise(function (resolve, reject) {
            ctx.canvas.toBlob(function (blob) {
                                resolve(blob);
            }, type);
        });
}
```

If you now try:

```
saveCanvas(ctx);
```

you will discover that a dialog box appears asking you to confirm the details of the save operation. There is, or there should be, no way to circumvent this dialog box. If you find one then you have broken the browser's security.

Response

There is a new promise-based way to read a file, the `Response` object, which provides a stream-based way to read data. A stream allows you to read or write chunks of data rather then the whole file at once, which can be useful when the data is being generated continuously or when the file in question is too large to fit into memory. You might consider that reading graphics files is a useful thing to do with large files, but for many graphics formats you can't process part of a graphics file, so streams are more difficult to use than you might think.

You can construct a `Response` object using:

```
var response=new Response(body, init);
```

where `body` is one of:

- `Blob`
- `BufferSource`
- `FormData`
- `ReadableStream`
- `URLSearchParams`
- `USVString`

and `init` sets a range of response properties, which can be ignored in most cases.

Once you have the `Response` object you can attempt to read the data defined by the body. You can do this as a stream, i.e. read chunks of data as they become ready, or you can use one of the methods that read to completion in a specified format:

- `arrayBuffer()`
- `blob()`
- `formData()`
- `json()`
- `text()`

None of these formats is particularly useful for a graphics file and it is generally easier to use an `Image` object to read and decode a file. For an example, let's implement the reading of a text file from the local file system:

```
async function displayFile() {
   var file = await getFile();
   var response= await new Response(file);
   var result = await response.text();
   console.log(result);
}
```

Notice that `text` is always treated as `UTF-8` and that `ReadFile` has an optional parameter that allows you to specify the encoding.

The `Response` object is a good alternative to using a `FileReader` simply because it is promise-based, but it is also useful when you really do want to work with a stream. It is also an integral part of the Fetch API.

Working with the Server - Basic Fetch

We can use the file input tag and the `fileReader` to read files on the local machine and the `HTMLAnchorElement` object to save them. Getting files from the remote file system, i.e. the server, is a much more common operation. We have already seen how to use the `Image` object to load any supported graphics file under program control. Sometimes, however, we need to access a file more directly.

The Fetch API is an implementation of the `XMLHttpRequest` object and can be used to download almost any file the browser has access to, and to send data to the server using GET or POST HTTP methods. You can still use `XMLHttpRequest`, but `fetch` is the modern way to do things and this is what will be described in this chapter.

The basic idea is really simple. All you have to do is use:

```
fetch("URL");
```

This performs a GET request for the URL specified and returns a `Promise` that eventually resolves to a `Response` object. The `fetch` function is available in the `Window` and `WorkerGlobal` contexts. Also notice that you can use the `URL` object to construct the URL you need to use, or you can simply use a string.

Most HTTP errors are also returned as a resolved promise and a response object that specifies the error. The reject state is reserved for communications errors. This means that you can use try-catch to deal with communications problems but you have to check the response object for "soft" errors.

You could use the promise's `then` method to specify what happens to the response, but it is much simpler to use `async` and `await`:

```
async function getText(){
        var response=await fetch('myFile.txt');
```

For a simple file retrieval this is almost all there is to using `fetch`. The `response` object returned has a set of methods and properties that allow you to discover the status of the request and retrieve the data.

For example, the `status` property returns the HTTP status code – usually `200`. As already mentioned HTTP errors such as 404 no such page are returned as resolved promises and you have to handle them as errors. You only get a rejected promise if there is something wrong that is more reasonably characterized as an exception. You can also retrieve the headers sent from the server using the `headers` property which returns a `Headers` object.

Notice that at this stage we only have the HTTP headers and status, the data are still to be fetched across the network.

The `Response.body` gives you access to a readable stream. This allows you to read the data in a `chunk` at a time. This is useful when, for example, you are trying to work with something that is too big to fit in memory or when data is being continuously generated. The Streams API is another new feature that makes use of Promises. To read the `Response` in chunks you would use something like:

```
var reader=Response.body.getReader();
```

Following this each time you use the `read` method a promise which resolves to the next chunk of the stream is returned:

```
var data=await reader.read();
```

The data is of the form:

```
{value:chunk,done:boolean}
```

where `value` is the data and `done` is true if this is the last `chunk` of data. You also need to know that a stream can only be read once unless it is recreated.

Streams are very low-level compared to what most people want to do with retrieved resources. For this reason the `Body` object also implements a set of higher-level stream readers. These return a `Promise` that resolves after the entire stream has been read to the data in a processed format.

As already explained, the currently supplied formatted readers are `arrayBuffer`, `blobform`, `Datajson`, and `text` and each returns a `Promise` which resolves to the type of data you have selected.

One subtle point is that you can only retrieve a response's data once. This is obvious if you keep in mind that the methods that retrieve the data are stream readers and you can only read a stream to the end once. However, it can cause problems if you mistakenly think of these methods as simply providing format conversion.

Consider, for example:

```
async function getText(){
        var response=await fetch('myFile.txt');
        console.log(response.status);
        console.log(await response.text());
}
```

This retrieves the data in the file as text. Once the response body has been retrieved or "used" you cannot repeat the operation. That is:

```
async function getText(){
        var response=await fetch('myFile.txt');
        console.log(response.status);
        console.log(await response.text());
        console.log(await response.text());
}
```

throws the exception:

```
Uncaught (in promise) TypeError: Already read
```

You can check to see if the body has been used via the `bodyUsed` property of either the `request` or the `response`. If you do want to access the data in more than one format then you have to make use of the `clone` method – see later.

Request Object

Things are only a little more complicated when you want to do something more than just a get. You can specify a second parameter, the init object, in the call to control the type of request made.

The init object has lots of properties, but the most important are:

- method – the request method e.g. GET, POST, PUT etc
- headers – a header object
- body – the body of the request which is sent to the server, which can be any of Blob, BufferSource, FormData, URLSearchParams, USVString or ReadableStream. You can find the full specification in the documentation.

If you want to repeatedly fetch the same resource it is better to create a Request object which has all of the properties of the init object plus a URL property. You can pass the Request object to fetch in place of the URL parameter and it acts as the init object as well.

So the previous fetch could be implemented as:

```
async function getText(){
        var request=new Request('myFile.txt',
                                {
                                    method:'GET'
                                });
        var response=await fetch(request);
```

Notice that you can reuse a Request object even if you have streamed the body data of its associated Response. However, as already commented, you cannot reuse a Response object after you have read its body data.

You can also obtain a duplicate Request or Response object using the clone method. This can be useful if you aren't sure that the response will be valid. For example, to first check to see if the response is valid json we could use:

```
var response = await fetch(request);
var res2 = response.clone();
try{
        console.log(await res2.json());
    } catch (e) {
        console.log(await response.text());
    }
```

If the response isn't valid json it is displayed as text. Notice you have to clone the response before trying to retrieve the body. You cannot clone a stream that has been read.

You can use a fluent style to make this look neater:

```
var response = await fetch(request);
try{
      console.log(await response.clone().json());
   }
catch (e) {
      console.log(await response.text());
   }
```

The `clone` method introduces a buffer into the equation and the data is streamed into a local buffer from where it can be accessed a second time. This has the side effect of keeping the data in memory until all of the copies are read or disposed of.

Downloading Graphics from the Server

Using `fetch` this is very easy. All you need is a call to `fetch` with the correct URL and then use one of the formatted reads to get the data. The problem is that there is no format provided that works simply with graphics data.

You can read the file as a blob but then you have to create an object URL, read the data into an `Image` object and draw to the canvas. For example:

```
async function fetchGraphic(url){
    var response=await fetch(url);
    var blob=await response.blob();
    return new Promise(
                function (resolve, reject) {
                    var url = URL.createObjectURL(blob);
                    var img = new Image();
                    img.addEventListener("load", function (e) {
                        resolve(img);
                        URL.revokeObjectURL(url);
                    }, false);
                    img.src = url;

                });
}
```

The only advantage of this overloading of the URL directly into the `Image` object is that the load occurs with the `fetch` rather than on setting the `src` attribute.

In fact the more direct:

```
async function fetchGraphic2(url) {
  return new Promise(
                function (resolve, reject) {
                    var img = new Image();
                    img.addEventListener("load", function (e) {
                                                resolve(img);
                                    }, false);
                    img.src = url;
                });
}
```

is also slightly faster because we don't have to load the file and then load the blob into the `Image` object.

Notice that this doesn't mean that `fetch` is useless as, while it isn't the best way to load graphics, it is completely general and it also works with `upload`. Sometimes we need to load the file as an array to do some work on it before using it as a graphic, see the PCX example at the end of the next chapter.

Uploading Local Graphics

The Fetch API can be used to upload a graphics file to the server using a POST or PUT request. In practice POST is generally easier as it doesn't require any extra configuration of the web server.

When you use the POST method the payload is in the body of the HTTP request as a stream of octets, i.e. bytes. At its most basic, POST simply sends the body to the server, complete with all its headers, and then the server retrieves the HTML page indicated by the URL in the request. In practice, what usually happens is that the URL references a program that runs and does something with the data in the body and generates the response HTML data. In this example we will assume that the programming language is PHP but there are similar facilities in other languages.

In most cases the POST method is handled differently by the server according to what MIME type is specified. This goes well beyond the basic POST method where the data is just a blob of bytes. For example, if the MIME type is `application/x-www-form-urlencoded` or `multipart/form-data` then PHP sets the `$_POST` array after processing the data. In both cases the data consists of key value pairs and the `$_POST` array is indexed by the key and returns the value. This is ideal for processing form data as by default it is URL encoded when submitted. So if you have a form with field names `name1`, `name2` and values `value1`, `value2` and so on then the `$_POST` array will have entries like `$_POST["name1"]` containing `value1` and so on.

The `application/x-www-form-urlencoded` MIME type is particularly simple and just consists of *name1=value1&name2=value2* and so on, that is the payload is just one large query string. This isn't suitable for transferring files or large quantities of data.

It is usually said that the correct way to send files is to use `multipart/form-data` and let the server extract the key value pairs – even when one of the keys is a filename and the value is the file contents. In this case each key value pair is a separate part of the payload. Parts are separated by a boundary separator, which is a set of bytes that must not occur in the value. If they did then the server would unintentionally interpret them as additional boundary separators and the POST would fail, or at best be truncated.

Each part also has a `Content-Disposition` header that gives its type and a name. For example:

```
Content-Type: multipart/form-data;boundary="boundary"
--boundary
Content-Disposition: form-data; name="field1"
value1
--boundary
Content-Disposition: form-data; name="field2";
filename="example.txt"
value2
--boundary--
```

The values can be encodings of the file content. If you use a form with file input tags and a POST submit method then the browser will automatically use `multipart/form-data` and will automatically create the appropriate body for you. If you are using PHP, not only will the key-value pairs be parsed and stored in the `$_POST` array, but any files will be copied to a temporary directory and details stored in the `$_FILES` array. For example, the client page to upload a single file of any type is:

```
<!DOCTYPE html>
<html>
  <head>
    <title>TODO supply a title</title>
      <meta charset="UTF-8">
      <meta name="viewport" content="width=device-width,
                                     initial-scale=1.0">
  </head>
  <body>
      <form action="http://server/fileHandler.php"
                    method="post" enctype="multipart/form-data">
        <p><input type="file" name="file1">
        <p><button type="submit">Submit</button>
      </form>
  </body>
</html>
```

Notice that we don't need any JavaScript since the file is encoded as
`multipart/form-data` and sent to the server without us getting involved. How
this is handled at the server depends on the language used, but PHP makes it
very easy to retrieve the file:

```php
<?php
 $fname = $_FILES["file1"]["name"];
 $tmpfname = $_FILES["file1"]["tmp_name"];
 move_uploaded_file($tmpfname, $fname);
?>

<!DOCTYPE html>
<html>
  <head>
    <title>TODO supply a title</title>
      <meta charset="UTF-8">
      <meta name="viewport" content="width=device-width,
                             initial-scale=1.0">
  </head>
  <body>
    <img src="<?php echo $fname ?>" />
  </body>
</html>
```

The `$_FILES` array has elements that give the name that the file has been
temporarily stored under and its original name and these can be used to move
the file to any location you want. In this case the file is copied to the same
directory as the page and then loaded into an `<img>` tag to show the file. In a
production program you would also have to check the file type and size,
provide error handling and possibly allow for multiple files to be uploaded at
a single go.

Using FormData

This is fine and very easy, but what if you want to save a file in a way that
doesn't lend itself to a form? The answer is you can use the new `FormData`
API. A `FormData` object contains the same key-value pairs as as a form but as
property-values that have get and set methods. You can create a `FormData`
object from a form and so take control of what happens when the user clicks
the submit button.

For example, to add some data to the form:

```
var formData = new FormData(form1);
formData.append("CustomField", "This is some extra data");
```

You can use get and set to modify fields. Once you have the form data you want to send you can use fetch to send the data as a multipart/form-data body. For example:

```
<!DOCTYPE html>
<html>
 <head>
   <title>TODO supply a title</title>
     <meta charset="UTF-8">
     <meta name="viewport" content="width=device-width,
                                    initial-scale=1.0">
 </head>
 <body>
   <form name="form1" action="http://server/fileHandler.php"
               method="post" enctype="multipart/form-data">
     <p><input type="file" name="file1">
     <p><input type="text" name="age">
     <p><button type="button" onclick="doSubmit()">Submit</button>
   </form>
   <script>
     async function doSubmit() {
       var form = document.forms.namedItem("form1");
       var formData = new FormData(form1);
       formData.append("CustomField", "This is some extra data");
       var url = new URL("fileHandler.php","http://server/");
       var request = new Request(url, {
                              method: "POST",
                              body: formData,
                              cache: "no-cache",
                              "Content-Type": "multipart/form-data"
                  });
       var response = await fetch(request);
     }
   </script>
 </body>
</html>
```

Notice that now the button in the form doesn't submit the form but calls the doSubmit function which uses the fetch object to send the data in the formData object. Notice that you don't have to change the server file for this to work – a temporary file is created and moved. However, as this is an AJAX call the current page isn't replaced so you don't see the graphics file displayed.

Upload Without a Form

You can append a file or blob to the `FormData` object using append:

```
formData.append("myfile", myFile, "filename.txt");
```

where the first parameter is the name of the field, the second the data, i.e. a `File` or `Blob` object, and the final parameter is the file name – which is optional. Of course, you can't get a `File` object that references a local file unless you use a file input field and allow the user to select it. In other words, you can't use this to upload a file unless the user has been made aware of it. However, you can use this method to upload the contents of a canvas object. For example, you can change the client page to read:

```html
<!DOCTYPE html>
<html>
  <head>
    <title>TODO supply a title</title>
        <meta charset="UTF-8">
        <meta name="viewport" content="width=device-width,
                                        initial-scale=1.0">
  </head>
  <body>
    <div id="myDiv">test </div>
    <script>
      function createCanvas(h, w) {
        var c = document.createElement("canvas");
        c.width = w;
        c.height = h;
        return c;
      }
      var ctx = document.body.appendChild(createCanvas(300, 300)).
                                        getContext("2d");
      ctx.fillStyle = '#fff';  /// set white fill style
      ctx.fillRect(0, 0, ctx.canvas.width, ctx.canvas.height);
      var myPath = new Path2D();
      myPath.moveTo(50, 50);
      myPath.lineTo(100, 100);
      myPath.lineTo(0, 100);
      myPath.lineTo(50, 50);
      myPath.moveTo(50, 110);
      myPath.lineTo(0, 60);
      myPath.lineTo(100, 60);
      myPath.lineTo(50, 110);
      ctx.stroke(myPath);
```

Notice that now we have some instructions to create a canvas with some contents that we can send as a file.

Next we call uploadCanvas to actually do the job:

```
uploadCanvas(ctx);
```

It converts the canvas to a blob, sends it using postGraphic and then displays the returned data in a <div> with id myDiv:

```
async function uploadCanvas(ctx) {
    var blob = await canvasToBlob(ctx, "image/png");
    var response = await postGraphic(blob);
    myDiv.innerHTML = await response.text();
}

function canvasToBlob(ctx, type) {
    return new Promise(function (resolve, reject) {
                       ctx.canvas.toBlob(function (blob) {
                       resolve(blob);
                   }, type);
            });

}
```

The interesting function is postGraphic:

```
async function postGraphic(blob) {
    var url = new URL("fileHandler.php", "http://server/fetchtest/");
    var file = new File([blob], "pond.png", {type: "image/png"});
    var formData = new FormData();
    formData.append("file1", blob, "pond.png");
    var request = new Request(url, {
                                method: "POST",
                                body: formData,
                                cache: "no-cache",
                              "Content-Type": "multipart/form-data"
                });
    var response = await fetch(request);
    return response;
}
  </script>
 </body>
</html>
```

This first converts the blob to a File with the correct name and MIME type. It then adds it to a FormData object and sends it using the same code that would be used if the FormData had been derived from a real form.

The PHP program is exactly the same, apart from now returning some HTML to display the file that has been created on the remote server. Notice that as this is an AJAX request, the original page is not replaced by a new one.

```php
<?php
 $fname = $_FILES["file1"]["name"];
 $tmpfname = $_FILES["file1"]["tmp_name"];
 move_uploaded_file($tmpfname, $fname);
?>
<img src="<?php echo $fname ?>" />
```

If you run this pair of programs you will find that the drawing in the canvas is successfully uploaded without the user being involved. You can use the same approach to upload multiple files simply by appending them to the FormData object.

Direct Binary Upload

Using multipart/form-data is relatively easy, but there is a more direct way of uploading a file which avoids the overheads and the potential error of the random boundary value being used as a separator should it happen to occur within the binary file.

To upload in pure binary you need to create a blob and then send it to the server as an octet stream:

```javascript
async function postGraphic(blob) {
  var url = new URL("fileHandler.php","http://server/fetchtest/");
  var request = new Request(url, {
                        method: "POST",
                        body: blob,
                        cache: "no-cache",
                      "Content-Type": "application/octet-stream"
            });
  var response = await fetch(request);
  return response;
}
```

No other changes to the client side program are required, but as the data is no longer being sent using multipart/form-data, in general the server will not know how to treat it. In other words, you cannot make use of $_POST or $_FILES. Instead you have to work with the raw POST data.

In PHP this is fairly easy:

```php
<?php
 $rawData = file_get_contents("php://input");
 $fname="pond.png";
 $fp = fopen('/var/www/temp/fetchtest/'+$fname, 'w');
 fwrite($fp, $rawData);
 fclose($fp);
?>
<img src="<?php echo $fname ?>" />
```

Notice that now we have to hard code the file name into the program as it isn't transmitted to the server as part of the POST data. We could arrange for it to be sent first and write a perfectly general program. Notice that this is a completely general method of transferring a binary file or binary data to the server and not restricted to an image file.

The Data URL

As well as the object URL, which can allow you to reference an object to supply the data, there is the data URL which stores the data as part of the URL. This is a useful trick, but it has many limitations. The data in a data URL is stored as text as part of the URL. If the data is binary then it is converted to a text representation called base64.

This is a very simple format that uses just 64 text characters that can be represented on almost any system. As there are 64 characters each can represent 6-bits. In most cases the characters are taken to be A to Z, a to z, 0 to 9 and + /. These are all representable as ASCII characters and as single byte in a UTF-8 encoding. What is important to realize is that it is not the character codes which are used to represent values but the index of the character in the list. That is, the ASCII code for A is 65 but in base64 it represents 0. In this way the encoding is fixed even if the character coding changes.

The only problem with base64 is that it uses four bytes to represent three. That is, each character takes a byte to represent but only encodes six bits of the original data. As four times six is 24 it takes four characters to code three eight-bit bytes and as a result a base64 encoding is larger, by about 33%, than the original binary data.

There are two JavaScript functions that work with base64:

- `atob()` takes a base64 string and decodes it
- `btoa()` takes a string and encodes it as a base64 string.

You can use base64 whenever you need to send binary data over a connection that can only reliably handle a limited range of characters using an uncertain character coding. However, it is most commonly encountered as part of a data URL which has the form:

```
data:MIMEtype;base64,data
```

The *MIMEtype* is an optional type specifier which defaults to `text/plain;charset=US-ASCII`. If you omit the `base64` parameter then the data is assumed to be text with the appropriate escapes and formatting according to the `MIMEtype`. For example:

```
data:,Hello%20World!
```

Notice the comma and the use of URL encoding.

You can use this data URL anywhere you can use a standard URL. For example:

```
<iframe src="data:,Hello%20World!"></iframe>
```

creates an `<iframe>` with the text `Hello World`.

You can create a data URL of the contents of a canvas using the `toDataURL` method:

```
canvas.toDataURL(MIMEtype,quality);
```

where `MIMEtype` is an optional parameter that determines the format of the data and `quality` (0 to 1) specifies the compression to be used if you specify a lossy format such as jpeg. The default `MIMEtype` is image/png.

For example:

```
var dataURL=ctx.canvas.toDataURL();
myImg.src=dataURL;
```

creates a data URL in the default `png` format and displays it in an `<img>` tag with `id myImg`.

When data URLs were first introduced they allowed you to do things that weren't possible by other methods. This is less true today as type arrays, blobs, object URLs and other facilities provide more direct ways of achieving many of the same results. One of the main uses of data URLs is to reduce the number of HTTP requests. Instead of a separate download of a graphics file, it can be "inlined" into the webpage as a data URL. The only problem is that a base64 graphics file is 33% larger, but generally this still results in a faster overall download time because individual HTTP requests are slower. It is worth noting that data URLs are limited in size according to the browser in use – 64K is a common limit for the size of a URL.

SVG To Canvas – HTML To Canvas

As another example of using `dataURLs` consider the example from Chapter 6 of using SVG to create text:

```
async function text(ctx,x,y, text, style) {
    var svg = '<svg xmlns="http://www.w3.org/2000/svg"
                                    height="80" width="800">';
    svg += '<text x="0" y="0" dominant-baseline="text-before-edge" ';
    svg += style + '>' + text + '</text>'+ '</svg>';
    svg = btoa(svg);
    var img = new Image();
    img.src = 'data:image/svg+xml;base64,' + svg;
    await imgLoaded(img);
    ctx.drawImage(img, x, y);
}
```

The basic idea is that an `Image` object can render SVG graphics and a data URL lets us create an SVG string and use it as the `src` property of an `Image` object. Notice the use of the `btoa` function to base64 encode the SVG string.

This is a general principle not limited to text. You can create a general SVG string and get an `Image` object to render it using a data URL. You can also use this SVG to canvas connection to draw any valid HTML onto the canvas. This is sometimes used to render an HTML UI to the canvas so that it can be modified.

The key to this trick is the `foreignObject` tag. This can be used to embed other XML tags within the SVG. How these tags are interpreted depends on the namespace assigned to them. If you use:

```
        xmlns="http://www.w3.org/1999/xhtml
```

then most browsers will interpret the tags as HTML and render them within the SVG code.

Using this it is quite easy to write a function that will render any HTML to a canvas:

```
async function html(ctx, x, y, html) {
 var svg = `<svg xmlns="http://www.w3.org/2000/svg"
                                    height="800" width="800">
            <foreignObject x="0" y="0" width="160" height="160">
             <body xmlns="http://www.w3.org/1999/xhtml">
               ${html}
             </body>
            </foreignObject>
          </svg>`;
 svg = btoa(svg);
 var img = new Image();
 img.src = 'data:image/svg+xml;base64,' + svg;
 await imgLoaded(img);
 ctx.drawImage(img, x, y);
}
```

The `imgLoaded` function is listed earlier:

```
function imgLoaded(img) {
    return new Promise(
                function (resolve, reject) {
                    img.addEventListener("load", function () {
                                    resolve(img);
                    });
                });
}
```

You can call this function with any legal HTML and, in principle, it will be rendered onto the canvas. This isn't a well used feature and exactly what works depends on the browser in use. You can render most HTML to Firefox and Chrome.

For example:

```
html(ctx, 0, 0, "<button>Click Me!</button>");

text(ctx,100,100,"Hello SVG Text!",'font-family="symbol"
                                    font-size="20pt"');
```

produces:

Click Me!

Ηελλο ΣςΓ Τεξτ!

Notice that the button is just a bitmap of what the button looks like – you can't click it!

Summary

- The `Blob` is essentially a file but without a filename or other properties. You can consider it an unstructured stream of data.

- A `File` is a blob with a filename and date and time of creation and use.

- The `FileReader` object can be used to read the data associated with a `File` or a `Blob`.

- You can open and read a file in the local file system but only if the user selects it via a File Open dialog box.

- You can write a file to the local file system but only if the user is made aware of it via a File Save dialog box.

- The `Response` object provides a stream-oriented and promise-based way of reading a file. For graphics data in most cases you would use the typed "read to the end" methods.

- The Fetch API is a promise-based replacement for `XMLHttpRequest`.

- The `Request` object customizes the request made by the Fetch API.

- In most cases the simplest and fastest way to download graphics from a server is to use the `Image` object to download and decode the file format.

- You can upload graphics data to the server with the help of a form and/or the `FormData` object. According to the MIME type you use this provides a great deal of automatic processing at the client and the server.

- If you want to be in complete control of what is happening, you can use a direct binary upload of a file, but then you usually have to do more work at the server to retrieve the file.

- A Data URL stores text or binary data within the URL itself. Binary data is stored as base64 encoded text.

- You can use a Data URL to establish a link to render both SVG and HTML onto a canvas object.

Chapter 13

Image Processing

In the early part of this book the emphasis was on creating graphics by drawing on the canvas. By contrast the latter part of the book is about loading graphics files into the canvas. Why would you want to do this as opposed to simply loading files into an `Image` object? If you only want to display the bitmaps then you should use an `image` object. The advantage of a canvas object is that you can manipulate the pixel values to change what is displayed. This is image processing and it is the subject of this chapter.

Getting at the Pixels

The `drawImage` method allows you to make the connection between a bitmap and the canvas object, but what about getting at the pixels of a bitmap?

You can do this quite easily with the help of the `ImageData` object.

There are two methods for creating an `ImageData` object:

- `ctx.createImageData(w,h)` creates an `ImageData` object with width w and height h
- `ctx.createImageData(IData)` creates an `ImageData` object the same size as the `ImageData` object specified by `IData`.

In both cases all pixels are set to transparent black, `i.e.` `R=0`, `G=0`, `B=0` and `A=0`.

These two methods correspond to constructors which can be used in a `Worker` where no canvas is available:

- `new ImageData(w,h)`
- `new ImageDate(IData)`

A third method creates an `ImageData` object from the pixels in a specified area of a canvas object:

- `ctx.getImageData(x,y,w,h)` creates an `ImageData` object from the pixels in the rectangle with top left corner at `x,y` and width w and height h.

To manipulate the pixels in the `ImageData` object you make use of its data property which is a `Uint8ClampedArray` (see Chapter11) of pixel values in the order `RGBA` for each pixel.

The first element of the array i.e. `data[0]` is the `R` value for the pixel in the top left corner. The pixels are stored in the array in row order with four elements to each pixel.

A few moments thought should convince you that the `R` value for the pixel at `x,y` in the rectangle of pixels is stored at:

```
data[(x+y*w)*4]
```

We can use this to write a method that allows direct access to the color information for the pixel at `x,y`. We can then use these methods to manipulate the pixel data and then write the result to the canvas using:

```
ctx.putImageData(ImageData,x,y);
```

which renders the `ImageData` object with its top left corner at `x,y`.

There is another more sophisticated `putImageData` method:

```
ctx.putImageData(ImageData,x,y,sx,sy,sw,sh)
```

which only transfers data from the `ImageData` object within the rectangle with top left corner at `sx,sy` and width `sw` and height `sh`.

This is more or less all we need to create and modify graphics working at the pixel level. Of course, it would be a good idea to implement some slightly higher-level methods and while this is easy it does raise the question of how best to package them to make them easy to use. One approach is simply to add them as ad-hoc methods to the `ImageData` object that you create. For example:

```
var ImDat=ctx.createImageData(100,100);
ImDat.getPixel=function(x,y){
  var i=(x+y*this.width)*4;
  return {R:this.data[i],
          G:this.data[i+1],
          B:this.data[i+2],
          A:this.data[i+3]
          }
 }
```

adds the `getPixel` method to the `ImDat` object to return an object with the properties R, G, B and A for the pixel at `x,y`.

You can add a similar `setPixel` method:

```
ImDat.setPixel=function(x,y,c){
  var i=(x+y*this.width)*4;
  this.data[i]=c.R;
  this.data[i+1]=c.G;
  this.data[i+2]=c.B;
  this.data[i+3]=c.A;
}
```

to set the pixel at `x,y` to the color specified by the `RGBA` properties of the `c` object. Of course, in a production system you would need to add checks that the parameters were of the correct type and that the values were all in the range `0` to `255`. You could also write other methods to work with color defined in other ways - CSS colors, color in the range `0` to `1` and so on.

This approach has two main problems. The first is that you have to augment each instance of the `ImageData` object in the same way. You also have to update it with each of the new methods you want to add to it. One way of making this easier is to write an augmentation function:

```
function augmentImageData(o){
   o.getPixel=function(x,y){
      var i=(x+y*this.width)*4;
      return {R:this.data[i],
              G:this.data[i+1],
              B:this.data[i+2],
              A:this.data[i+3]
             };
   };
   o.setPixel=function(x,y,c){
      var i=(x+y*this.width)*4;
      this.data[i]=c.R;
      this.data[i+1]=c.G;
      this.data[i+2]=c.B;
      this.data[i+3]=c.A;
   };
};
```

This will add the two methods to any instance of the `ImageData` object. To do the job properly, you could even add a `createAugmentedImageData` method to the canvas object. So now we can simply write:

```
var ImDat=ctx.createImageData(100,100);
augmentImageData(ImDat);
```

and use the `getPixel` and `setPixel` methods on `ImDat`.

For example:

```
for(var x=0;x<100;x++){
  for (var y = 0; y < 100; y++) {
    ImDat.setPixel(x, y, {
                            R: 0,
                            G: 255,
                            B: 0,
                            A: 255});
  }
}
```

sets every pixel to green.

To see this we can put the `ImageData` object to the canvas:

```
ctx.putImageData(ImDat,0,0);
```

Of course, this is a complex way of drawing a green square and the canvas
already has a perfectly easy to use way of doing the same job in the form of
`fillRectangle`.

In general, there is never much point in using an uninitialized `ImageData`
object to draw regular shapes that could just as easily be drawn using the
standard canvas methods. However, there are some things that are easier to
do directly in terms of pixels. For example, to create a completely random
background:

```
var ImDat=ctx.createImageData(300,300);
augmentImageData(ImDat);
for(var x=0;x<300;x++){
 for (var y = 0; y < 300; y++) {
 ImDat.setPixel(x, y, {
 R: Math.floor(Math.random()*256),
 G: Math.floor(Math.random()*256),
 B: Math.floor(Math.random()*256),
 A: 255});
 }
}

ctx.putImageData(ImDat,0,0);
```

A Special Effects Filter

As an example of loading and modifying an existing image, let's implement a simple "embossed" effect filter.

First we create a canvas object:

```
function createCanvas(h, w) {
 var c = document.createElement("canvas");
 c.width = w;
 c.height = h;
 return c;
}
async function draw(){
   var ctx =document.body.appendChild(createCanvas(400,400))
                                        .getContext("2d");
```

Now we have a canvas ready to use, next we load the image file to be processed:

```
var img = new Image();
var url = new URL("jeep.jpg", "http://localhost:8383/Filter/");
img.src = url;
await imgLoaded(img);
ctx.drawImage(img, 0, 0, 400, 300);
```

Getting the **ImageData** is just a repeat of what we did in the previous example:

```
var ImDat = ctx.getImageData(0, 0, 400, 300);
augmentImageData(ImDat);
```

At this point we can now process the image data using the augmented methods:

```
for (var x = 0; x < 400; x++) {
  for (var y = 0; y < 300; y++) {
    var c1 = ImDat.getPixel(x, y);
    var c2 = ImDat.getPixel(x, y + 3);
    var r = Math.abs(c1.R - c2.R) + 128;
    var g = Math.abs(c1.G - c2.G) + 128;
    var b = Math.abs(c1.B - c2.B) + 128;
    var gray = (r + g + b) / 3;
    ImDat.setPixel(x, y,{R: gray, G: gray, B: gray, A: c1.A});
  }
}
```

The two for loops simply scan through every pixel in the image and compute the difference between the pixel's color value and the color value of the pixel three to the right. The 128 is added to make the difference have an average of 128 rather than 0 and then the color values are converted to a gray level, i.e. the average of the three color values. Finally the new pixel data is stored back in the ImageData object without changing the A value.

When the `for` loops come to an end all that remains is to put the pixel data
back in the canvas, or into a different canvas if you want to display both the
input and the result:

```
    ctx.putImageData(ImDat,0,0);
}
draw();
```

The complete program is:

```html
<!DOCTYPE html>
<html>
  <head>
    <title>TODO supply a title</title>
    <meta charset="UTF-8">
    <meta name="viewport" content="width=device-width,
                                    initial-scale=1.0">
  </head>
  <body>
   <script>
     function createCanvas(h, w) {
       var c = document.createElement("canvas");
       c.width = w;
       c.height = h;
       return c;
     }

     function imgLoaded(img) {
       return new Promise(
                   function (resolve, reject) {
                     img.addEventListener("load", function () {
                                                 resolve(img);
                     });
               });
     }
```

```javascript
    function augmentImageData(o) {
      o.getPixel = function (x, y) {
        var i = (x + y * this.width) * 4;
        return {R: this.data[i],
                G: this.data[i + 1],
                B: this.data[i + 2],
                A: this.data[i + 3]
              }
      }
      o.setPixel = function (x, y, c) {
        var i = (x + y * this.width) * 4;
        this.data[i] = c.R;
        this.data[i + 1] = c.G;
        this.data[i + 2] = c.B;
        this.data[i + 3] = c.A;
      }
  }

  async function draw() {
   var ctx = document.body.appendChild(createCanvas(400, 400)).
                                        getContext("2d");
   var img = new Image();
   var url = new URL("jeep.jpg", "http://server/Filter/");
   img.src = url;
   await imgLoaded(img);
   ctx.drawImage(img, 0, 0, 400, 300);
   var ImDat = ctx.getImageData(0, 0, 400, 300);
   augmentImageData(ImDat);
   for (var x = 0; x < 400; x++) {
    for (var y = 0; y < 300; y++) {
      var c1 = ImDat.getPixel(x, y);
      var c2 = ImDat.getPixel(x, y + 3);
      var r = Math.abs(c1.R - c2.R) + 128;
      var g = Math.abs(c1.G - c2.G) + 128;
      var b = Math.abs(c1.B - c2.B) + 128;
      var gray = (r + g + b) / 3;
      ImDat.setPixel(x, y,{R: gray, G: gray, B: gray, A: c1.A});
    }
    }
   ctx.putImageData(ImDat,0,0);
  }

  draw();
   </script>
 </body>
</html>
```

A Security Problem

You can try loading images for this filter from the local file system, but if you do you will discover that it doesn't work. You cannot access the pixels of an image that has been loaded from a different URL and accessing pixels of a local file is strictly forbidden. If you download the file from a server with the same URL as the script then there's no problem.

To allow for testing, Chrome has a command line switch that turns off the security check - no doubt other browsers have similar features. All you have to do is locate the shortcut that you use to launch Chrome and change the target to read:

```
"C:\Program Files\Google\Chrome\Application\chrome.exe"
--allow-file-access-from-files
```

Alternatively simply use the command from the command prompt or add:

```
--allow-file-access-from-files
```

to whatever command initiates Chrome. With this command line switch it all works and you can see the result of the effect.

The Filter API

SVG has long had a set of filter functions and these are now being migrated to Canvas in the Filter API. Note, however, that not all browsers support the Filter API at the time of writing, in particular Safari and Opera don't.

The basic idea is that you can set a list of filters on a context which modifies what you draw to it.

The basic filter method is:

```
ctx.filter = "filter1 ... filterN";
```

where the filters are any of:

- `none` No filter is applied and this has the effect of removing filters.

- `url(url)` - a url referencing an SVG filter element, see later.

- `blur(amount)` Applies a Gaussian blur to the drawing with amount giving the standard deviation i.e. the extent of the blur. A value of 0 leaves the input unchanged.

- `brightness(percent)` A value under 100% darkens the image, while a value over 100% brightens it. A value of 0% will create an image that is completely black, while a value of 100% leaves the input unchanged.

- ◆ `contrast(percent)` Adjusts the contrast of the drawing. A value of `0%` will create a drawing that is completely black. A value of `100%` leaves the drawing unchanged.

- ◆ `grayscale(percentage)` Converts the drawing to grayscale. A value of `100%` is completely grayscale. A value of `0%` leaves the drawing unchanged.

- ◆ `invert(percentage)` Inverts the drawing. A value of `100%` means complete inversion. A value of `0%` leaves the drawing unchanged.

- ◆ `opacity(percentage)` Applies transparency to the drawing. A value of `0%` means completely transparent. A value of `100%` leaves the drawing unchanged.

- ◆ `saturate(percentage)` Saturates the drawing. A value of `0%` means completely unsaturated. A value of `100%` leaves the drawing unchanged.

- ◆ `sepia(percentage)` Converts the drawing to sepia. A value of `100%` means completely sepia. A value of `0%` leaves the drawing unchanged.

- ◆ `hue-rotate(angle)` Applies a hue rotation on the drawing. A value of `0` degrees leaves the input unchanged.

- ◆ `Drop-shadow()` This function takes up to five arguments:

`offset-x`	Specifies the horizontal distance of the shadow.
`offset-y`	Specifies the vertical distance of the shadow.
`Blur-radius`	The larger this value, the bigger the blur, so the shadow becomes bigger and lighter.
`Cclor`	CSS color specification

There isn't much to say about using these specific filters – they are generally adjusted by trial and error and they either do what you want or they don't. For example:

```
async function draw() {
    var ctx = document.body.appendChild(createCanvas(400, 400)).
                                        getContext("2d");
    var img = new Image();
    var url = new URL("jeep.jpg", "http://server/Filter/");
    img.src = url;
    await imgLoaded(img);
    ctx.filter = "grayscale(100%)invert(75%)";
    ctx.drawImage(img, 0, 0, 400, 300);
}
```

produces:

Notice that the range of filters that you can apply is limited but the url filter lets you use any filter that is defined or can be defined using SVG. You can find a complete list of SVG filters in the documentation and to use them you first define the SVG filter as if you were going to use it in an SVG drawing:

```
<feBlend>
<feColorMatrix>
<feComponentTransfer>
<feComposite>
<feConvolveMatrix>
<feDiffuseLighting>
<feDisplacementMap>
<feDropShadow>
<feFlood>
<feGaussianBlur>
<feImage>
<feMerge>
<feMorphology>
<feOffset>
<feSpecularLighting>
<feTile>
<feTurbulence>
```

For example to apply the SVG `<feGaussianBlur>` filter to a canvas:

```
<svg aria-hidden="true" style="position: absolute;
                width: 0; height: 0; overflow: hidden;"
                        xmlns="http://www.w3.org/2000/svg">
 <filter id="blurMe">
   <feGaussianBlur stdDeviation="5"/>
 </filter>
</svg>
```

This has to be included in the body of the page. Notice that it doesn't display anything. To use it in with Canvas you would simply write:

```
ctx.filter = "url(#blurMe)";
```

where the URL is a reference to the id. You could save the SVG in a separate file and use that as the URL.

Convolution Filter

Many of the SVG filters are already available as canvas filters. The notable exception is the convolution filter. Convolution sounds like a very complex operation, but in fact it is very simple. You simply specify an array of numbers. For example:

$$\begin{pmatrix} 1 & 0 & -1 \\ 0 & 0 & 0 \\ 0 & 0 & 0 \end{pmatrix}$$

Imagine that the pixel of interest is the one in the middle of the array. Now take each of the pixels that surround it and multiply by the corresponding number and replace the pixel by the sum. In other words, the convolution mask given above replaces every pixel in the image by the difference between the pixel to its top left and top right.

As another example consider the mask:

$$\begin{pmatrix} 1 & 1 & 1 \\ 1 & 0 & 1 \\ 1 & 1 & 1 \end{pmatrix}$$

This replaces each pixel by the sum of the pixels surrounding it. You can try this out by defining the following SVG filter:

```
<svg aria-hidden="true" style="position: absolute;
                width: 0; height: 0; overflow: hidden;"
                    xmlns="http://www.w3.org/2000/svg">
  <filter id="average">
    <feConvolveMatrix order="3"
        preserveAlpha="true"
        kernelMatrix="1 1 1
                      1 0 1
                      1 1 1"/>
  </filter>
</svg>
```

The order attribute sets the size of the matrix, 3 by 3 in this case. The preserveAlpha attribute when set to "true" removes the alpha channel from the convolution. To keep the values within the normal range the convolution is divided by the sum of the matrix elements. Thus, in this case, the sum is divided by 8 and so the center pixel is replaced by the average of the eight surrounding pixels. You can change the divisor by setting the `divisor` attribute.

There is a small problem about what to do when processing a pixel right at the edge of the image. The problem is that the pixel will lack some of the neighbors used in the mask. You can set the value of the edge attribute so that the missing values are either treated as 0 (`none`), assumed to the be same as the values actually on the edge (`duplicate`) or taken from the edge on the other side of the image (`wrap`).

You can implement your own convolution filter using direct pixel manipulation and of course you can go beyond what convolution offers.

As a final example, the mask:

```
kernelMatrix="1  1  1
              0  0  0
             -1 -1 -1"
```

replaces every pixel by the average difference between the three pixels above and the three below. It is a horizontal edge finder:

Notice that it only shows horizontal edges that have a positive difference. Negative values are mapped to 0 and values larger than 255 are mapped to 255.

Custom Convolution

You can implement your own convolution in JavaScript. It is slower, but you can customize it more than the SVG convolution filter.

For example, to implement the edge finder filter in the previous section:

```
async function draw() {
  var ctx = document.body.appendChild(createCanvas(400, 400)).
                                            getContext("2d");
  var img = new Image();
  var url = new URL("jeep.jpg", "http://server/");
  img.src = url;
  await imgLoaded(img);
  ctx.drawImage(img, 0, 0, 400, 300);
  var ImDat1 = ctx.getImageData(0, 0, 400, 300);
  augmentImageData(ImDat1);
  var ImDat2 = ctx.createImageData(400, 300);
  augmentImageData(ImDat2);

  var mask = [[-1, -1, -1], [0, 0, 0], [1, 1, 1]];
  var m = 3;
  var n = 3;

 for (var x = m; x < 400 - m; x++) {
   for (var y = n; y < 300 - n; y++) {
     var pixel = {R: 0, G: 0, B: 0, A: 0};

     for (var i = 0; i < m; i++) {
       for (var j = 0; j < n; j++) {
         var c1 = ImDat1.getPixel(x + Math.floor(i - m / 2),
                                  y + Math.floor(j - n / 2));
         pixel.R += mask[j][i] * c1.R;
         pixel.G += mask[j][i] * c1.G;
         pixel.B += mask[j][i] * c1.B;
       }
     }

     pixel.A = ImDat1.getPixel(x, y).A;
     pixel.R = Math.abs(pixel.R);
     pixel.G = Math.abs(pixel.G);
     pixel.B = Math.abs(pixel.B);

     ImDat2.setPixel(x, y, pixel);
   }
 }
 ctx.putImageData(ImDat2, 0, 0);
}
```

The first two `for` loops step through the image file x,y and for each pixel the two inner loops form the sum of the product with each pixel and the mask. Notice that we need two `ImageData` objects as we cannot modify the image while working on it because the old values are needed after the new values are calculated. When the inner loops finish the mask has been convolved at a single x,y location. We next take the absolute value to convert negative gradients into positive values and store the pixel value in the second `ImageData` object. When all of the loops complete we show the result. Notice that in this case we avoid processing the edge of the image.

Reading a PCX File

One of the less common, but more demanding, tasks is to write a JavaScript program that will read in and render a graphics file format that isn't supported by the browser. PCX format graphics files were very common until more modern formats replaced them. As well as having an archival importance, they are still the basis of the file format used by fax machines, which are still in use in many niche organizational situations.

Using typed arrays and some new facilities in the File API and Canvas we can read in almost any format file - as long as we know its format. PCX files are reasonably well documented by the company that created the format at: `http://bespin.org/~qz/pc-gpe/pcx.txt`

For the demonstration it is easier to allow the user to select a local file to be loaded and processed, but in principle you could use any of the techniques described in Chapter 12 to obtain the file.

Start a new HTML page and add the tag:

```
<input type='file' id="files">
```

This displays a Choose File button. When the user clicks it they are shown a file selection dialog box. When they finally select a file, the input object fires a change event. In principle the user can select multiple files, but for this example it is easier to suppose that they select a single PCX file.

In order to use `async` and `await` we need two simple wrapper functions that replace the usual event handlers:

```
 function getFile(files) {
    return new Promise(function (resolve, reject) {
       files.addEventListener("change", function (e) {
                              var file = e.target.files[0];
                              resolve(file);
                          });
       });
}


function readFile(file) {
    return new Promise(function (resolve, reject) {
                 var fileReader = new FileReader();
                 fileReader.addEventListener("load", function (e) {
                                      resolve(e.target.result);
                                  }, false);
                 fileReader.readAsArrayBuffer(file);
           });
}
```

The function that is going to do the work is `processImage`. This simply prompts the user to select a PCX file, reads it into an `ArrayBuffer` and then calls `getPCX` to decode the file into an `ImageData` object:

```
async function processImage() {
    var file = await getFile(files);
    var buffer = await readFile(file);
    var imageData = getPCX(buffer);
}
```

As we already have `getFile` and `readFile`, all we need to write is `getPCX` and to do this we need to know the format of a PCX file.

Processing the PCX File

For simplicity, it is assumed that the user has selected a valid PCX file. For testing the simplest thing to do is to use Gimp, or your favorite graphics program, to create a small PCX file, say 128 by 128 pixels and to save it in 24-bit color format, as this is the only format the demo program decodes. It is also the only format that Gimp creates.

There are many other PCX formats, but this is just a minimal viable program to illustrate how things work. A PCX file starts with 128-byte header:

```
typedef struct _PcxHeader
{
 0 BYTE  Identifier;        /* PCX Id Number (Always 0x0A) */
 1 BYTE  Version;           /* Version Number */
 2 BYTE  Encoding;          /* Encoding Format */
 3 BYTE   BitsPerPixel;     /* Bits per Pixel */
 4 WORD  XStart;            /* Left of image */
 6 WORD  YStart;            /* Top of Image */
 8 WORD  XEnd;              /* Right of Image
 10 WORD  YEnd;             /* Bottom of image */
 12 WORD  HorzRes;          /* Horizontal Resolution */
 14 WORD  VertRes;          /* Vertical Resolution */
 16 BYTE  Palette[48];      /* 16-Color EGA Palette */
 64 BYTE  Reserved1;        /* Reserved (Always 0) */
 65 BYTE  NumBitPlanes;     /* Number of Bit Planes */
 66 WORD  BytesPerLine;     /* Bytes per Scan-line */
 68 WORD  PaletteType;      /* Palette Type */
 70 WORD  HorzScreenSize;   /* Horizontal Screen Size */
 72 WORD  VertScreenSize;   /* Vertical Screen Size */
 74 BYTE  Reserved2[54];    /* Reserved (Always 0) */
} PCXHEAD;
```

The data follows the header. We don't need to read most of the header as its information isn't used. The raw data starts at offset 128 and the rest of the header from 74 to 127 is padding.

We can read in some of the header's data using a `DataView`:

```
function getPCX(buffer) {
    var datav = new DataView(buffer);
    var Identifier = datav.getUint8(0, true);
    var Version = datav.getUint8(1, true);
    var Encoding = datav.getUint8(2, true);
    var BitsPerPixel = datav.getUint8(3, true);
    var XStart = datav.getUint16(4, true);
    var YStart = datav.getUint16(6, true);
    var XEnd = datav.getUint16(8, true);
    var YEnd = datav.getUint16(10, true);
    var NumBitPlanes =   datav.getUint8(65, true);
    var BytesPerLine =   datav.getUint16(66, true);

    var rawData = new Uint8Array(buffer, 128);
```

Notice that the final "endian" parameter has to be `true` because PCX files are always stored in little endian order and this has to be converted into whichever order the machine that the program is running on uses.

Notice also that we have also created a typed array for the raw data. Using these fields we can compute some important parameters. First, we need the width and height of the image in pixels:

```
var ImageWidth = XEnd - XStart + 1;
var ImageHeight = YEnd - YStart + 1;
```

Next, we need the length of a scan line, i.e. one horizontal row of pixels in bytes:

```
var ScanLineLength = NumBitPlanes * BytesPerLine;
```

and the number of padding bytes at the end of each scan line:

```
var Padding = ScanLineLength - ImageWidth * NumBitPlanes;
```

Our next job is to unpack the raw data into an `ImageData` object. This is a slightly difficult task because of the way that compression is implemented. Whereas the raw data are run length encoded. This means that:

- ◆ If you read a byte and the most significant bits are zeros then the lower six bits are the pixel value.

- ◆ If you read a byte and the most significant bits are ones then the pixel value is in the next byte and the lower six bits are the number of times it should be repeated.

Thus every pixel has a `count` and a `data` value. For example, in this unpacking:

```
if (!(~rawData[position] & 0xC0)) {
    count = rawData[position] & 0x3F;
    position++;
} else {
    count = 1;
}
data = rawData[position];
position++;
```

the if statement tests for the most significant bits to be ones and extracts the count from the lower six bits if they are. Otherwise the `count` is 1 and the data is the single byte that was read. The way that `position` in the PCX file is incremented means `data` is either the original byte or the next byte and `position` is incremented ready to read the next byte to begin another `count`/`data` read. Notice that if the pixel value is greater than can be represented in six bits, it has to be coded as two bytes with a count of 1. For example, if you read a byte `0x3F` then `count` is 1 and `data` is `0x3F`, i.e.=63. If you read a byte `0xCF` then `count` is `0xF`, i.e =15 and `data` is in the next byte.

Now that we have the count and pixel values we need to transfer it to its correct location according to its `x,y` position and its color. The pixels are stored in scan lines, each of which has a set of bit planes. In our case we are assuming 8-bits per pixel and three bit planes, Red, Green and Blue. What this means is that the first row of pixels you read are the Red values for the first row of the image. Next come the Green and the third row gives the Blue. The only complication is that the image row ends when we have read the `ImageWidth` values, but the row is padded with extra values that mean we have to actually read `BytesPerLine` bytes before moving on to the next row.

So we can convert the PCX file by reading `value` and `count` from it, setting `count` pixels to that `value` and checking to see when we reach the end of a line. When we do we can set x back to 0 and increment `color` to set the next color on the line of pixels. When we have set three colors we can increment the y value to process the next set of three colors.

So our algorithm is roughly, in pseudo code:

```
set x, y and color equal to zero
repeat until y= ImageHeight
      read a count and value from the PCX file.
      Repeat count times:
             if(x< ImageWidth) pixel at x,y,color = value
             increment x
             if(x=== BytesPerLine) x=0, increment color
                     if color===3 color=0 increment y
```

Notice that, even though we only update pixel values up to `ImageWidth`, we have to continue to process data until we reach `BytesPerLine` to deal with padding as there may be bytes we have to unpack even if they are not used.

This is a difficult algorithm to implement because if things are even slightly out order the result is a set of jumbled pixels. There is also the small matter that we have to remember to set the alpha channel to `0x255` for all of the pixels as the PCX file doesn't include opacity data. This is rectified by:

```javascript
var ctx = document.body.appendChild(
        createCanvas(ImageWidth, ImageHeight)).getContext("2d");
var imageData = ctx.createImageData(ImageWidth, ImageHeight);
for (var y = 0; y < ImageHeight; y++) {
   for (var x = 0; x < ImageWidth; x++) {
       imageData.data[(x + y * ImageWidth) * 4 + 3] = 0xFF;
   }
}
```

Now we can ignore the A channel and focus on computing R, G and B.

Translating the pseudo code to JavaScript gives:

```javascript
while (y < ImageHeight) {
  if (!(~rawData[position] & 0xC0)) {
    count = rawData[position] & 0x3F;
    position++;
  } else {
    count = 1;
  }
  data = rawData[position];
  position++;
  for (var r = 0; r < count; r++) {
    if (x < ImageWidth)
      imageData.data[(x + y * ImageWidth) * 4 + color] = data;
    x++;
    if (x === BytesPerLine) {
      color++;
      if (color === 3) {
        color = 0;
        y++;
      }
      x = 0;
    }
  }
}
```

Notice that `position` gives the current position in reading the PCX file, x and y give the current position in the `ImageData` and `color` gives the color we are currently processing.

Finally we can view the image and return the result:

```
 ctx.putImageData(imageData, 0, 0);
 return imageData;
}
```

If you now try the program out you will find that you can read a PCX file and display it, but notice it only works for 24-bit PCX files – i.e. `BitsPerPixel` equal to 8 and `NumBitPlanes`equal to 3 and you should add tests for this if you are planning to try PCX files that might be in alternative formats.

Listing - Read a PCX File

```
<!DOCTYPE html>
<html>
 <head>
   <title>PCX Reader</title>
     <meta charset="UTF-8">
     <meta name="viewport" content="width=device-width,
                                    initial-scale=1.0">

   </head>
   <body>
     <input type="file" id="files">
     <script>
       function createCanvas(h, w) {
         var c = document.createElement("canvas");
         c.width = w;
         c.height = h;
         return c;
       }
       function imgLoaded(img) {
         return new Promise(
                 function (resolve, reject) {
                       img.addEventListener("load", function () {
                              resolve(img);
                       });
                 });
       }
       function getFile(files) {
         return new Promise(function (resolve, reject) {
                 files.addEventListener("change", function (e) {
                       var file = e.target.files[0];
                       resolve(file);
                 });
             });
       }
```

```javascript
function readFile(file) {
        return new Promise(function (resolve, reject) {
                        var fileReader = new FileReader();
                        fileReader.addEventListener("load",
                                function (e) {
                                        resolve(e.target.result);
                        }, false);
                        fileReader.readAsArrayBuffer(file);
                });
        }


        async function processImage() {
          var file = await getFile(files);
          var buffer = await readFile(file);
          var imageData = getPCX(buffer);
        }
        function getPCX(buffer) {
          var datav = new DataView(buffer);
          var Identifier = datav.getUint8(0, true);
          var Version = datav.getUint8(1, true);
          var Encoding = datav.getUint8(2, true);
          var BitsPerPixel = datav.getUint8(3, true);
          var XStart = datav.getUint16(4, true);
          var YStart = datav.getUint16(6, true);
          var XEnd = datav.getUint16(8, true);
          var YEnd = datav.getUint16(10, true);
          var NumBitPlanes =   datav.getUint8(65, true);
          var BytesPerLine =   datav.getUint16(66, true);

          var rawData = new Uint8Array(buffer, 128);

          var ImageWidth = XEnd - XStart + 1;
          var ImageHeight = YEnd - YStart + 1;
          var ScanLineLength = NumBitPlanes * BytesPerLine;
          var Padding = ScanLineLength - ImageWidth * NumBitPlanes;
          var ctx = document.body.appendChild(
            createCanvas(ImageWidth, ImageHeight)).getContext("2d");
          var imageData = ctx.createImageData(
                                ImageWidth, ImageHeight);
          for (var y = 0; y < ImageHeight; y++) {
            for (var x = 0; x < ImageWidth; x++) {
              imageData.data[(x + y * ImageWidth) * 4 + 3] = 0xFF;
            }
          }
```

```javascript
      var color = 0;
      var y = 0;
      var x = 0;
      var position = 0;
      var count;
      var data;

      while (y < ImageHeight) {
        if (!(~rawData[position] & 0xC0)) {
          count = rawData[position] & 0x3F;
          position++;
        } else {
          count = 1;
        }
        data = rawData[position];
        position++;
        for (var r = 0; r < count; r++) {
          if (x < ImageWidth)imageData.data[(x + y * ImageWidth)
                                            * 4 + color] = data;

          x++;
          if (x === BytesPerLine) {
            color++;
            if (color === 3) {
              color = 0;
              y++;
            }
            x = 0;
          }
        }
      }
      ctx.putImageData(imageData, 0, 0);
      return imageData;
      }
      processImage();
    </script>
  </body>
</html>
```

Summary

- The `ImageData` object allows direct access to the pixel data within a bitmap.

- The pixel data is stored in the data array property which is a `Uint8ClampedArray` in RGBA order.

- With direct access to the pixel data you can write filters which change the bitmap in controlled ways using functions formed from the surrounding pixels.

- The new Filter API provides a range of predefined filters that you can use.

- You can also use any of the SVG filters via the url filter.

- The SVG filters include a general convolution filter which can be used to implement many standard and custom linear filters.

- A convolution filter replaces the current pixel value with a weighted average of it and the pixels that surround it. The weighted average is specified as a convolution matrix or mask.

- It is also fairly easy to implement a convolution filter directly using `ImageData` and direct pixel manipulation.

- You can also arrange to read and process any graphics file format that you have the specification for using the standard techniques of reading files, bit manipulation and `ImageData`.

Chapter 14

3D WebGL

This book has so far been about 2D graphics with Canvas using the standard graphics context. You will hear people say that if you want to do 2D graphics then a good way is to use WebGL. The reason is that WebGL is GPU-accelerated and hence has the potential to provide very fast animation. It also provides 3D graphics and animation. As a result learning it seems like a good investment – and it is, but only if you are serious about graphics. There is a steep learning curve associated with WebGL and in this chapter we start from the very basics and work up to some simple graphics with the intention of letting you see how involved it all is. In the next chapter we look at the slightly simpler problem of using WebGL for 2D graphics.

Using WebGL isn't easy for several reasons. Generally, the documentation isn't WebGL specific and simply refers you to the OpenGL/ES documentation pointing out differences. Even if you do know OpenGL, there are some surprising and unwelcome differences between it and the slightly more primitive WebGL. It all makes it difficult to get started on a 3D project.

The project we are about to make a start on, to draw a simple triangle, is going to presented as a single long function and it is not going to use any "helper" functions or any elaborate ways of doing things. The purpose of this example is to show you how things work with code that is simple and direct. While this is good from the point of view of understanding what is happening, when you start work on a real program you need to break it down into sensible functions, you need helper functions to keep the code compact and an "elaborate" way of doing something may turn out to be the best.

You can use any WebGL-supporting browser, but this example is based on using the latest Chrome.

The Canvas and the Viewport

There is a lot of initialization to do before you can start drawing anything and this is the case with most 3D programs. WebGL is particularly bad when it comes to lengthy initialization - there is nothing much that can be done about this. The first thing to do is set up a web page complete with a canvas object that we can use to draw on:

```
function createCanvas(h, w) {
  var c = document.createElement("canvas");
  c.width = w;
  c.height = h;
  return c;
}

function draw3d(){
  var gl= document.body.appendChild(createCanvas(400,400)).
                                    getContext("webgl");
```

You should now test that the variable gl really does have a reference to the WebGL object, but for the sake of simplicity let's just assume it does.

The webgl context will return a WebGL 1 or WebGL 2 context depending on what the browser supports. WebGL 1 is supported by all major browsers apart from Safari. WebGL 2 uses a slightly modified form of shader language, but unless you enable this it is backward compatible with WebGL1. For this reason the rest of this chapter uses WebGL 1 and its shader language, even though there are some efficiency improvements in WebGL 2.

Finally we have to set the WebGL viewport to the area of the Canvas object that we want to use to render the 3D graphics. In most cases this is the whole of the Canvas:

```
gl.viewport(0, 0, canvas.width, canvas.height);
```

Shader Theory

The next standard initialization task is to set up a vertex and pixel shader. If you have used other 3D frameworks you might not be used to this idea, but modern graphics hardware has a programmable pipeline and WebGL and OpenGL support this.

There are no default rendering modes that you can fall back on - you have to specify how you want to process the 3D points and you have have to specify how to render them. There are no lights, no lighting effects and so on, unless you provide the shader code for it. This can make getting started more difficult, but in practice you can "borrow" standard shaders to create the

lighting and rendering effects you want. When you become an expert then
working out new shaders simply adds to the fun.

In most cases you have to supply two shaders - a vertex shader and a pixel, or
fragment, shader. The vertex shader is all about how the point that you
specify in 3D space is converted to the point that is plotted on the screen. It
provides the transformation and projection processing and generally you use
it to apply transformation and projection matrices onto the raw 3D data. The
fragment shader is responsible for setting the color of the pixels that are
within the area specified by the vertices. Exactly how it does this can be as
simple as assigning a fixed color or as complex as working out what the color
should be based on what light is falling on the surface in a 3D scene.

The whole point is that everything that happens is programmable using the
shader code. In addition it is worth knowing that your shader code is
executed in parallel by hundreds of processors – this is why GPU graphics are
much faster than CPU graphics.

Vertex Shader

The key idea here is that the WebGL drawing context is 2D. If you want to
render 3D graphics then you have to supply the math that converts the 3D
points to 2D canvas points. The only co-ordinate system that WebGL uses is
shown in the diagram below:

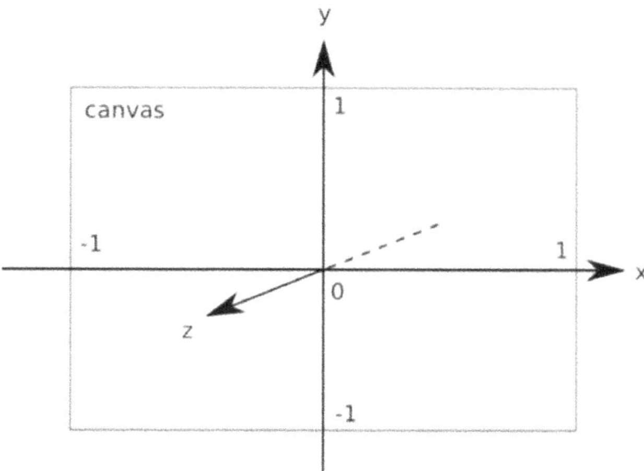

You can work with other co-ordinate systems by applying a transformation,
but this is the final co-ordinate system everything is mapped to. The
z co-ordinate isn't used for positioning, it simply determines which pixel will

be drawn on top of which pixel. It is exactly like the z-order for an HTML page and you can set up the hardware to control how it affects what is in front of what.

The first shader that you have to set up, the vertex shader, controls how the co-ordinate system you are working with is mapped to the canvas. In general, it has to reduce the 3D co-ordinates that you are using in "model space" to the 2D co-ordinates. This is usually done in two steps. First a "projection" matrix is used to convert the 3D points to a 2D representation that "looks correct". In most cases a perspective transformation is applied giving a 2D representation where objects that are further away in the z dimension are smaller. After this a 2D transformation is used to scale, rotate and skew the model co-ordinates into the canvas co-ordinates.

You also need to know that WebGL works with homogeneous co-ordinates. That is, any point you want to plot on the canvas is specified as:

`(x,y,z,1)`

If you look back to Chapter 5 you will see that the 2D context also uses this form of position and for the same reason. Homogeneous co-ordinates make it possible to use a single matrix to specify scaling, skew and rotation and translation.

For example, a transformation matrix like:

$$T = \begin{pmatrix} 1 & 0 & 0 & cx \\ 0 & 1 & 0 & cy \\ 0 & 0 & 1 & cz \\ 0 & 0 & 0 & 1 \end{pmatrix}$$

when multiplied by a homogeneous vector, gives:

$$\begin{pmatrix} 1 & 0 & 0 & cx \\ 0 & 1 & 0 & cy \\ 0 & 0 & 1 & cz \\ 0 & 0 & 0 & 1 \end{pmatrix} \begin{pmatrix} x \\ y \\ z \\ 1 \end{pmatrix} = \begin{pmatrix} x+cx \\ y+cy \\ z+cz \\ 1 \end{pmatrix}$$

You can see that the effect is to move the point by `cx,cy,cz`. Without homogeneous co-ordinates you would have to deal with translation as a special case.

There is a second reason for working with homogeneous co-ordinates. As a final step before the `x.y` values are plotted in 2D they are divided by the fourth dummy co-ordinate. As in standard form a homogeneous co-ordinate has a fourth co-ordinate that is **1** this usually makes no difference, but a perspective transformation produces a final co-ordinate that is different from 1 and in this case the division does make a difference. In general in a transformation that attempts to represent depth on a 2D canvas, the fourth co-ordinate is proportional to z and so things that are further away, large z, are divided by a larger fourth co-ordinate and so are drawn smaller, more about this a little later.

The vertex shader we are going to use at first is one you will find in most introductions to WebGL and is a perspective transformation followed by a co-ordinate transformation:

```
Canvas coordinates = Perspective Transformation *
                     Model Transformation * vertex coordinates
```

Shaders are specified using GLSL (OpenGL Shading Language) which is basically C with additional data types and standard functions. We don't have space to go into the details of GLSL, but you should be able to understand roughly what our basic shaders are doing. Notice that WebGL1 supports GLSL ES 1.0 whereas WebGL2 supports both GLSL ES 1.0 and GLSL ES 3.0. These are all older than the current version of GLSL used in modern OpenGL systems and there are differences. As already stated, for reasons of compatibility and because Safari doesn't currently support WebGL2, the rest of this chapter uses GLSL ES 1.0. The differences are minor.

Our "standard" vertex shader is:

```
attribute vec3 vertexPosition;
uniform mat4 modelViewMatrix;
uniform mat4 perspectiveMatrix;
void main(void) {
 gl_Position = perspectiveMatrix * modelViewMatrix *
                               vec4(vertexPosition, 1.0);
}
```

The first three lines define some data structures. The `vertexPosition` is a 3D vector, `vec3`, which specifies a location in model space.

If you are using WebGL 2 then the shader is:

```
#version 300 es
in vec3 vertexPosition;
uniform mat4 modelViewMatrix;
uniform mat4 perspectiveMatrix;
void main(void) {
  gl_Position = perspectiveMatrix * modelViewMatrix *
                                vec4(vertexPosition, 1.0);
}
```

where attributes are now declared as in variables. Note that `#version 300 es` is required and has to be the very first line.

An attribute is a value that is supplied to the shader from your program via a buffer. Buffers are arrays of data that you supply to WebGL and are used when you ask it to draw the buffer. Attributes determine how to read that data and your vertex shader is called repeatedly to process the items of data in the buffer. You can think of this as an implied loop reading the data in the buffer and processing it until the buffer is used up.

There are a number of predefined attributes, but in this case we are going to supply these attributes after we create the buffer defined as the `x,y,z` co-ordinates that specifies the points to be drawn.

The two matrices are also going to be supplied to the shader later. The `uniform` qualifier means that these quantities don't vary with the vertices being read from an attribute buffer. That is, they are very much like simple parameters passed to the vertex shader in the sense a `uniform` has the same value each time the shader is called to process an item of data in the buffer associated with an attribute. If the attribute is like an implied `for` loop reading and processing the buffer, then a uniform is a variable that is constant for the entire loop.

There is one `modelViewMatrix` and one `perspectiveMatrix` for each call of the shader while it is processing the items in the buffer associated with vertexPosition. The `gl_Position` variable is standard and supplied by the system that sets the position of the vertex using the fundamental co-ordinate system.

As well as uniforms and attributes, there are other types of data you can pass into your shaders and you can also use simple local variables within a shader as temporary storage. Notice the uniforms and attributes are read-only in the shader.

To be clear, when you ask WebGL to draw the contents of a buffer, the vertex shader is called for each element in the buffer with the same values for the uniforms.

Fragment Shader

The most basic shape in WebGL is the triangle. The vertex shader works out where the points in the buffer are to be plotted on the canvas. Usually groups of three points are taken to define a triangle, the interior of which is to be colored by the fragment shader. This means that when the fragment shader is called it works out the colors to be assigned to each of the pixels within each of the triangles. This can be a sophisticated calculation that involves the colors assigned to each of the vertices and the angle that the 3D fragment makes with a given direction – this is how lighting effects are added. You can also specify bitmaps which are processed by the shader to render a texture on the fragment, see the next chapter. For our first example, however, the simplest possible fragment shader just assigns a constant color:

```
void main(void) {
   gl_FragColor = vec4(0.0, 1.0, 0.0, 1.0);
}
```

Setting the standard variable `gl_FragColor` to an RGBA value sets every pixel within the triangle to that color. In this case the color is green. Now that `gl_FragColor` has been deprecated in GLSL ES 3.0, you should use your own variable defined using:

```
#version 300 es\n
 precision mediump float;
 out vec4 outColor;
 void main(void) {
   outColor= vec4(0.0, 1.0, 0.0, 1.0);
 }
```

Although triangles are the fundamental fragment in WebGL, you can also use lines and points and how these are handled is slightly different. But for most 3D graphics, the triangle is the workhorse.

Shader practice

Now we have our two shaders how do we get them into the WebGL object? The answer to this question is specific to JavaScript and WebGL as we have to write the shaders within JavaScript and somehow load them into the GPU.

The shader code is first stored as a string in a suitable variable. It is then stored in a shader object of the correct type and compiled. This has to be done for both the vertex and fragment shader. Then the two shaders are combined into a single program that the GPU can run to render our 3D model.

So starting with the vertex shader, first we have to store the code into a string:

```
var vsScript = `attribute vec3 vertexPosition;
                uniform mat4 modelViewMatrix;
                uniform mat4 perspectiveMatrix;
                void main(void) {
                  gl_Position = perspectiveMatrix *
                    modelViewMatrix * vec4(vertexPosition, 1.0);
                }`;
```

Notice that we are using a template string, which lets us write a multi-line string, and the "quotes" are back-ticks or grave accent characters.

The fragment shader, using a string template, is simply:

```
var fsScript = `void main(void) {
                  gl_FragColor = vec4(0.0, 1.0, 0.0, 1.0);
                }`;
```

Now we have both shaders as strings, we have to create a shader object of the correct type from each string:

```
var vertexShader = gl.createShader( gl.VERTEX_SHADER);
```

Next add it with the code to the WebGL object and compile the shader:

```
gl.shaderSource(vertexShader, vsScript);
gl.compileShader(vertexShader);
```

As long as there are no syntax errors in the code, we now have a compiled shader ready to be used. However, syntax errors are common so we need to check that it worked and print any errors to the console:

```
if(!gl.getShaderParameter(vertexShader, gl.COMPILE_STATUS)) {
 alert("Error in vertex shader");
 var compilationLog = gl.getShaderInfoLog(vertexShader);
 console.log('Shader compiler log: ' + compilationLog);
 gl.deleteShader(vertexShader);
}
```

We have to repeat the whole thing over again to enter and compile the fragment shader. Rather than splitting the steps down, it is more reasonable simply to present the code that creates both shaders in a function which will be used to compile both shaders from now on:

```
function createShaders(gl, vs, fs) {
  var vertexShader = gl.createShader(gl.VERTEX_SHADER);
  gl.shaderSource(vertexShader, vs);
  gl.compileShader(vertexShader);
  if (!gl.getShaderParameter(vertexShader, gl.COMPILE_STATUS)) {
    alert("Error in vertex shader");
    var compilationLog = gl.getShaderInfoLog(vertexShader);
    console.log('Shader compiler log: ' + compilationLog);
    gl.deleteShader(vertexShader);
    return;
  }
  var fragmentShader = gl.createShader(gl.FRAGMENT_SHADER);
  gl.shaderSource(fragmentShader, fs);
  gl.compileShader(fragmentShader);
  if (!gl.getShaderParameter(fragmentShader, gl.COMPILE_STATUS)) {
    alert("error in fragment shader");
    var compilationLog = gl.getShaderInfoLog(fragmentShader);
    console.log('Shader compiler log: ' + compilationLog);
    gl.deleteShader(fragmentShader);
    return;
  }
  return [vertexShader, fragmentShader];
}
```

This function accepts the drawing context and two strings that define the vertex and fragment shader. It returns an array with the first element (0) the `vertexShader` and the second (1) the `fragmentShader`.

Now we are almost done with the shaders. All that remains is to link them together into a single program that the GPU can run. This always follows the same steps. First create a program object, attach the compiled shaders to it and then link them together. It makes sense to write a function that does the job using the array of shaders returned by the previous function:

```
function createProgram(gl,shaders) {
  var program = gl.createProgram();
  gl.attachShader(program, shaders[0]);
  gl.attachShader(program, shaders[1]);
  gl.linkProgram(program);
  if (!gl.getProgramParameter(program, gl.LINK_STATUS)) {
   alert("Error in shaders");
   gl.deleteProgram(program);
   gl.deleteProgram(vertexShader);
   gl.deleteProgram(fragmentShader);
   return;
  }
  return program;
}
```

Finally we have to tell the GPU to use the program:
```
gl.useProgram(program);
```

Setting up the shaders always follows these fairly tedious steps and you can mostly forget how these function do their jobs. You always define and create two shaders and use these to construct the GPU's program object. In more advanced uses you can define multiple shaders and multiple programs. You can tell the GPU to use a given program before you render an object, so varying how the object is rendered.

The Matrices - Connecting with the Shaders

At some point in working with WebGL you have to define the matrices used in the shader. In general, you have to make connections between all of the variables used in the shaders and objects in the JavaScript program.

For a uniform follow the same three steps:

1. Get a reference to the uniform variable in the shader that can be used in JavaScript.

2. Construct a JavaScript object that will supply the data to be used by the shader variable.

3. Make the connection between the JavaScript object and the uniform variable in the shader.

In this case you have to connect the use of:

```
uniform mat4 modelViewMatrix;
uniform mat4 perspectiveMatrix;
```

in the vertex shader and two JavaScript matrices that specify the transformations. At this point in most tutorials we have to take a detour to explain how the two matrices are constructed. In full OpenGL there are a lot of handy helper functions that will build and manipulate matrices and construct perspective transformations from "camera-like" specifications. These aren't available in WebGL and while there are alternatives, let's keep things simple.

To make things even more simple we are going to use predefined transformation matrices. How they are constructed isn't difficult, but it takes us away from the main part of the story. The model view matrix might as well just be the identity matrix, i.e. no transformation of the 3D co-ordinates is performed:

```
var mvMatrix = [1, 0, 0, 0,
                0, 1, 0, 0,
                0, 0, 1, 0,
                0, 0, 0, 1 ];
```

Using this matrix means we are working with the fundamental co-ordinate system. The JavaScript matrix is a one-dimensional array even though it specifies a 2D matrix in the shader.

Making the connection between the JavaScript data and the vertex shader uniform follows the same standard steps using methods provided by the WebGL object. First get the reference to the shader object:

```
var shaderMVMatrix = gl.getUniformLocation(program,
                                    "modelViewMatrix");
```

You have to specify the program and the variable within the program that you want the reference to. The reference is in fact an index into a table of variables. Next you make the connection, there are a set of methods that you can use depending on the data type being transferred to the shader. In this case the method we need is:

```
gl.uniformMatrix4fv(shaderMVMatrix, false,
                            new Float32Array(mvMatrix));
```

You can see that this copies the data in `mvMatrix` to the specified shader variable. From this point on the shader will use the specified matrix.

There are many "uniform" functions which transfer data from the JavaScript program to the uniform in the shader and they differ according to the data type involved. In this case you can see that the data being transferred is a `Matrix4`, with float elements and it is a vector. If you have a uniform that is a single float you would use `uniform1f` and so on.

Perspective Transformation

The procedure is the same for the perspective matrix:

```
var pMatrix = [
            3, 0, 0, 0,
            0, 3, 0, 0,
            0, 0, 1, 2,
            0, 0,-1, 0
            ];
var shaderpMatrix = gl.getUniformLocation(program,
                                    "perspectiveMatrix");
gl.uniformMatrix4fv(shaderpMatrix, false,
                            new Float32Array(pMatrix));
```

You can see that we define the JavaScript array, get the location of the attribute and then use a method to transfer the data to the attribute.

This is all you need to know about making the connection between the JavaScript object and the shader uniform variable. However, it is worth spending a few moments considering what the perspective transform is doing. If you know your 3D theory you can skip this section.

The perspective matrix provided is simply one that results in a reasonable view of the simple object we are going to draw - you can worry about how to work out what the perspective matrix has to be in any particular situation later. The key to understanding the perspective transform is to know that there is a little more to homogeneous co-ordinates than simply implementing a transformation. Before the co-ordinates are plotted, they are converted to normal co-ordinates by dividing by the last component. That is, if you specify:

```
[x,y,z,w]
```

then, before being plotted, the system converts this to:

```
[x/w,y/w,z/w]
```

and the pixel is rendered at x/w, y/w. The z value is used to determine what is in front of what. Notice that the division isn't part of the matrix multiplication. It is how all homogeneous co-ordinates are treated before being plotted in 2D. Also notice that when w equals 1, which it does for all of the homogeneous vectors you create, then the division has no effect. The perspective transformation, however, creates a vector with w different from 1.

Consider:

$$T = \begin{pmatrix} 3 & 0 & 0 & 0 \\ 0 & 3 & 0 & 0 \\ 0 & 0 & 1 & 2 \\ 0 & 0 & -1 & 0 \end{pmatrix} \begin{pmatrix} 0.5 \\ 0.5 \\ 1 \\ 1 \end{pmatrix} = \begin{pmatrix} 1.5 \\ 1.5 \\ 3 \\ -2 \end{pmatrix}$$

You can see that the final 1 is now -2 and after division this gives:

$$\begin{pmatrix} -0.75 \\ -0.75 \\ -1.5 \end{pmatrix}$$

which is a point within the fundamental co-ordinate system. As the z co-ordinate of the point varies, the perspective transformation alters x and y so that things that are further away get smaller. Notice that this transformation can result in points that are outside of the canvas drawing area if z is small. This corresponds to zooming in really close to an object. There is a lot more to creating perspective transformations, but this is enough to get started.

Vertex Data

We have spent a lot of time setting up the transformation matrices, but there is still the matter of providing the 3D vertex data that provides the geometry of the model to be rendered. To do this we have to make another connection between data in our JavaScript program and in the vertex shader. In this case, however, the connection is to an array of vertex data in the JavaScript and an attribute in the shader.

As in most first examples, we are going to pass a 3D array to the shader that gives the position of each vertex, but it is important to know that you can pass data that is something other than position. You can even pass multiple arrays to different attributes. Each attribute is read one element at a time when the vertex shader is run. Think of a `for` loop processing two or more arrays in parallel.

Making the connection between a JavaScript object and an attribute follows a standard set of steps:

1. Get a reference to the shader attribute that can be used by JavaScript
2. Create a buffer within the GPU
3. Bind the newly created buffer so that it is used as a buffer within the GPU

4. Describe the buffer's content so that the GPU can work out what an element is and how to read it from the buffer

5. Create the JavaScript data object that will be used as elements of the buffer

6. Connect the JavaScript data with the buffer

7. Enable the attribute

8. Optionally draw the buffer

This is more complicated than processing a uniform, but we are creating and using an array of data.

In this simple case the only vertex attribute that the shader processes is its position. The shader has a variable called:

```
attribute vec3 vertexPosition;
```

and we have to deal with making the connection between this and the vertex position attribute that we are going to specify in the JavaScript. First we need to get a reference to `vertexPosition`:

```
var vertexPos = gl.getAttribLocation( program, "vertexPosition");
```

For it to behave like an array attribute we have to associate it with a buffer in the GPU. To do this we first have to create a buffer object - this is a completely general buffer without any particular structure - and bind it to the WebGL object's array buffer:

```
var vertexBuffer = gl.createBuffer();
gl.bindBuffer(gl.ARRAY_BUFFER,vertexBuffer);
```

After this we have a buffer in the GPU, but it isn't associated with any attribute in the vertex shader. To associate the structure-less, name-less buffer we have just created with the attribute in the vertex shader we need to use:

```
gl.vertexAttribPointer(vertexPos,
                       3.0,
                       gl.FLOAT,
                       false,
                       0, 0);
```

This says that the `vertexPos` attribute is a three-component entity of type `gl.FLOAT`, and they should be un-normalized. The final two parameters are rarely used. The first specifies the stride of the data, i.e. the amount of storage allocated to each element, and the second specifies the offset, i.e. where the data starts. For standard JavaScript arrays both are set to `0` to indicate tight packing and no offset.

The buffer that we have just created is an internal buffer in the sense that WebGL uses it to store and display whatever vertex data you have transferred to it. At this point we have a buffer set up and associated with an attribute and we can transfer data from the JavaScript program and then expect it to be used by the shader when the model is rendered.

Let's draw a single triangle to get started:

```
var z = 4;
var vertices = new Float32Array(
                            [-0.5,  0.5, z,
                              0.5,  0.5, z,
                              0.5, -0.5, z]);
gl.bufferData(gl.ARRAY_BUFFER, vertices, gl.STATIC_DRAW);
```

You can vary z to see the effect of the perspective transformation. The JavaScript array vertices is loaded into the buffer that is currently bound to `ARRAY_BUFFER`. You can repeat this entire procedure to define additional attributes each with their own buffer.

The `bufferData` method transfers the vertex data in the JavaScript object to the WebGL object's buffer. The `STATIC_DRAW` states that we are only going to write to this buffer very infrequently and the system can optimize for this situation. It doesn't stop us from writing to the buffer again, but it might not be as efficient. Finally at some point before you draw the data in the buffer you need to enable it:

```
gl.enableVertexAttribArray(vertexPos);
```

If you enable it, WebGL will use its data whenever you ask for a draw or re-draw of the scene. If you don't enable it then the attribute will behave like a uniform and you can set it in the usual way.

Final Setup and Drawing

Now we are almost ready to render the model, but there are still some very simple initialization steps we need to take. The first is to set the value that the color will be cleared to:

```
gl.clearColor(0.0, 0.0, 0.0, 1.0);
```

This doesn't clear the buffer, it just sets the default color that it will be cleared to. Next we set the way that "culling" is performed.

```
gl.enable(gl.DEPTH_TEST);
gl.depthFunc(gl.LEQUAL);
```

These two methods set up the system to remove pixels that are behind other pixels in the 2D rendered scene. Without them you would be able to see distant objects mixed in with closer objects. Now we can clear the buffers using the values we just set:

```
gl.clear(gl.COLOR_BUFFER_BIT | gl.DEPTH_BUFFER_BIT);
```

and finally we can ask the system to draw the triangle, or in general whatever is in the buffer:

```
gl.drawArrays(gl.TRIANGLES,  0, vertices.length / 3.0);
gl.flush();
}
```

Notice that we have to specify the number of vertices that are in the buffer as the last parameter.

The result is a fairly unimpressive green triangle. However, it is a 3D green triangle. For example, if you change the z value the triangle changes its size. If you change the z value for different vertices then the triangle changes its appearance as it becomes skewed. Don't expect any lighting effects or shadows because we haven't used a shader that creates them.

From here you need to create more sophisticated shaders, use matrix operations to set up the view and position, define more complex models with color and texture attributes and experiment with lighting and animation.

You can see a complete listing of this program at www.iopress.info.

A 3D Cube

Although our example is enough to introduce most of the aspects of using WebGL in 3D, we need something slightly more realistic to demonstrate the possibilities. The usual first example is a 3D cube. This is easy enough, but first we need to create a better and more flexible perspective transform. The usual way to think of a perspective transform is as a camera positioned within the 3D space, looking at a particular point and with an adjustable angle, which corresponds to the focal length of the camera lens and a front and back clipping plane which limits what is drawn:

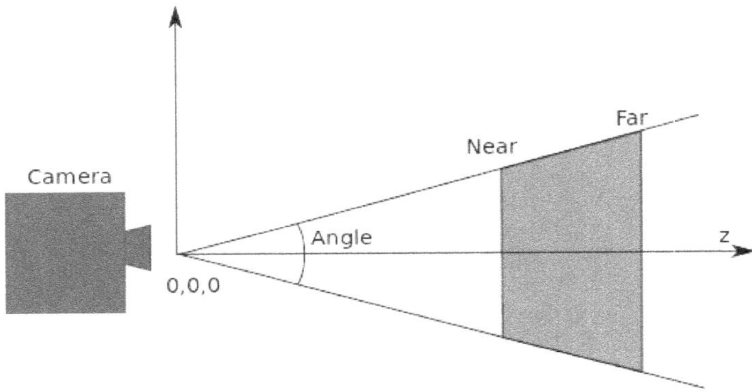

The transformation is generally arranged so that the viewpoint is at the origin and looking along the z axis into the screen. You can easily create a function to generate a perspective transformation from these parameters:

```
function perspective(angle, aspect, zMin, zMax) {
   var tan = Math.tan(angle*Math.PI/180);
   var A = -(zMax + zMin) / (zMax − zMin);
   var B = (-2 * zMax * zMin) / (zMax - zMin);
   return [
         .5 / tan,                      0, 0, 0,
            0, .5 * aspect / tan, 0, 0,
            0,                      0, A, -1,
            0,                      0, B,  0
      ];
}
```

You can look up how this is derived in almost any book on 3D graphics. The aspect is included so that you can adjust the ratio of x to y.

A reasonable projection is:

```
var pMatrix = perspective(20, 1,0.1, 100);
```

Given that the "camera" is now positioned at the origin you might think that it is required to draw things positioned away from the origin so that they can be seen. This is not a good idea and generally we follow the same principle as used in 2D graphics – draw a unit-sized object centered on the origin and use a transformation to position it.

To draw our unit cube we need a set of vertices:

```
var vertices = new Float32Array(
 [
  // Front face
  -1.0, -1.0, 1.0,
   1.0, -1.0, 1.0,
   1.0, 1.0, 1.0,
  -1.0, 1.0, 1.0,
  // Back face
  -1.0, -1.0, -1.0,
  -1.0, 1.0, -1.0,
   1.0, 1.0, -1.0,
   1.0, -1.0, -1.0,
  // Top face
  -1.0, 1.0, -1.0,
  -1.0, 1.0, 1.0,
   1.0, 1.0, 1.0,
   1.0, 1.0, -1.0,
  // Bottom face
  -1.0, -1.0, -1.0,
   1.0, -1.0, -1.0,
   1.0, -1.0, 1.0,
  -1.0, -1.0, 1.0,
  // Right face
   1.0, -1.0, -1.0,
   1.0, 1.0, -1.0,
   1.0, 1.0, 1.0,
   1.0, -1.0, 1.0,
  // Left face
  -1.0, -1.0, -1.0,
  -1.0, -1.0, 1.0,
  -1.0, 1.0, 1.0,
  -1.0, 1.0, -1.0,
]);
```

This is a lot of data, but a cube has six faces and each face has four defining points. You might be puzzled as to why we only need four points if each face is made up of two triangles. The answer is that we specify that the vertex data is in the form of a triangle strip. A triangle strip starts off with three vertices that define the first triangle. After this each additional vertex defines a triangle with the previous two vertices:

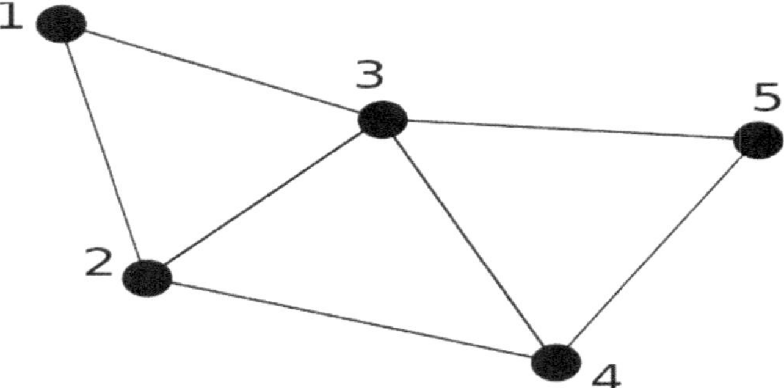

In the diagram you can see that vertices 1, 2 and 3 define the first triangle, 2, 3 and 4 the second, and 3, 4 and 5 the third. This saves having to repeat vertices. Each rectangle is defined by four vertices. For example, the front face is:

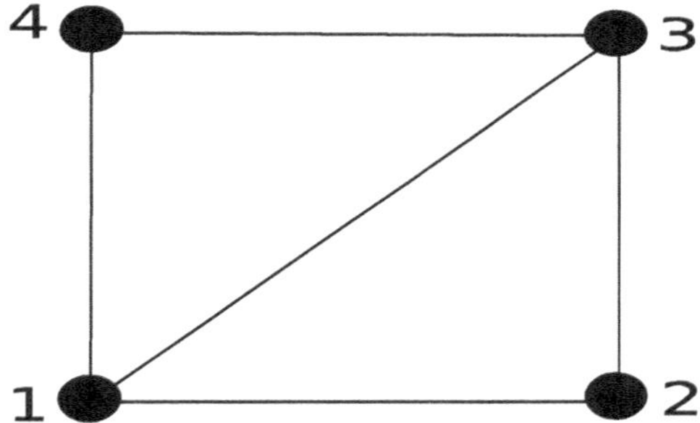

Notice that the face is defined in an anti-clockwise order. This is important because it defines the front facing side of the triangles.

Once we have the unit cube defined we need to create a transform to move it to a new location and add a rotation so that we can see more than the front face:

```
var angle = 45*Math.PI/180;
var sy = Math.sin(angle);
var cy = Math.cos(angle);

var mvMatrix = [
                cy, 0, sy, 0,
                 0, 1,  0, 0,
                -sy, 0, cy, 0,
                 0, 0, -6, 1
                ];
```

The only other change needed to the draw instruction is:
```
gl.drawArrays(gl.TRIANGLE_STRIP, 0, vertices.length / 3.0);
```

Without coloring or lighting the faces, this is as good as it gets.

It is easy to create a rotating cube by defining a run function that is called in a `requestAnimationFrame`. This updates the transformation matrix to give a new rotation angle, clears the canvas and redraws the cube:

```
var theta = 0;
var vertices;
var gl;
function run(t) {
  var angle = theta++ * Math.PI / 180;
  var sy = Math.sin(angle);
  var cy = Math.cos(angle);
  var mvMatrix = [
                   cy, 0, sy, 0,
                    0, 1,  0, 0,
                  -sy, 0, cy, 0,
                    0, 0, -6, 1
                 ];

  var shaderMVMatrix = gl.getUniformLocation(gl.
         getParameter(gl.CURRENT_PROGRAM),"modelViewMatrix");
  gl.uniformMatrix4fv(shaderMVMatrix, false,
                                   new Float32Array(mvMatrix));
  gl.clear(gl.COLOR_BUFFER_BIT | gl.DEPTH_BUFFER_BIT);
  gl.drawArrays(gl.TRIANGLE_STRIP, 0, vertices.length / 3.0);
  gl.flush();
  requestAnimationFrame(run);
}
```

To allow the function to use some of the objects they have to be converted into global variables.

Listing - Rotating Cube

The complete listing for the rotating cube, after slight cleaning up is:

```
<!DOCTYPE html>
<html>
  <head>
    <title>JavaScript Graphics</title>
    <meta charset="UTF-8">
    <meta name="viewport" content="width=device-width,
                                   initial-scale=1.0">

  </head>
  <body>
    <script>
function createCanvas(h, w) {
  var c = document.createElement("canvas");
  c.width = w;
  c.height = h;
  return c;
}
function createShaders(gl, vs, fs) {
  var vertexShader = gl.createShader(gl.VERTEX_SHADER);
  gl.shaderSource(vertexShader, vs);
  gl.compileShader(vertexShader);
  if (!gl.getShaderParameter(vertexShader, gl.COMPILE_STATUS)) {
   alert("Error in vertex shader");
   var compilationLog = gl.getShaderInfoLog(vertexShader);
   console.log('Shader compiler log: ' + compilationLog);
   gl.deleteShader(vertexShader);
   return;
  }
  var fragmentShader = gl.createShader(gl.FRAGMENT_SHADER);
  gl.shaderSource(fragmentShader, fs);
  gl.compileShader(fragmentShader);
  if (!gl.getShaderParameter(fragmentShader, gl.COMPILE_STATUS)) {
   alert("error in fragment shader");
   var compilationLog = gl.getShaderInfoLog(fragmentShader);
   console.log('Shader compiler log: ' + compilationLog);
   gl.deleteShader(fragmentShader);
   return;
  }
  return [vertexShader, fragmentShader];
 }
```

```javascript
function createProgram(gl, shaders) {
  var program = gl.createProgram();
  gl.attachShader(program, shaders[0]);
  gl.attachShader(program, shaders[1]);
  gl.linkProgram(program);
  if (!gl.getProgramParameter(program, gl.LINK_STATUS)) {
    alert("Error in shaders");
    gl.deleteProgram(program);
    gl.deleteProgram(vertexShader);
    gl.deleteProgram(fragmentShader);
    return;
  }
  return program;
}

function perspective(angle, aspect, zMin, zMax) {
  var tan = Math.tan(angle * Math.PI / 180);
  var A = -(zMax + zMin) / (zMax - zMin);
  var B = (-2 * zMax * zMin) / (zMax - zMin);
  return [.5 / tan,                0, 0, 0,
              0, .5 * aspect / tan, 0, 0,
              0,                0,  A,-1,
              0,                0,  B, 0
        ];
}

function draw3d() {
 gl = document.body.appendChild(createCanvas(400, 400)).
                                    getContext("webgl2");
 if (!gl)
  alert("no webgl2");
 gl.viewport(0, 0, gl.canvas.width, gl.canvas.height);

 var vsScript = `attribute vec3 vertexPosition;
              uniform mat4 modelViewMatrix;
              uniform mat4 perspectiveMatrix;
              void main(void) {
                gl_Position = perspectiveMatrix *
                      modelViewMatrix * vec4(vertexPosition, 1.0);
              }`;

 var fsScript = `void main(void) {
                gl_FragColor = vec4(0.0, 1.0, 0.0, 1.0);
              }`;

 var shaders = createShaders(gl, vsScript, fsScript);
 var program = createProgram(gl, shaders);
 gl.useProgram(program);
```

```javascript
var pMatrix = perspective(20, 1, 0.1, 100);
var shaderpMatrix = gl.getUniformLocation(program,
                                "perspectiveMatrix");
gl.uniformMatrix4fv(shaderpMatrix, false,
                              new Float32Array(pMatrix));
var vertexPos = gl.getAttribLocation(program, "vertexPosition");
var vertexBuffer = gl.createBuffer();
gl.bindBuffer(gl.ARRAY_BUFFER, vertexBuffer);
gl.vertexAttribPointer(vertexPos,
                       3.0,
                       gl.FLOAT,
                       false,
                       0, 0);
vertices = new Float32Array(
               [
                // Front face
                -1.0, -1.0, 1.0,
                 1.0, -1.0, 1.0,
                 1.0, 1.0, 1.0,
                -1.0, 1.0, 1.0,
                // Back face
                -1.0, -1.0, -1.0,
                -1.0, 1.0, -1.0,
                 1.0, 1.0, -1.0,
                 1.0, -1.0, -1.0,
                // Top face
                -1.0, 1.0, -1.0,
                -1.0, 1.0, 1.0,
                 1.0, 1.0, 1.0,
                 1.0, 1.0, -1.0,
                // Bottom face
                -1.0, -1.0, -1.0,
                 1.0, -1.0, -1.0,
                 1.0, -1.0, 1.0,
                -1.0, -1.0, 1.0,
                // Right face
                 1.0, -1.0, -1.0,
                 1.0, 1.0, -1.0,
                 1.0, 1.0, 1.0,
                 1.0, -1.0, 1.0,
                // Left face
                -1.0, -1.0, -1.0,
                -1.0, -1.0, 1.0,
                -1.0, 1.0, 1.0,
                -1.0, 1.0, -1.0
               ]);
```

```javascript
  gl.bufferData(gl.ARRAY_BUFFER, vertices, gl.STATIC_DRAW);
  gl.enableVertexAttribArray(vertexPos);
  gl.clearColor(0.8, 0.8, 0.8, 1.0);
  gl.enable(gl.DEPTH_TEST);
  gl.depthFunc(gl.LEQUAL);
  gl.clear(gl.COLOR_BUFFER_BIT | gl.DEPTH_BUFFER_BIT);
  requestAnimationFrame(run);
}

var theta = 0;
var vertices;
var gl;
function run(t) {
  var angle = theta++ * Math.PI / 180;
  var sy = Math.sin(angle);
  var cy = Math.cos(angle);
  var mvMatrix = [
                   cy, 0, sy, 0,
                    0, 1, 0, 0,
                  -sy, 0, cy, 0,
                    0, 0, -6, 1
                  ];

  var shaderMVMatrix = gl.getUniformLocation(
          gl.getParameter(gl.CURRENT_PROGRAM),"modelViewMatrix");
  gl.uniformMatrix4fv(shaderMVMatrix, false,
                                  new Float32Array(mvMatrix));
  gl.clear(gl.COLOR_BUFFER_BIT |   gl.DEPTH_BUFFER_BIT);
  gl.drawArrays(gl.TRIANGLE_STRIP, 0, vertices.length / 3.0);
  gl.flush();
  requestAnimationFrame(run);
}
draw3d();
  </script>
 </body>
</html>
```

Summary

- Canvas supports WebGL 1 and 2 but only version 1 is well supported.

- WebGL is a 2D rendering system implemented in hardware. It has enough flexibility to implement 3D graphics, but nothing is provided as standard.

- You have to supply two shaders to control how graphics are rendered. The vertex shader modifies the co-ordinates of the points you supply, which are used to define triangles. The fragment shader is called for each of the interior pixels to set its color.

- A vertex and fragment shader go together to form a program. You can have more than one program, but only one is active at any given time.

- You load shaders from JavaScript strings into the GPU.

- Vertices are specified to the vertex shader in attribute arrays. The shader is called once for each element in the buffer associated with the attribute.

- Uniforms are shader variables that can be set from JavaScript. They remain constant during the processing of the elements in the vertex buffer.

- Before you can draw anything you have to set up connections between the JavaScript data and the uniforms and attributes in the shaders.

- Uniforms are easy to use, but attributes take more setting up and definition.

- For 3D graphics there is a standard set of matrices used to convert a 3D point to 2D. The most common perform rotation, scaling and translation, followed by a perspective transformation.

- You can think of a perspective transformation as being like a camera with a given focal length lens positioned at the origin and looking down the z axis.

- You can draw 3D objects at unit size and centered on the origin and then move them to the desired location in front of the "camera" using the transformation matrix.

Chapter 15

2D WebGL

The preceding example is typical of "getting started with WebGL" tutorials. It shows you how to do what most people using WebGL want to do, i.e. 3D graphics. As already explained, WebGL is in fact a very general 2D graphics system that can be used to display in 3D if the appropriate transformations are made to render 3D points in 2D. However, in many cases all you want is a 2D graphics environment and in this case we can design a simple 2D vertex shader, develop functions that draw standard 2D shapes, and even use bitmaps.

Notice that in this chapter we are using many of the functions developed in the previous chapter unmodified.

A 2D Vertex Shader

A simple 2D vertex shader takes a 2D vector and assigns it a full 4D homogeneous co-ordinate:

```
var vsScript = `attribute vec2 vertexPosition;
                void main(void) {
                  gl_Position = vec4(vertexPosition,0.0,1.0);
                }`;
```

With this we can supply 2D co-ordinates and have them converted to fundamental WebGL co-ordinates with z set to 0. Of course we also have to change the way the geometry is defined as now it is 2D as far as the JavaScript is concerned. For example, the co-ordinates of a triangle are now:

```
var vertices = new Float32Array(
                    [-0.5, 0.5,
                      0.5, 0.5,
                      0.5,-0.5]);
```

and no z co-ordinate is required.

We also have to change the way the vertex buffer is defined because now an element consists of just two floats:

```
var vertexPos = gl.getAttribLocation(program, "vertexPosition");
var vertexBuffer = gl.createBuffer();
gl.bindBuffer(gl.ARRAY_BUFFER, vertexBuffer);
gl.enableVertexAttribArray(vertexPos);
gl.vertexAttribPointer(vertexPos,
                       2.0,
                       gl.FLOAT,
                       false,
                       0, 0);
```

The only differences are that now the vertex array is 2D and the definition of `vertexPosition` has to state that just two values are to be used per vertex. To make this more general, we can supply an input parameter to the fragment shader to set the color of the triangle we are about to draw:

```
var fsScript = `precision mediump float;
                uniform vec4 f_color;
                void main(void) {
                   gl_FragColor= f_color;
                }`;
```

The only new statement is the use of `precision` to let the GPU know how accurate you want the calculation to be. You don't always need this as the precision can often be deduced, but in this case you do. Of course, we still need to make the connection between the JavaScript program and the shader:

```
var color = gl.getUniformLocation(program, "f_color");
gl.uniform4f(color, 1.0, 0.0,0.0, 1);
```

sets the color to red.

Now we have all of the components we need to write some functions that draw simple shapes. For example, a function that draws a triangle:

```
function triangle(gl, color, p1, p2, p3) {
 var vertices = new Float32Array([p1[0], p1[1],
                                  p2[0], p2[1],
                                  p3[0], p3[1]]);
 var fcolor =gl.getUniformLocation(
                 gl.getParameter(gl.CURRENT_PROGRAM),"f_color");
 gl.uniform4f(fcolor, color[0], color[1], color[2], color[3]);
 gl.bufferData(gl.ARRAY_BUFFER, vertices, gl.STATIC_DRAW);
 gl.drawArrays(gl.TRIANGLES, 0, 3);
}
```

Notice the way that the values are stored in the shader variables and the use of `gl.getParameter(gl.CURRENT_PROGRAM)` to avoid having to pass in a reference to program.

Once you have this function you can use it to draw multiple triangles:

```
var color = [0, 1, 0, 1];
triangle(gl, color, [-0.5, 0.5], [.5, .5], [0.5, -0.5]);
color = [1, 1, 0, 1];
triangle(gl, color, [-0.6, 0.2], [-0.6, -.5], [0.8, 0.8]);
gl.flush();
```

Changing the values in the vertex array is not the usual way that multiple shapes would be drawn, but it is simple. The alternative is to create a single vertex array for the shape centered on (0,0) and then use a transformation to draw the shape at a new location and scale. To use this method we need to first implement a transformation.

Transformations

So far we have worked in fundamental co-ordinates, but it is quite easy to add a transformation so that we can work in any co-ordinate system or implement an active transformation on what we draw.

As we are working in 2D we want to define and work with a 3D matrix to perform the transformation on a 3D homogeneous vector. That is, the transformation is of the form:

$$x' = ax + cy + e$$
$$y' = bx + dy + f$$

and the matrix transform is:

$$T = \begin{pmatrix} a & c & e \\ b & d & f \\ 0 & 0 & 1 \end{pmatrix} \begin{pmatrix} x \\ y \\ 1 \end{pmatrix}$$

This gives a 3D homogeneous vector (x',y',1), just as in Chapter 5. The only problem is that we need to convert this to a 4D vector (x',y',0,1), i.e. a homogeneous vector with z equal to 0. This can be done relatively easily by picking out the x,y co-ordinates from the 3D homogeneous co-ordinates:

```
var vsScript=`attribute vec2 vertexPosition;
                uniform mat3 transform;
                void main(void) {
                 vec2 temp= vec2(transform*vec3(vertexPosition,1.0));
                 gl_Position = vec4(temp,0.0,1.0);
                }`;
```

Notice that we are using a local variable `temp` to hold the 2D vector (x',y') before conversion to the 4D vector. This is done for clarity, there is nothing stopping us from writing everything on a single line.

Of course, we need to define the transformation matrix and connect it to the shader variable:

```
var T = [1, 0, 0,
         0, 1, 0,
         0, 0, 1
        ];

var TMatrix = gl.getUniformLocation(program, "transform");
gl.uniformMatrix3fv(TMatrix, false, new Float32Array(T));
```

If you run the modified program you will find that nothing has changed because we have used an identity matrix.

If you want to change the co-ordinate system to a range xmin-xmax and ymin-ymax then you can use:

```
var T = [ 2 / (xmax - xmin), 0,                   0,
          0,                 2 / (ymax - ymin), 0,
          -1,                -1,                  1
        ];
```

For example if you want to work in pixel co-ordinates use:

```
var T = [2 / canvas.width, 0,                 0,
         0,                2 / canvas.height, 0,
         -1,               -1,                1
        ];
```

Notice that you can change the transformation before drawing an object, just as you can change the color, and this allows you to draw everything at 0,0 and translate it to its new location. For example:

```
var color = [0, 1, 0, 1];
triangle(gl, color, [0, .25], [.25, -.25], [-0.25,-0.25]);
```

draws a green triangle about the center point (0,0) but if you set the transform before this to;

```
gl.uniformMatrix3fv(TMatrix, false, new Float32Array([  1,    0, 0,
                                                        0,    1, 0,
                                                      0.5,  0.5, 1
                                                      ]));
var color = [0, 1, 0, 1];
triangle(gl, color, [0, .25], [.25, -.25], [-0.25, -0.25]);
```

the triangle is moved to (0.5,0.5). What this means is that, instead of having to write a new set of vertices to the vertex buffer, we can simply use the standard set and transform.

Triangles

Now we have everything set up to make it worth creating some functions that draw standard shapes. To make things efficient, we have to first set up a buffer and store the vertex data in it. That is, we need an initialization stage:

```
triangle.init = function (gl) {
    var prog=gl.getParameter(gl.CURRENT_PROGRAM);
    triangle.vertexPos = gl.getAttribLocation(prog,"vertexPosition");
    triangle.vertexBuffer = gl.createBuffer();
    gl.bindBuffer(gl.ARRAY_BUFFER, triangle.vertexBuffer);
    var vertices = new Float32Array([0, 1, 1, -1, -1, -1]);
    gl.bufferData(gl.ARRAY_BUFFER, vertices, gl.STATIC_DRAW);
    triangle.fcolor = gl.getUniformLocation(prog,"f_color");
    triangle.T = gl.getUniformLocation(prog, "transform");
};
```

You can see what is happening. The attribute is retrieved, a buffer created and vertex data loaded into it. Finally the uniforms, f_color and the transform, are retrieved and stored as properties.

This is such a standard set of actions that we can write a utility function to make it easier:

```
function initShape(gl, shape, vert) {
  var prog=gl.getParameter(gl.CURRENT_PROGRAM);
  shape.vertexPos = gl.getAttribLocation(prog, "vertexPosition");
  shape.vertexBuffer = gl.createBuffer();
  gl.bindBuffer(gl.ARRAY_BUFFER, shape.vertexBuffer);
  gl.enableVertexAttribArray(shape.vertexPos);
  gl.bufferData(gl.ARRAY_BUFFER, vert, gl.STATIC_DRAW);
  shape.fcolor = gl.getUniformLocation(prog,  "f_color");
  shape.T = gl.getUniformLocation(prog, "transform");
}
```

With this utility function we can now write the `triangle.init` as:

```
triangle.init = function (gl) {
  var vertices = new Float32Array([0, 1, 1, -1, -1, -1]);
  initShape(gl, this, vertices);
};
```

We can use the same approach to initialize other shapes. All we have to do is compute the vertex array and then pass it to the `initShape` function.

Once we have initialized the shape we can create a function to draw it:

```
function triangle(gl, color, p, s) {
  gl.uniformMatrix3fv(triangle.T, false,
          new Float32Array([    s,     0, 0,
                                0,     s, 0,
                             p[0], p[1], 1
                          ]));
  gl.uniform4f(triangle.fcolor,
               color[0], color[1], color[2], color[3]);
  gl.bindBuffer(gl.ARRAY_BUFFER, triangle.vertexBuffer);
  gl.vertexAttribPointer(triangle.vertexPos,
                         2.0,
                         gl.FLOAT,
                         false,
                         0, 0);
  gl.enableVertexAttribArray(triangle.vertexPos);
  gl.drawArrays(gl.TRIANGLES, 0, 3);
 }
```

You can see the basic idea, it is very simple. First we create the transformation matrix for a scale factor of s and a translation to p and use these to set the uniforms, the locations of which are already stored. Finally we make the buffer that we have already set up the current buffer and draw it.

Using this you can draw as many triangles as you like without having to reload the vertex data:

```
triangle.init(gl);
triangle(gl, [0, 1, 0, 1], [.25, .25], .5);
triangle(gl, [1, 0, 0, 1], [-0.6, 0.2], .25);
triangle(gl, [0, 0, 1, 1], [0.6, -0.6], .25);
```

Rectangles

You can create similar functions for other shapes.

For example, for a rectangle:

```
function rect(gl, color, p, h, w) {
  gl.uniformMatrix3fv(rect.T, false, new Float32Array(
                  [  w,    0, 0,
                     0,    h, 0,
                   p[0], p[1], 1
              ]));
  gl.uniform4f(rect.fcolor, color[0], color[1], color[2], color[3]);
  gl.bindBuffer(gl.ARRAY_BUFFER, rect.vertexBuffer);
  gl.vertexAttribPointer(rect.vertexPos,
                    2.0,
                    gl.FLOAT,
                    false,
                    0, 0);
 gl.drawArrays(gl.TRIANGLE_STRIP, 0, 4);
}
```

```
rect.init = function (gl) {
  var vertices = new Float32Array(
                                 [-1,   1,
                                   1,   1,
                                  -1,  -1,
                                   1,  -1
                                 ]);
  initShape(gl, this, vertices);
};
```

Notice that we are now using a `TRIANGLE_STRIP`, see the previous chapter, and
hence only need four points in the vertex array. Also notice that the rectangle
is specified by top left corner and its height and width and the transformation
to produce this is automatically created.

Adding:

```
rect.init(gl);
rect(gl, [1, 1, 0, 1], [-.2, -.3], 0.25, 0.5);
rect(gl, [0, 1, 1, 1], [.1, .5], 0.15, 0.5);
rect(gl, [1, 0, 1, 1], [.2, -.6], 0.25, 0.5);
```

to the previous program produces:

Circles - Triangle Fan

Finally let's draw a circle. There are no curves in WebGL, only straight lines and triangles. We can use the approach outlined in Chapter 3 based on approximations by polygons – only now we will use triangles:

```
function circle(gl, color, p, r) {
  gl.uniformMatrix3fv(circle.T, false,
                      new Float32Array([
                                          r,    0, 0,
                                          0,    r, 0,
                                        p[0], p[1], 1
                                      ]));
  gl.uniform4f(circle.fcolor,color[0],color[1],color[2],color[3]);
  gl.bindBuffer(gl.ARRAY_BUFFER, circle.vertexBuffer);
  gl.enableVertexAttribArray(circle.vertexPos);
  gl.vertexAttribPointer(circle.vertexPos,
                         2.0,
                         gl.FLOAT,
                         false,
                         0, 0);
  gl.drawArrays(gl.TRIANGLE_FAN, 0, circle.noVert);
}

circle.init = function (gl) {
  var temp = [];
  temp[0] = 0;temp[1] = 0;
  var i = 2;
  var inc = 0.1;
  for (t = 0; t < 2 * Math.PI; t = t + inc) {
    temp[i++] = Math.sin(t);
    temp[i++] = Math.cos(t);
  }
  temp[i++] = temp[2];
  temp[i] = temp[3];
  var vertices = new Float32Array(temp);
  circle.noVert = vertices.length / 2;
  initShape(gl, this, vertices);
};
```

An increment of 0.1 provides a smooth enough circle for most applications.

The only new feature is the use of TRIANGLE_FAN which takes the first vertex as the third point of all of the triangles drawn:

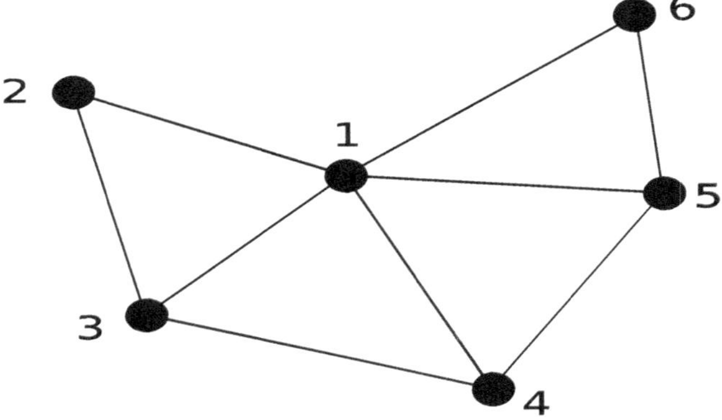

To add a red disk to the drawing:

```
circle.init(gl);
circle(gl, [1, 0, 0, 1], [0.8, 0.5], .2);
```

You can carry on like this creating as many shapes as you need. In practice it is more difficult to get beyond the basic shapes manually and you generally need to use a program that will give you the co-ordinates of the points.

It is worth pointing out that as well as these filled drawing modes there are also:

- ◆ `gl.POINTS`   Draws a series of points
- ◆ `gl.LINES`   To draw a series of unconnected line segments
- ◆ `gl.LINE_STRIP`   To draw a series of connected line segments
- ◆ `gl.LINE_LOOP`   To draw a series of closed connected line segments.

Listing - Shapes Program

```
<!DOCTYPE html>
<html>
 <head>
   <title>TODO supply a title</title>
   <meta charset="UTF-8">
   <meta name="viewport" content="width=device-width,
                                   initial-scale=1.0">
</head>
<body>
 <script>
  function createCanvas(h, w) {
    var c = document.createElement("canvas");
    c.width = w;
    c.height = h;
    return c;
  }
  function createShaders(gl, vs, fs) {
    var vertexShader = gl.createShader(gl.VERTEX_SHADER);
    gl.shaderSource(vertexShader, vs);
    gl.compileShader(vertexShader);
    if (!gl.getShaderParameter(vertexShader, gl.COMPILE_STATUS)) {
      alert("Error in vertex shader");
      var conpilationLog = gl.getShaderInfoLog(vertexShader);
      console.log('Shader compiler log: ' + compilationLog);
      gl.deleteShader(vertexShader);
      return;
    }
    var fragmentShader = gl.createShader(gl.FRAGMENT_SHADER);
    gl.shaderSource(fragmentShader, fs);
    gl.compileShader(fragmentShader);
    if (!gl.getShaderParameter(fragmentShader, gl.COMPILE_STATUS)) {
      alert("error in fragment shader");
      var compilationLog = gl.getShaderInfoLog(fragmentShader);
      console.log('Shader compiler log: ' + compilationLog);
      gl.deleteShader(fragmentShader);
      return;
    }
    return [vertexShader, fragmentShader];
  }
```

```javascript
function createProgram(gl, shaders) {
  var program = gl.createProgram();
  gl.attachShader(program, shaders[0]);
  gl.attachShader(program, shaders[1]);
  gl.linkProgram(program);
  if (!gl.getProgramParameter(program, gl.LINK_STATUS)) {
    alert("Error in shaders");
    gl.deleteProgram(program);
    gl.deleteProgram(vertexShader);
    gl.deleteProgram(fragmentShader);
    return;
  }
 return program;
}

function initShape(gl, shape, vert) {
 var prog = gl.getParameter(gl.CURRENT_PROGRAM);
 shape.vertexPos = gl.getAttribLocation(prog, "vertexPosition");
 shape.vertexBuffer = gl.createBuffer();
 gl.bindBuffer(gl.ARRAY_BUFFER, shape.vertexBuffer);
 gl.enableVertexAttribArray(shape.vertexPos);
 gl.bufferData(gl.ARRAY_BUFFER, vert, gl.STATIC_DRAW);
 shape.fcolor = gl.getUniformLocation(prog, "f_color");
 shape.T = gl.getUniformLocation(prog, "transform");
}


function triangle(gl, color, p, s) {
 gl.uniformMatrix3fv(triangle.T, false,
                     new Float32Array([   s,     0, 0,
                                          0,     s, 0,
                                       p[0], p[1], 1
                                      ]));
 gl.uniform4f(triangle.fcolor,
                      color[0],color[1],color[2], color[3]);
 gl.bindBuffer(gl.ARRAY_BUFFER, triangle.vertexBuffer);
 gl.vertexAttribPointer(triangle.vertexPos,
                    2.0,
                    gl.FLOAT,
                    false,
                    0, 0);
 gl.enableVertexAttribArray(triangle.vertexPos);
 gl.drawArrays(gl.TRIANGLES, 0, 3);
}
triangle.init = function (gl) {
  var vertices = new Float32Array([0, 1, 1, -1, -1, -1]);
  initShape(gl, this, vertices);
};
```

```javascript
function rect(gl, color, p, h, w) {
  gl.uniformMatrix3fv(rect.T, false,
                  new Float32Array([   w,    0, 0,
                                       0,    h, 0,
                                    p[0], p[1], 1
                                  ]));
  gl.uniform4f(rect.fcolor,
                    color[0], color[1], color[2], color[3]);
  gl.bindBuffer(gl.ARRAY_BUFFER, rect.vertexBuffer);
  gl.vertexAttribPointer(rect.vertexPos,
                         2.0,
                         gl.FLOAT,
                         false,
                         0, 0);
  gl.drawArrays(gl.TRIANGLE_STRIP, 0, 4);
}
rect.init = function (gl) {
  var vertices = new Float32Array([-1, 1, 1, 1, -1, -1, 1, -1]);
  initShape(gl, this, vertices);
};

function circle(gl, color, p, r) {
  gl.uniformMatrix3fv(circle.T, false,
                  new Float32Array([   r,    0, 0,
                                       0,    r, 0,
                                    p[0], p[1], 1
                                  ]));
  gl.uniform4f(circle.fcolor,
                    color[0], color[1], color[2], color[3]);
  gl.bindBuffer(gl.ARRAY_BUFFER, circle.vertexBuffer);
  gl.enableVertexAttribArray(circle.vertexPos);
  gl.vertexAttribPointer(circle.vertexPos,
                         2.0,
                         gl.FLOAT,
                         false,
                         0, 0);
  gl.drawArrays(gl.TRIANGLE_FAN, 0, circle.noVert);
}
```

```javascript
circle.init = function (gl) {
  var temp = [];
  temp[0] = 0;
  temp[1] = 0;
  var i = 2;
  var inc = 0.1;
  for (t = 0; t < 2 * Math.PI; t = t + inc) {
    temp[i++] = Math.sin(t);
    temp[i++] = Math.cos(t);
  }
  temp[i++] = temp[2];
  temp[i] = temp[3];
  var vertices = new Float32Array(temp);
  circle.noVert = vertices.length / 2;
  initShape(gl, this, vertices);
};

function draw2d() {
  var gl = document.body.appendChild(createCanvas(400, 400)).
                                       getContext("webgl2");
  if (!gl)
    alert("no webgl2");
  gl.viewport(0, 0, gl.canvas.width, gl.canvas.height);
  var vsScript =
            `attribute vec2 vertexPosition;
             uniform mat3 transform;
             void main(void) {
                 vec2 temp= vec2(transform*vec3(vertexPosition,1.0));
                 gl_Position = vec4(temp,0.0,1.0);
             }`;

  var fsScript = `precision mediump float;
                  uniform vec4 f_color;
                  void main(void) {
                   gl_FragColor= f_color;
                  }`;

  var shaders = createShaders(gl, vsScript, fsScript);
  var program = createProgram(gl, shaders);
  gl.useProgram(program);

  gl.clearColor(0.8, 0.8, 0.8, 1.0);
  gl.clearDepth(1.0);
  gl.clear(gl.COLOR_BUFFER_BIT | gl.DEPTH_BUFFER_BIT);

  triangle.init(gl);
  triangle(gl, [0, 1, 0, 1], [.25, .25], .5);
  triangle(gl, [1, 0, 0, 1], [-0.6, 0.2], .25);
  triangle(gl, [0, 0, 1, 1], [0.6, -0.6], .25);
```

```
    rect.init(gl);
    rect(gl, [1, 1, 0, 1], [-.2, -.3], 0.25, 0.5);
    rect(gl, [0, 1, 1, 1], [.1, .5], 0.15, 0.5);
    rect(gl, [1, 0, 1, 1], [.2, -.6], 0.25, 0.5);

    circle.init(gl);
    circle(gl, [1, 0, 0, 1], [0.8, 0.5], .2);
    gl.flush();
}
draw2d();
    </script>
  </body>
</html>
```

Multiple Objects

One of the problems of getting to grips with WebGL is that while you might
make progress in seeing how to draw a single object, drawing and managing
multiple objects is harder.

There are two general approaches.

The first is the most obvious. Simply create all the buffers you require and
then upload the new data every time you need to, and draw the buffers. The
only problem with this is the need to upload the vertex and other data each
time you need a new object. This becomes a problem as the amount of vertex
data increases.

The alternative is to set up multiple buffers one or more per object that you
want do draw. This is the approach we have been using in our triangle,
rectangle and circle drawing programs and it corresponds to:

1. Initialize everything including shaders, programs, uniforms and
    attributes, and the buffers you want to use.

2. Compute and load the data into the buffers.

Then the rendering loop becomes:

1. Clear the canvas

2. For each object you want to draw set the program that will render it

3. Set up attributes (don't reload the data)

4. Set up uniforms including transforms which alter how the shape will
    be drawn

5. Finally call `drawArrays`.

Notice that you can also have multiple shaders defined in multiple programs and pick which one to use for a given object using `gl.useProgram`. This makes it possible to custom render each object. This is the basic principle of any 3D or 2D graphics engine you might use.

Notice that things are slightly more complicated because you can also use the transformations to set where your shape is rendered. This means you have one buffer for multiple instances of a shape. In other words, the single set of vertices used to define a circle can be used to draw many circles at different locations. This approach is faster than computing the vertices, uploading them and drawing them each time they are needed.

Animation

You can use the approach of upload the vertices, set transform and draw to implement fast animation. In this case we have to be careful how things are set up and we need to move a number of variables to be global so that the animate event handler can access them. There are better ways to organize things, see Chapter 8, but this simple approach makes it clear what is happening.

The `animate` function works in the same way as the ones given earlier. It uses the `requestAnimationFrame` function to update the graphics once per frame:

```
function animate(t) {
  if (typeof t !== "undefined") {
    temp = 0.8 * temp + 0.2 * (t - tp);
    tp = t;
  }
  count++;
  if (count === 120) {
    fps.value = (1000 / temp).toFixed(2);
    temp = 0;
    count = 0;
  }
  gl.clear(gl.COLOR_BUFFER_BIT | gl.DEPTH_BUFFER_BIT);
  for (var i = 0; i < noballs; i++) {
    pos[i][0] += vel[i][0];
    pos[i][1] += vel[i][1];
    if (pos[i][0] + r > 1) {
      vel[i][0] = -vel[i][0];
      pos[i][0] = 1 - r;
    }
    if (pos[i][1] + r > 1) {
      vel[i][1] = -vel[i][1];
      pos[i][1] = 1 - r;
    }
```

```
    if (pos[i][0] - r < -1) {
     vel[i][0] = -vel[i][0];
     pos[i][0] = r - 1;
    }
    if (pos[i][1] - r < -1) {
     vel[i][1] = -vel[i][1];
     pos[i][1] = r - 1;
    }
    circle(gl, [1, 0, 0, 1], pos[i], r);
  }
  requestAnimationFrame(animate);
}
```

You can see we have the usual position and velocity update followed by the draw of the next circle.

We also need some global variables:

```
var r = 0.05;
var noballs = 50;
var pos = [];
var vel = [];
var gl;
var tp = 0;
var temp = 0;
var count = 0;

for (var i = 0; i < noballs; i++) {
  pos[i] = [Math.random() * (2 - r) - 1,
                            Math.random() * (2 - r) - 1];
  vel[i] = [Math.random() * 0.01 + 0.005,
                            Math.random() * 0.01 + 0.005];
}
```

If you try this out you will find that it works but you might find that the WebGL approach is actually slower than the direct Canvas 2D approach. It also shows glitches as the browser is loaded. The reason is that the WebGL updates are still dependent on JavaScript running on the UI thread. You would at least have to move the update code to a worker thread to make it smooth. What is slowing down the update is the need to keep sending data to the GPU.

You can see a complete listing of this program at www.iopress.info.

Bitmaps in WebGL

Although WebGL works in terms of vertices and triangles it is possible to load and work with bitmaps. This ability is used in 3D to apply texture to 3D solids by mapping bitmaps to each of the faces. In our case we are going to make use of texture bitmaps as bitmaps, but you should be able to see how to apply the same ideas to 3D texture mapping.

There are some key new ideas and one of them is a varying. This is a variable that is used by the fragment shader to determine the property of a pixel that isn't positioned at one of the vertices of the triangle. The idea is simply that a varying takes a value that is a weighted average of the values at the vertices that surround the pixel. The weights are simply the distances to each of the vertices. So a varying that is halfway between two vertices will have the average of the value at each vertex. More generally the pixel shown in the diagram below will have a value that is the average of the values at A, B and C weighted by the distance from each of the vertices.

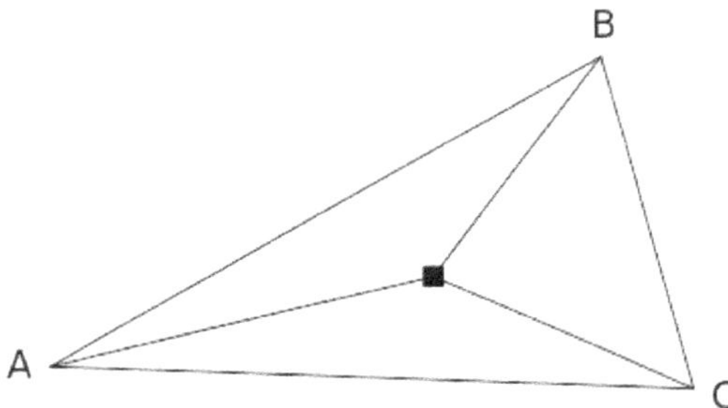

The most common example of a varying is assigning a color to each of the three points and then allowing the fragment shader to color the interior of the fragment in a gradient fill. A more usual practice use is to obtain a co-ordinate for the pixel based on the co-ordinates assigned to the vertices.

For example, if we have a right-angled triangle and assign the co-ordinates as shown, then the pixel equidistant from each vertex has a value (`0.5,0.5`) and pixels at intermediate positions have a proportional co-ordinate. This is the basic idea of a texture co-ordinate. Notice that the co-ordinates assigned to the vertices are not their actual position.

You can assign texture co-ordinates as you please as they are only used to provide the pixels within the triangle co-ordinates. To keep the distinction between co-ordinates that fix the position of the vertices and assigned texture co-ordinates we usually use x,y for position and u,v for texture co-ordinates.

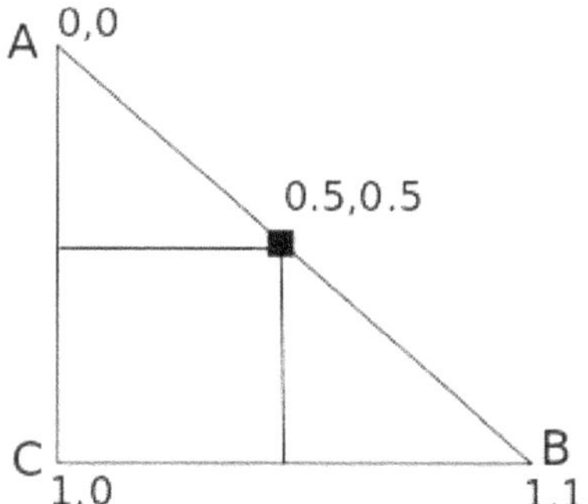

What has all this got to do with bitmaps? The answer is that we are going to load a bitmap, usually referred to as a texture map, into the GPU. A GPU bitmap has a standard co-ordinate system (0,0) to (1,1)

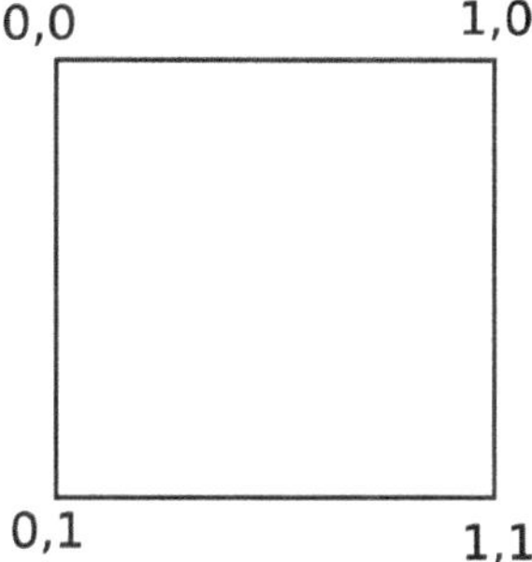

By applying texture co-ordinates to the vertices of a fragment, we can sample pixels within the texture bitmap to set the color of the fragment's pixel. To do this we need new shaders. The vertex shader becomes:

```
var vsScript =
        `attribute vec2 a_texCoord;
        varying vec2 v_texCoord;
        attribute vec2 vertexPosition;
        uniform mat3 transform;
        void main(void) {
         vec2 temp= vec2(transform*vec3(vertexPosition,1.0));
         gl_Position = vec4(temp,0.0,1.0);
         v_texCoord = a_texCoord;
        }`;
```

The new features are the two additional `texCoord` variables, one an attribute and one a varying. At the end of the shader, the attribute is passed to the varying which is automatically passed to the fragment shader. Vertex shaders can read and write varyings and they are automatically passed to the fragment shader where they are read only:

```
var fsScript = `precision mediump float;
                uniform vec4 f_color;
                uniform sampler2D u_image;
                varying vec2 v_texCoord;
                void main(void) {
                 gl_FragColor = texture2D(u_image, v_texCoord);
                }`;
```

You can see that in the fragment shader we now have an image variable and the `textCoord` variable which is passed in from the vertex shader. The varying changes its value according to the position of the pixel being processed and the final line samples the color of the pixel in the bitmap at the specified texture co-ordinate.

To make this work we now need to load the bitmap into the GPU and set the texture co-ordinates on a suitable set of vertices. Loading the image into the GPU is a standard operation:

```
function loadBitmap(gl,img) {
  var texture = gl.createTexture();
  gl.bindTexture(gl.TEXTURE_2D, texture);
  gl.texParameteri(gl.TEXTURE_2D, gl.TEXTURE_WRAP_S,
                                       gl.CLAMP_TO_EDGE);
  gl.texParameteri(gl.TEXTURE_2D, gl.TEXTURE_WRAP_T,
                                       gl.CLAMP_TO_EDGE);
  gl.texParameteri(gl.TEXTURE_2D, gl.TEXTURE_MIN_FILTER, gl.LINEAR);

  gl.texImage2D(gl.TEXTURE_2D, 0, gl.RGBA, gl.RGBA,
                                   gl.UNSIGNED_BYTE, img);
}
```

The first two instructions create the texture. The next three set how it will be handled if it is sampled at different resolutions and outside of its borders. The final instruction associates the image object holding the bitmap with the texture. You can see that you have to specify its color format.

Now we have the bitmap we need to create the texture co-ordinates and the vertex co-ordinates. For the shape that the bitmap will be mapped onto we will use a rectangle composed of two triangles that fill the entire canvas:

```
var vertexPos = gl.getAttribLocation(program, "vertexPosition");
var vertexBuffer = gl.createBuffer();
gl.bindBuffer(gl.ARRAY_BUFFER, vertexBuffer);
            gl.bufferData(gl.ARRAY_BUFFER,  new Float32Array([
                                                -1,  1,
                                                -1, -1,
                                                 1,  1,
                                                 1,  1,
                                                -1, -1,
                                                 1, -1
                                             ]),
                                             gl.STATIC_DRAW);
gl.vertexAttribPointer(vertexPos,2.0,gl.FLOAT,false,0, 0);
```

You should recognize the steps to set up the vertex buffer. Next we set up the texture co-ordinates for each vertex and you have to be careful to assign the correct texture co-ordinate to each of the corners to get the image to map correctly:

```
var texCoord = gl.getAttribLocation(program, "a_texCoord");
var texCoordBuffer = gl.createBuffer();
gl.bindBuffer(gl.ARRAY_BUFFER, texCoordBuffer);
gl.bufferData(gl.ARRAY_BUFFER, new Float32Array([
                                        0.0, 0.0,
                                        0.0, 1.0,
                                        1.0, 0.0,
                                        1.0, 0.0,
                                        0.0, 1.0,
                                        1.0, 1.0
                                     ]),
                                     gl.STATIC_DRAW);
gl.vertexAttribPointer(texCoord, 2, gl.FLOAT, false, 0, 0);
```

Again, all of the steps should be familiar, but they are now associating the buffer with the `texCoord` attribute.

Finally all we have to do is enable the attributes and draw the triangles:

```
gl.enableVertexAttribArray(texCoord);
gl.enableVertexAttribArray(vertexPos);
gl.drawArrays(gl.TRIANGLES, 0, 6);
```

You should now see the image displayed in the canvas. You can make sure that you understand the texture co-ordinates by changing them and seeing the effect.

As the transformation matrix is still in the program, you can now scale and position the bitmap just as you would any collection of vertices. The only difference is that now the fragments are being shaded using the bitmap as a source.

You can see a complete listing of this program at www.iopress.info.

A GPU Convolution

Now that we can display an image in WebGL, the next question is can we process it? The answer is very easy. All we have to do is translate pixel co-ordinates to texture co-ordinates in the range (0,0) to (1,1). To do this we need to pass the shader the size of a pixel in texture co-ordinates:

```
var pixelStep = gl.getUniformLocation(program, "pixelStep");
gl.uniform2f(pixelStep,1.0/img.width,1.0/img.height);
```

The shader has to be modified to use this uniform and to implement the [1,1,1,0,0,0,-1,-1,-1] horizontal edge-finding mask implemented in Chapter 13:

```
var fsScript = `precision mediump float;
                uniform vec2 pixelStep;
                uniform sampler2D u_image;
                varying vec2 v_texCoord;

                void main(void) {
                 vec4 color= texture2D(u_image,
                       v_texCoord+vec2(-pixelStep.x,-pixelStep.y));
                 color+=texture2D(u_image,
                       v_texCoord+vec2(0,-pixelStep.y));
                 color+= texture2D(u_image,
                       v_texCoord+vec2(+pixelStep.x,-pixelStep.y));

                 color-= texture2D(u_image,
                       v_texCoord+vec2(-pixelStep.x,pixelStep.y));
                 color-= texture2D(u_image,
                       v_texCoord+vec2(0,pixelStep.y));
                 color-= texture2D(u_image,
                       v_texCoord+vec2(+pixelStep.x,pixelStep.y));

                 color=abs(color);

                 gl_FragColor = vec4(color.rgb,1);
                }`;
```

You can see that the convolution is first computed into the variable color and then it is stored in gl_FragColor after setting the alpha channel, A, to 1. Notice the use of "swizzlers". You can access array elements using syntax like v.x for the x component i.e. v[0] and v.xy which is a 2D vector made up of the x and y components.

If you try this out the result is:

You can use the same technique to implement a complete custom convolution program. Simply pass in a uniform for the mask and write shader code to work out the convolution of the mask and the bitmap.

Listing – Bitmap Convolution

```html
<!DOCTYPE html>
<html>
  <head>
    <title>TODO supply a title</title>
    <meta charset="UTF-8">
    <meta name="viewport" content="width=device-width,
                                    initial-scale=1.0">

  </head>
  <body>
    <script>
      function createCanvas(h, w) {
        var c = document.createElement("canvas");
        c.width = w;
        c.height = h;
        return c;
      }

      function createShaders(gl, vs, fs) {
       var vertexShader = gl.createShader(gl.VERTEX_SHADER);
       gl.shaderSource(vertexShader, vs);
       gl.compileShader(vertexShader);
       if (!gl.getShaderParameter(vertexShader, gl.COMPILE_STATUS)){
        alert("Error in vertex shader");


        var compilationLog = gl.getShaderInfoLog(vertexShader);
        console.log('Shader compiler log: ' + compilationLog);
        gl.deleteShader(vertexShader);
        return;
      }

      var fragmentShader = gl.createShader(gl.FRAGMENT_SHADER);
      gl.shaderSource(fragmentShader, fs);
      gl.compileShader(fragmentShader);
      if (!gl.getShaderParameter(fragmentShader, gl.COMPILE_STATUS){
        alert("error in fragment shader");
        var compilationLog = gl.getShaderInfoLog(fragmentShader);
        console.log('Shader compiler log: ' + compilationLog);
        gl.deleteShader(fragmentShader);
        return;
      }
     return [vertexShader, fragmentShader];
     }
```

```javascript
function createProgram(gl, shaders) {
  var program = gl.createProgram();
  gl.attachShader(program, shaders[0]);
  gl.attachShader(program, shaders[1]);
  gl.linkProgram(program);
  if (!gl.getProgramParameter(program, gl.LINK_STATUS)) {
    alert("Error in shaders");
    gl.deleteProgram(program);
    gl.deleteProgram(vertexShader);
    gl.deleteProgram(fragmentShader);
    return;
          }
  return program;
}

function imgLoaded(img) {
  return new Promise(
    function (resolve, reject) {
      img.addEventListener("load", function () {
                              resolve(img);
                            });
    });
}
function loadBitmap(gl, img) {
  var texture = gl.createTexture();
  gl.bindTexture(gl.TEXTURE_2D, texture);
  gl.texParameteri(gl.TEXTURE_2D, gl.TEXTURE_WRAP_S,
                                  gl.CLAMP_TO_EDGE);


  gl.texParameteri(gl.TEXTURE_2D, gl.TEXTURE_WRAP_T,
                                  gl.CLAMP_TO_EDGE);
  gl.texParameteri(gl.TEXTURE_2D, gl.TEXTURE_MIN_FILTER,
                                      gl.LINEAR);
  gl.texImage2D(gl.TEXTURE_2D, 0, gl.RGBA, gl.RGBA,
                                  gl.UNSIGNED_BYTE, img);
}
```

```javascript
async function draw2d() {
  gl = document.body.appendChild(createCanvas(600, 600)).
                                  getContext("webgl2");
  if (!gl)
   alert("no webgl2");
   gl.viewport(0, 0, gl.canvas.width, gl.canvas.height);

   var vsScript =
         `attribute vec2 a_texCoord;
          varying vec2 v_texCoord;
          attribute vec2 vertexPosition;
          uniform mat3 transform;
          void main(void) {
           vec2 temp= vec2(transform*vec3(vertexPosition,1.0));
           gl_Position = vec4(temp,0.0,1.0);
           v_texCoord = a_texCoord;
         }`;

   var fsScript = `
       precision mediump float;
       uniform vec2 pixelStep;
       uniform sampler2D u_image;
       varying vec2 v_texCoord;
       void main(void) {
             vec4 color= texture2D(u_image,
                   v_texCoord+vec2(-pixelStep.x,-pixelStep.y));
             color+=texture2D(u_image,
                              v_texCoord+vec2(0,-pixelStep.y));
             color+= texture2D(u_image,
                   v_texCoord+vec2(+pixelStep.x,-pixelStep.y));

             color-= texture2D(u_image,
                   v_texCoord+vec2(-pixelStep.x,pixelStep.y));
             color-= texture2D(u_image,
                              v_texCoord+vec2(0,pixelStep.y));
             color-= texture2D(u_image,
                   v_texCoord+vec2(+pixelStep.x,pixelStep.y));
             color=abs(color);

             gl_FragColor = vec4(color.rgb,1);
       }`;


  var shaders = createShaders(gl, vsScript, fsScript);
  var program = createProgram(gl, shaders);
  gl.useProgram(program);
```

```javascript
gl.clearColor(0.8, 0.8, 0.8, 1.0);
gl.clearDepth(1.0);
gl.clear(gl.COLOR_BUFFER_BIT | gl.DEPTH_BUFFER_BIT);

var url = new URL("jeep.jpg", "http://server/");
var img = new Image();
img.src = url;
await imgLoaded(img);
loadBitmap(gl, img);

var pixelStep = gl.getUniformLocation(program, "pixelStep");
gl.uniform2f(pixelStep, 1.0 / img.width, 1.0 / img.height);

var T = gl.getUniformLocation(program, "transform");
gl.uniformMatrix3fv(T, false, new Float32Array([1, 0, 0,
                                                0, 1, 0,
                                                0, 0, 1
                                               ]));

var vertexPos = gl.getAttribLocation(program, "vertexPosition");
var vertexBuffer = gl.createBuffer();
gl.bindBuffer(gl.ARRAY_BUFFER, vertexBuffer);

gl.bufferData(gl.ARRAY_BUFFER, new Float32Array([
                                                -1,  1,
                                                -1, -1,
                                                 1,  1,
                                                 1,  1,
                                                -1, -1,
                                                 1, -1
                                               ]), gl.STATIC_DRAW);
gl.vertexAttribPointer(vertexPos,2.0,gl.FLOAT,false,0, 0);

var texCoord = gl.getAttribLocation(program, "a_texCoord");
var texCoordBuffer = gl.createBuffer();
gl.bindBuffer(gl.ARRAY_BUFFER, texCoordBuffer);
gl.bufferData(gl.ARRAY_BUFFER, new Float32Array([
                                                0.0, 0.0,
                                                0.0, 1.0,
                                                1.0, 0.0,
                                                1.0, 0.0,
                                                0.0, 1.0,
                                                1.0, 1.0
                                               ]), gl.STATIC_DRAW);
```

```
    gl.vertexAttribPointer(texCoord, 2, gl.FLOAT, false, 0, 0);

    gl.enableVertexAttribArray(texCoord);
    gl.enableVertexAttribArray(vertexPos);

    gl.drawArrays(gl.TRIANGLES, 0, 6);
  }
  draw2d();
  </script>
 </body>
</html>
```

WebGL for 2D Graphics?

If you want to use WebGL then, unless you are planning something special, it
is better to adopt a library such as three.js. However, most of these specialize
in 3D graphics and 2D is an afterthought, if it is mentioned at all. A notable
exception is pixi.js. You can learn to do things directly using the WebGL API,
but this generally requires a bigger investment of time. The 2D Canvas API is
much easier and for simple graphics is much closer in performance to WebGL
than is generally accepted. However, this said, it is not so difficult to
implement very efficient 2D bitmap graphics using WebGL once you have the
basic ideas.

Summary

- WebGL is just a 2D rendering system which makes use of the GPU hardware that most machines have.

- If you just want to work in 2D you can simplify the vertex shader to accept 2D vertex data.

- Using a transformation matrix you can use the standard method of drawing a 2D shape centered on the origin and transform it to the size and position you need.

- It if fairly easy to create functions which draw standard shapes without having to load the vertex data every time you need to draw something.

- Animation in WebGL works in the usual way via the `requestAnimationFrame` function and setting a transformation.

- WebGL can work with bitmaps which are referred to as textures because of their use in 3D graphics.

- A varying is a shader variable that is set to a weighted average of the values at the vertices of a fragment according to the distance from each of the current pixels.

- Bitmaps loaded into the GPU always have a `0,0` (top left corner) to `1,1` (bottom right corner) co-ordinate system.

- Texture co-ordinates are a 2D vector of varyings that interpolate the texture co-ordinates assigned to the vertices.

- Texture co-ordinates are used to sample the pixel value in the texture bitmap and use that as the pixel's color.

- The fragment shader can do image processing by forming functions of the colors of neighboring pixels in the texture bitmap.

Index

Other Books by Ian Elliot

JavaScript Async: Events, Callbacks, Promises and Async Await
ISBN: 9781871962567

Asynchronous programming is essential to the modern web and at last JavaScript programmers have the tools to do the job – the Promise object and the async and await commands. These are so elegant in their design that you need to know about them if only to be impressed. It is likely that other languages will incorporate similar facilities in the future. While async and await make asynchronous code as easy to use as synchronous code there are a lot of subtle things going on and to really master the situation you need to know about Promises and you need to know how the JavaScript dispatch queue works.

Written for experienced JavaScript developers who want to get to grips with the complexities of the language, *JavaScript Async* guides you through the story of async. It starts with Events, which is where asynchronous programming originates, but it quickly becomes apparent that you need additional ways of dealing with long running tasks. The most basic solution is the callback and this is where async programming starts to become difficult. JavaScript used to be a single-threaded language, but with the introduction of the Web Worker you can write multi-threaded programs. Promises are the pinnacle of async programming in JavaScript and putting them together with the dispatch queue provides further advances. The way that async and await work with Promises is nothing short of amazing. The book concludes with a look at how async and await integrate with some of the latest JavaScript APIs that are based on the Promise object. The Service Worker is possibly the biggest change in the way JavaScript can be used to create programs that are just as happy being offline as online.

Working with async can be confusing and disorienting, but by combining code examples and lucid explanations Ian Elliot presents a coherent explanation. If you want to work with async read this book first.

Just JavaScript: An Idiomatic Approach
ISBN: 9781871962574

Just JavaScript is an attempt to understand JavaScript for what it really is - a very different language that should not be compared to Java or dismissed as simply a scripting language. It looks at the ideas that originally motivated the JavaScript approach and also at the additions over time that have produced modern JavaScript/ECMAScript.

It isn't a complete introduction to JavaScript and isn't for the complete beginner to programming. It has been written for those who are familiar with the basic constructs used in any programming language and have already encountered JavaScript.

After a brief overview of its history, we come to the key idea in JavaScript: it is object-based. Everything in JavaScript is an object and three chapters are used to introduce objects before we meet the Function Object. The many different ways of creating a JavaScript function tends to hide the fact that they are indeed all objects with properties and a lifetime that is different from local variables. This is the reason closure is natural. Having explored JavaScript's unique approach to parameters we are ready to consider how functions become methods. After this factory functions and constructors seem obvious as does the prototype chain. The final three chapters tackle the issues that are usually seen as problems for JavaScript and which are now reconciled within the idiomatic approach.

After reading Ian Elliot's account, you will have an understanding how and why JavaScript is unique and the way in which you can exploit its strengths.

Just jQuery: The Core UI
ISBN:9781871962505

jQuery is a library of functions for JavaScript that provides easy and sophisticated access to the HTML in a web page. Originally intended to smooth over the differences in the way browsers interact with JavaScript, it has developed into a much more powerful tool that fully lives up to its motto of "write less, do more". As a result jQuery is compact and can seem cryptic until you get used its common idioms.

Written for JavaScript developers working with web page layout, *Just jQuery: The Core UI* enables you to use jQuery easily and efficiently. It also cuts through its seeming complexity, by presenting enough explanation at every stage for you to understand what is happening.

After outlining what jQuery is, how to obtain it and why you should use it, early chapters deal with the essential jQuery - its selectors, filters and DOM traversal functions. Next we look at how to modify existing HTML elements and how to create completely new elements. Next we look at more advanced aspects of the UI - storing data and working with forms. jQuery also provides simple animation functions and to understand these we look at function queues and asychronous animation. Adding custom elements, both to the jQuery UI and to jQuery itself, is the next major topic. The book closes with an explanation of how jQuery's unit testing package, QUnit, lets you write tests to make sure that your JavaScript code works and continues to work.

If you program in JavaScript in a web environment Ian Elliot's approach will help you write code that makes sense and works across browsers without causing problems.

Just jQuery: Events, Async & Ajax

ISBN: 9781871962529

jQuery is the closest thing JavaScript has to a standard library, yet many programmers never venture beyond its most obvious facilities. As well as having easy to use and very powerful DOM manipulation features, described in the companion book *Just jQuery: The Core UI*, it also offers an improved JavaScript event system, help with writing asynchronous code in the form of Promises, and easy to use and powerful AJAX functions.

Written for JavaScript developers working with advanced web pages, *Just jQuery: Events, Async & AJAX* covers the parts of jQuery not associated with the DOM. Specifically it is about how to make use of jQuery's event functions, Deferred and Promise functions and its AJAX functions. While not every programmer will need these advanced features in the early stages of using JavaScript, they are unavoidable aspects of modern web programming and sooner or later you will find a need to master them all.

This book is about ideas. Ian Elliot shows you how to use jQuery, but mainly by explaining how jQuery approaches the task. Once you understand this there is little need to go over complicated examples where the problem is seeing the big ideas because the small detail is overwhelming.